Normality and Disability

Hotly contested, normality remains a powerful, complex category in contemporary law and culture. What is little realized are the ways in which disability underpins and shapes the operation of norms and the power dynamics of normalization.

This pioneering collection explores the place of law in political, social, scientific and biomedical developments relating to disability and other categories of 'abnormality'. The contributors show how law produces cultural meanings, norms, representations, artefacts and expressions of disability, abnormality and normality, as well as how law responds to and is constituted by cultures of disability. The collection traverses a range of contemporary legal and political issues including human rights, mercy killing, reproductive technologies, hate crime, policing, immigration and disability housing. It also explores the impact and ongoing legacies of historical practices such as eugenics and deinstitutionalization.

Of interest to a wide range of scholars working on normality and law, the book also creates an opening for critical scholars and activists engaged with other marginalized and denigrated categories, notably contesting institutional violence in the context of settler colonialism, neoliberalism and imperialism, to engage more richly and politically with disability.

This book was originally published as a special issue of *Continuum: Journal of Media & Cultural Studies.*

Gerard Goggin is Professor of Media and Communications and ARC Future Fellow at the University of Sydney, Australia. He has published widely on the social and cultural dynamics of disability, including *Disability in Australia* (2005) and *Digital Disability* (2003) (both with Christopher Newell), *Disability and the Media* (2015, with Katie Ellis), *Routledge Companion to Disability and Media* (2018, with Katie Ellis and Beth Haller) and *Listening to Disability: Voices of Democracy* (2018, with Cate Thill and Rosemary Kayess).

Linda Steele is a Senior Lecturer in Law at the University of Technology Sydney, Australia. Her research explores the intersections of disability, law and injustice. She has published in journals across law, criminology and, gender and cultural studies.

Jessica Robyn Cadwallader is an independent scholar with an abiding interest in corporeal differences and its significance in contemporary culture, especially medical and legal cultures. Her doctoral thesis focused on experiences of suffering and how these are bound up with medical 'solutions' of normalization, while her postdoctoral project explored therapeutic forgetting, a response to trauma. Her work has been published in numerous international journals, including *Social Semiotics, Australian Feminist Studies, International Journal of Feminist Approaches to Bioethics* and *Somatechnics.*

Normality and Disability

Intersections among Norms, Law, and Culture

Edited by
Gerard Goggin, Linda Steele and Jessica Robyn Cadwallader

Routledge
Taylor & Francis Group

LONDON AND NEW YORK

First published 2018 by Routledge

2 Park Square, Milton Park, Abingdon, Oxfordshire OX14 4RN
52 Vanderbilt Avenue, New York, NY 10017

Routledge is an imprint of the Taylor & Francis Group, an informa business

First issued in paperback 2019

British Library Cataloguing in Publication Data
A catalogue record for this book is available from the British Library

ISBN 13: 978-1-138-30248-8 (hbk)
ISBN 13: 978-0-367-89150-3 (pbk)

Typeset in Myriad Pro
by RefineCatch Limited, Bungay, Suffolk

Publisher's Note
The publisher accepts responsibility for any inconsistencies that may have
arisen during the conversion of this book from journal articles to book chapters,
namely the possible inclusion of journal terminology.

Disclaimer
Every effort has been made to contact copyright holders for their permission to
reprint material in this book. The publishers would be grateful to hear from any
copyright holder who is not here acknowledged and will undertake to rectify
any errors or omissions in future editions of this book.

Contents

CONTENTS

Citation Information

The chapters in this book were originally published in *Continuum: Journal of Media & Cultural Studies*, volume 31, issue 3 (June 2017). When citing this material, please use the original page numbering for each article, as follows:

For any permission-related enquiries please visit:
http://www.tandfonline.com/page/help/permissions

Notes on Contributors

Nicole L. Asquith is an Associate Professor of Policing and Criminal Justice at Western Sydney University, Australia, the Co-Director of the Vulnerability, Resilience and Policing Research Consortium, and a university associate with the Tasmanian Institute of Law Enforcement Studies.

Jessica Robyn Cadwallader is an independent scholar with an abiding interest in corporeal differences and its significance in contemporary culture, especially medical and legal cultures.

Peter Cryle is an emeritus professor in the Institute for Advanced Studies in the Humanities at the University of Queensland, Australia.

Leanne Dowse is an associate professor and chair in Intellectual Disability Behaviour Support at the University of NSW, Sydney, Australia.

Gerard Goggin is Professor of Media and Communications and ARC Future Fellow at the University of Sydney, Australia.

Piers Gooding is a postdoctoral research fellow at the Melbourne Social Equity Institute and Melbourne School of Law, the University of Melbourne, Australia.

Isabel Karpin is a professor in the Faculty of Law at the University of Technology Sydney, Australia.

Melania Moscoso is a social anthropologist currently working at the University of the Basque Country UPV/EHU, Spain.

Roxanne Mykitiuk is an associate professor and director of the Disability Law Intensive clinical program at Osgoode Hall Law School, York University, UK.

Karen O'Connell is a senior lecturer in the Faculty of Law at the University of Technology Sydney, Australia.

R. Lucas Platero is a researcher at the VOSATEC project funded by the Spanish R&D Programme of MINECO (2016–18).

Kate Seear is a Senior Lecturer in Law at Monash University, Australia, and an Australian Research Council DECRA Fellow.

Claire Spivakovsky is a Senior Lecturer in Criminology at Monash University, Australia.

Linda Steele is a Senior Lecturer in Law at the University of Technology Sydney, Australia.

Elizabeth Stephens is an Associate Professor of Cultural Studies and Deputy Head of School (Research) in the School of Arts and Social Sciences at Southern Cross University, Australia.

NOTES ON CONTRIBUTORS

Frankie Sullivan is a graduate from the University of Sydney Law School, where they undertook an honours thesis investigating legal responses to instances of domestic and family violence against people with disability.

Ryan Thorneycroft is a final year PhD candidate, and a research assistant in the School of Social Sciences and Psychology at Western Sydney University, Australia.

Dinesh Wadiwel is a lecturer and director of the Master of Human Rights at the University of Sydney, Australia.

Penelope Weller is director of the Juris Doctor Program in the Graduate School of Business and Law at RMIT University in Melbourne, Australia.

Stephanie K. Wheeler is an assistant professor at the University Central Florida in Orlando, Florida, USA.

Normality and disability: intersections among norms, law, and culture

This special issue of *Continuum* is published in a conjuncture where there is increased scholarly attention to the positioning as 'abnormal' of people designated as disabled, as well as people designated to other marginalized and denigrated categories (such as queer, chronic illness, racial and Indigenous minorities, poverty and criminality). Scholars have critiqued the cultural and material role of technologies of diagnosis and therapy, and discourses of biomedicine and science, in the construction of abnormality, as well as the significant and primary role of disability in positioning as abnormal certain bodies and subjects designated to other marginalized and denigrated categories (for example, through medicalizing and biologizing). The role of law in codifying, challenging, perpetuating and amending historical, material and institutional constructions of disability has also been the subject of much research, particularly highlighting the continuities and discontinuities with key other cultural conditions including settler-colonialism, imperialism, eugenics, reproductive rights, violence and torture, and contemporary forms of neoliberalism.

In critiquing abnormality, scholars are drawing attention to the converse: normality.[1] Normality is a privileged, yet strikingly vacant and difficult to define, category which gains its existence and status from its relationship to the constitutive disavowal of abnormality (Tremain 2005; Campbell 2009; Shildrick 2009). As Shakespeare (1994) puts it, disability functions as a 'dustbin for disavowal' for the category of normality.

At the same time as this increased scholarly attention to disability, abnormality and normality, there have been complex and often contradictory political and legal developments. There has been recognition of individuals designated as disabled as entitled to enhanced human rights and legal protections, reflected in the United Nations *Convention on the Rights of Persons with Disabilities* and various domestic law reform inquiries. Survivor and self advocates have been particularly active in the disability rights movement and scholarship in engaging with rights discourses to reclaim and subvert 'abnormality', for instance, in 'mad studies' (LeFrançois, Menzies, and Reaume 2013). Yet, at a domestic, political and legal level discrimination, violence and disadvantage persists. Law also has the capacity to support the development and availability of technologies that support access for people with disability and for others, but in many circumstances law may also deny or limit their availability. There are a number of contemporary circumstances that might explain these political developments.

One set of circumstances is that technological advancements, together with an increase in epistemological authority granted to scientific knowledge, are increasing the use of 'objective', scientific classification and certification of individuals as abnormal, frequently entrenching existing normative designations in the dominant cultural imaginary. Another set is geopolitical conditions such as the ongoing impacts of settler-colonialism, armed conflict, forced migration and international development that are themselves generating disability, extreme poverty and dislocation. A third set of circumstances is shifting political and policy conditions which are demanding the measurement of the economic worth and productivity of abnormal individuals and categories. Together these circumstances are placing people designated as disabled and other 'abnormal' individuals in situations of greater precariousness and legitimating their subjection to ongoing regulations and control (McRuer 2012), as well as violent interventions in their lives and bodies even to the point of death or prevention of existence.

Against this background, the central aim of this anthology of papers is to consider the place of law in these political, social, scientific and biomedical developments relating to disability and other categories of 'abnormality'. The papers consider how categories of abnormality relate to the privileged and frequently unmarked position of 'normality' and how legal interventions in abnormality relate to existing normative designations in the dominant cultural imaginary. The contributions explore how law produces cultural meanings, norms, representations, artefacts and expressions of disability, abnormality and normality, as well as how law responds to and is constituted by cultures of disability, abnormality and normality circulating in society more broadly.

What is striking about this collection of papers is the range of disciplinary approaches they contain. In conceiving the project, we were mindful of the gulfs among different areas of research, still distinct theoretical traditions, concepts, approaches and methods, and, equally salient, the apparently discrete domains of culture, law and norms. We strongly believe it is imperative to bring together, nurture and cross-fertilize research that is fit for purpose when it comes to the urgent need to acknowledge, trace, critically examine and transform the relationships among law, disability, abnormality and normality. A number of these papers originated from panels at the 2015 *Complicities* Law, Literature and the Humanities Association of Australasia Conference held in Sydney, Australia, one of the important meeting places and supporting infrastructure for these kinds of intersections. Other papers presented at this conference will be published in a kindred special issue of the journal *Law in Context*, underscoring the important role that socio-legal scholarship plays in fostering work across law, justice, social sciences and humanities.

Many of the papers in this special issue also draw their energies from, and are deeply engaged in international disability studies research and theory. Disability scholars and students are keenly aware of the germinal work on normalcy by leading figures such as Berubé (2013), Berubé (2016), Campbell (2009), Clare ([1999] 2015), Davis (1995), Davis (2013), Garland-Thomson (1997), Garland-Thomson (2009), Meekosha and Dowse (1997), Michalko and Titchkosky (2009), Mitchell and Snyder (2000), Mitchell and Snyder (2015), Oliver ([1990] 2012), Shildrick (2009), McRuer (2006), Tremain (2005), Shakespeare (2014), Siebers (2008), Wendell (1996) and many others. Such work deserves to be much more widely combined and cross-referenced with the works on norms and normalcy that are influential elsewhere. However, it is highly significant that it is on the fertile and cross-disciplinary groundwork laid by cultural studies, and especially in this antipodean cultural studies journal *Continuum*, that this collection takes shape.

Law, justice, equality, rights and democracy have long been preoccupations for cultural studies. So too have matters of gender, sexuality, race and class. Disability is a more recent entrant into the field of cultural studies, surprisingly belated perhaps – but, as this special issue shows with all sorts of crossovers, borrowings, conflicts, amplifications, clashes and fertile admixtures possible. Indeed, as Stevens and Cryle, as well as Wheeler demonstrate in their papers for this special issue, the status of disability as a contemporary state of abnormality has historical underpinnings inextricably linked with race, gender and other categories of degeneracy and unfitness bound up in ideas of the nation state and conformity to authority. *Continuum* is notable for recognizing the importance of cultural studies engagement with disability by publishing pioneering papers on disability in cultural and media studies. The journal exemplifies the best of contemporary cultural studies in its openness to the manifold operations of culture across many domains and disciplinary terrains, and the importance of exploring how institutional cultures impact and inflect other cultural dynamics. Normality is such a central, obvious yet unmarked, highly wrought, much researched and debated concept. As a heated recent debate in queer studies reveals, normality remains at the heart of things (see, for instance, Wiegman and Wilson 2015, Jagose 2015 and response from Halberstam 2015).

Against such a backdrop, we would highlight that some papers in the special issue, notably Karpin and Mykitiuk, as well as O'Connell, open up the contemporary debates around normalcy and disability to question assumed orderings and boundaries of this dichotomy through examinations of 'fitting in' and 'eccentricity'. Moreover, other papers in the special issue use, such as Wadiwel, Wheeler, Sullivan and Steele an exploration of disability, normality and abnormality as a basis for exploring material practices that have resulted in the positioning of disabled bodies and populations for interventions, control, regulation and violence – at heightened or exceptional ways as compared to the 'normal' body – and, simultaneously, the negation of these practices. Other papers by Dowse, Gooding, Spivakovsky and Seear explore how law is complicit in both the representations of normality and abnormality as deviant, dangerous and disordered and in the lawful practices themselves that respond to these 'problems' – troubling ideas of law and the state as non-violent and as always saving, protecting or empowering people with disability (and society at large). Papers by Moscoso and Lucas Platero, and Thorneycroft and Asquith problematize the simultaneous mobilization and marginalization of disability in 'progressive' social justice movements – drawing connections and tensions between disability and other anti-oppression movements.

Together, these papers reveal the important ways that disability, in its diverse incarnations, operations and histories, shapes and fissures normality, in relation to law, policing, violence, genetics and eugenics, eccentricity and other categories, institutions and practices. As much as anything what the papers underscore is that we all have a deep stake in the operation of norms and the power relations of normalization, and that to understand these, we need to understand how disability plays into this, especially through the intertwined dynamics of culture and law. As well as providing a contribution to cultural studies in terms of a new body of work conversant in disability and normalcy, this special issue also creates an opening for cultural studies and other critical scholars and activists engaged with other marginalized and denigrated categories, notably contesting institutional violence in the context of settler colonialism, neoliberalism and imperialism, to engage more richly and politically with disability and to begin to form alliances and scholarship across institutional, epistemological and political divides .

Note

1. In line with much contemporary scholarship, we are happy to use the terms 'normality' and 'abnormality' roughly interchangeably with 'normalcy' and 'abnormalcy'.

Acknowledgement

The editors and authors are very grateful to Rosemary Curtis for her superb research and editorial assistance in preparing these papers for press. We also wish to thank the various reviewers across many disciplines for their critical acumen and generous feedback on the papers.

Disclosure statement

No potential conflicts of interest were reported by the authors.

References

Berubé, M. 2013. "Genetics, Disability, and Democracy." In *Disability Studies Reader*. 4th ed., edited by L. J. Davis, 201–225. London: Routledge.

Berubé, M. 2016. *The Secret Life of Stories: From Don Quixote to Harry Potter, How Understanding Intellectual Disability Transforms The Way We Read*. New York: New York University Press.

Campbell, F. K. A. 2009. *Contours of Ableism: The Production of Disability and Ableness*. London: Palgrave.

Clare, E. [1999] 2015. *Exile and Pride: Disability, Queerness, and Liberation*. [Originally published in 1999]. 2015 ed. Durham, NC: Duke University Press.

Davis, L. J. 1995. *Enforcing Normalcy: Disability, Deafness, and the Body*. London: Verso.

Davis, L. J. 2013. *The End of Normal – Identity in a Biocultural Era*. Ann Arbour: University of Michigan Press.

Garland-Thomson, R. 1997. *Extraordinary Bodies: Figuring Physical Disability in American Culture and Literature*. New York: Columbia University Press.

Garland-Thomson, R. 2009. *Staring: How We Look*. Oxford: Oxford University Press.

Halberstam, J. 2015. "Straight Eye for the Queer Theorist: A Review of 'Queer Theory without Normativity.'" *Bully Bloggers*, September 12. https://bullybloggers.wordpress.com/2015/09/12/straight-eye-for-the-queer-theorist-a-review-of-queer-theory-without-antinormativity-by-jack-halberstam/.

Jagose, A. 2015. "The Trouble with Antinormativity." *Differences* 26 (1): 26–47.

LeFrançois, B. A., R. Menzies, and G. Reaume, eds. 2013. *Mad Matters: A Critical Reader in Canadian Mad Studies*. Toronto: Canadian Scholars' Press.

Meekosha, H., and L. Dowse. 1997. "Enabling Citizenship: Gender, Disability and Citizenship in Australia." *Feminist Review* 57 (1): 49–72.

Michalko, R., and T. Titchkosky, eds. 2009. *Rethinking Normalcy: A Disability Studies Reader*. Toronto: Canadian Scholars' Press.

Mitchell, D. T., and S. Snyder. 2000. *Narrative Prosthesis: Disability and the Dependencies of Discourse*. Ann Arbor: University of Michigan Press.

Mitchell, D. T., and S. L. Snyder. 2015. *The Biopolitics of Disability: Neoliberalism, Ablenationalism, and Peripheral Embodiment*. Ann Arbor: University of Michigan Press.

McRuer, R. 2006. *Crip Theory: Cultural Signs of Queerness and Disability*. New York: New York University Press.

McRuer, R. 2012. "Cripping Queer Politics, or the Dangers of Neoliberalism." *The Scholar and Feminist Online* 10 (1–2), http://sfonline.barnard.edu/a-new-queer-agenda/cripping-queer-politics-or-the-dangers-of-neoliberalism/.

Oliver, M. [1990] 2012. *The New Politics of Disablement*. [Originally published as The Politics of Disablement, 1990]. 2nd ed. Houndsmills: Palgrave Macmillan.

Shakespeare, T. 1994. "Cultural Representation of Disabled People: Dustbins for Disavowal?" *Disability and Society* 9 (3): 283–299.

Shakespeare, T. 2014. *Disability Rights and Wrongs Revisited*. 2nd ed. London: Routledge.

Shildrick, M. 2009. *Dangerous Discourses of Disability, Subjectivity, and Sexuality*. Basingstoke: Palgrave Macmillan.

Siebers, T. 2008. *Disability Theory*. Ann Arbor: University of Michigan Press.

Tremain, S., ed. 2005. *Foucault and the Government of Disability*. Ann Arbor: University of Michigan Press.

Wiegman, R., and E. A. Wilson. 2015. "Introduction: Antinormativity's Queer Conventions." *Differences* 26 (1): 1–25.

Wendell, S. 1996. *The Rejected Body: Feminist Philosophical Reflections on Disability*. New York: Routledge.

Gerard Goggin

Linda Steele

Jessica Robyn Cadwallader

Fit or fitting in: deciding against normal when reproducing the future

Roxanne Mykitiuk and Isabel Karpin ⓘD

ABSTRACT

'Normal' is a contentious term. Descriptively, 'normal' represents 'what is' as a statistical average. However, the term also represents normative or prescriptive content about what is 'right' or 'what should be'. Correspondingly, abnormality is a deviation from the norm. It is both a factual exception to the average and a value judgement about what is a 'wrong' state of being. Pursuing 'normal' or deciding against it can be a defining moment in the high technology environment of assisted reproduction. Here, we explore notions of normalcy articulated through legal and policy regimes around screening and testing of gamete and embryo donors. We draw on the work of disability scholars and the diversity of responses to the idea of normal that were registered by four women interviewed in our studies. Three of the interviewees had used or were intending to use donated gametes and the fourth had intended to donate her embryos. We demonstrate how the choice of a particular donor may reveal ingrained or structural prejudice that reconstructs difference as disability. Equally, however, it may reveal a multitude of ways in which difference or deviation from a normative standard is incorporated as a *normal* part of family formation.

Introduction

'Normal' is a contentious term. Descriptively, 'normal' is a way of representing 'what is' as a statistical average, however, the term also represents normative or prescriptive content about what is 'right' or 'what should be'. Correspondingly, abnormality is a deviation from the norm. It is both a factual exception to the average and a value judgement about what is a 'wrong' state of being (Taylor and Mykitiuk 2001). Pursuing 'normal' or deciding against it can be a defining moment in the high technology environment of assisted reproduction. In this article, we explore notions of normalcy articulated through legal and policy regimes regarding screening and testing of gamete and embryo donors. To do this, we draw on the work of disability scholars and the diversity of responses to the idea of normal that were registered by four women interviewed in studies undertaken by the authors. (ARC DP 986213: *Enhancing Reproductive Opportunity 2009–2013*; ARC DP 15010157: *Regulating Relations* 2015–2018). Three of the women were interviewed because they had used, or were intending to use, donated gametes and the fourth had intended to donate her embryos. All four had encounters with donor selection systems and genetic testing regimes. Our research suggests that in some cases, the choice of a particular donor may reveal ingrained or structural prejudice that reconstructs difference as abnormality. Equally, however, it may reveal a multitude of ways in which difference or deviation from a normative standard is incorporated as a *normal* part of family formation.

Screening and testing protocols for donated gametes

Assisted Reproductive Technology (ART) clinic testing and screening protocols for donors exist to ensure they and/or their gametes are unaffected by genetic anomaly, infectious disease or psychological illness. They are often more rigorous for donors than for people who reproduce with ART using their own gametes. These guidelines and practices reflect a conception of what, in the clinical context, is considered to be 'normal' in both the descriptive and prescriptive sense. Nevertheless, screening and testing practices vary quite markedly across clinics and jurisdictions suggesting that there is no clear consensus about what constitutes a 'normal' or 'healthy' donor or donated gamete.

Australian clinics have both a domestic and imported supply of gametes for reproductive use and must comply with the Australian Reproductive Technology Accreditation Committee Code of Practice, the National Health and Medical Research Council guidelines on Assisted Reproduction and State based legislation. Apart from standard disease transmission controls there are no specific requirements regarding testing or screening though most clinics have extensive screening and testing regimes. IVF Australia, for instance, tests sperm donors' chromosomes and for genetic conditions such as cystic fibrosis, sickle cell disease, and other conditions depending on ethnic background (http://www.ivf.com.au/fertility-treatment/donor-program/require-a-sperm-donor). In the United States, the UK, and Europe a range of protocols and regulations operate for donated gametes. In Europe, for instance, under the European Union Directive on Human Tissues and Cells, 'gamete donors should be screened (tested) "for autosomal recessive genes known to be prevalent (…) in the donor's ethnic background"' (Commission Directive 2006; Dondorp et al. 2014, 2). In the US, screening and testing for certain autosomal conditions is recommended by the American Society for Reproductive Medicine (ASRM) regardless of ethnicity for the entire population, including carrier testing for Spinal Muscular Atrophy (Prior 2008 cited in Dondorp et al. 2014, 1355) and Cystic Fibrosis (ACOG 2011). While, the ASRM do not require karyotyping for chromosomal translocations, the French Centre d'Etude et de Conservation des Oeufs et du Sperme Humains and British guidelines of the Association of Biomedical Andrologists (Dondorp et al. 2014) recommend it. In comparison, in Germany and the Netherlands, there is an active recommendation against karyotyping (Dondorp et al. 2014). Finally, some protocols go so far as to recommend against using a donor who tests positive as a carrier for a heterozygous autosomal recessive disorder (requiring two copies of the gene for the disorder to materialize) (Dondorp et al. 2014). This is despite the fact that, as Sara Wienke et al., report, '[i]t is estimated that each individual is a carrier of between zero and seven severe childhood recessive conditions with an average of 2.8 found in one study' (2014, 191). This has led McGowan, Cho, and Sharp to suggest that 'identification as a carrier [is] the new normal' (2013, 9).

From this brief summary it is apparent that there is no consensus about testing/ screening protocols for donated gametes. Rather, they reflect a range of views about what constitutes a 'normal' or 'healthy' gamete. In the United States, where there is a commercial market for gametes, preconception screening and testing of donors is comprehensive. The World Egg Bank for instance, advertises next generation massive sequencing (NGS) which they describe as 'a powerful new technology that can examine the entire genetic code of a female donor, and predict how her DNA, or genetic code, will interact with the genetic information of the male partner before conception.' (http://www.theworldeggbank.com/next-generation-testing/). Testing is not limited to genetic analysis, but often includes comprehensive psychological testing alongside analysis of the medical history of the donor's immediate family (parents, grandparents and siblings) including any familial experience of conditions such as depression, mood swings, anxiety, and more. Though not required by any professional guidelines, a number of US IVF clinics use personality tests when screening potential donors. One clinic, the New York University Fertility Centre, has undertaken a study of its own practices using what they called 'enhanced genetic and psychological testing,' and reported excluding 31 percent of potential donors based on genetic and psychological factors. The report states: 'Enhanced genetic screening with universal testing for Tay-Sachs, Fragile X and karyotype excluded 25 candidates' (Reh et al. 2010, 2300). However it goes on to say '….those excluded for a personal or family medical history had histories suggestive of an unacceptable transmissible genetic trait such as dyslexia, early cardiac disease and aggressive cancers' (2300). These potential candidates were not identified (and excluded) by genetic testing but based on family histories. Further, exclusions occurred based on what was described as 'basic psychological screening.' Reh notes that 'depression was the most common factor for exclusion and alcoholism was the most common factor identified in family history of psychological disorder' (2300). But people were also excluded for attention deficit disorder, obsessive-compulsive disorder, family history of schizophrenia, suicide, bipolar disorder and other conditions (2302). Enhanced psychological testing, where even more candidates were excluded for 'unfavourable behaviour', followed this including for: dishonesty, non-compliance, immaturity, criminal history, hostility toward staff and refusal to disclose donation to spouse.

The testing and screening practices described above suggest an acceptance of the heritability of not only single gene conditions but of complex psychological conditions and socially undesirable personal characteristics as well as those regarded to be desirable. Daniels and Heidt-Forsythe equate this geneticization with a modern eugenics movement and state:

> The belief that idealized (and often nonbiological) human traits are transmitted genetically is one historical characteristic of the eugenics movement and …. [w]e argue that sperm and egg donation practices in the American reproductive industry mirror positive eugenic beliefs in new and more subtle forms. (Daniels and Heidt-Forsythe 2012, 720)

However, if these screening and testing processes are in lock step with an ideology of improvement it is by no means clear, as our research demonstrates below, that the people who access them have a shared understanding of what is 'better' or indeed what is 'normal'.

Diverse normality and normal disability

In *The End of Normal,* Lennard Davis describes 'diversity' as the new normal but as a constrained concept (Davis 2013) under conditions of neoliberalism. As a neoliberal concept, Davis argues, diversity is shaped by a commitment to the self-authorizing individual and 'implies celebration, choice'(8) and malleability (5). However, disabled bodies are conventionally imagined as 'fixed' (6, 7), in need of fixing and an identity that is not chosen (by oneself or others) (11, 14). Thus, for Davis, the neo-liberal diverse subject, cannot incorporate disability. This caveat is an important corrective to an uncritical embrace of the concept of diversity among those who might otherwise see it as a means to achieve radical inclusion. Davis states 'the concept of diversity, currently is rendered operative largely by excluding groups that might be thought of as abject or hypermarginalised' (4). Disability, therefore, 'reveals the state of exception' in the neoliberal diversity paradigm, 'by being continuously connected with the exception to the norm.'(9). Thus, Davis' contention is that the very difference of disability – its abjectness, immutability and *unchoseness* – is the necessary category of the not normal against which a self-chosen and malleable diversity can be inscribed as normative (14).

We suggest, and our research demonstrates below, that within the context of ART, where a neoliberal consumerist model increasingly proliferates, diversity nevertheless has a more expansive meaning than that suggested by Davis. We have found that some users of ART re/construct disability within a more capacious and diverse understanding of normalcy – what we might call diverse normality. Indeed, for some users of ART, a neo-liberal construction of diversity is neither accepted nor desired.

The idea that disability can be regarded as 'a new normal' has been proposed by Ginsburg and Rapp (2015). On their account, the increased growth of the (American) population with disabilities and its projected rise in the future, signals an opportunity for 'a refiguring of notions of typicality that we think of as "a new normal" in which the inclusion of disability is no longer considered exceptional but is simply taken for granted ….' (2015). Integral to this shift to a 'new normal' are the requisite accommodations of disability together with accessible and inclusive futures in which persons with a panoply of disabilities are accommodated as full participants.

As we highlight below, in the context of utilizing donated gametes and embryos, users of ART not only display an expansive understanding of what constitutes disability and what we are terming diverse normality, but in some instances do appear to choose disability or, at least, to place it on a continuum of normalcy. One of the distinct features of our study is the significance of the contingent and changing context of kin-making within which users of donor gametes are confronting issues of disability and normalcy. The use of genetic testing/screening is a practice which typically reinforces and apply a bio-medical model of disability in a context of desired family formation using donated gametes. However, these donor gamete practices, protocols, and regulations ignore the contingency of the process of kin-making. Payne notes for instance that the provision of a list of donors to choose from for people undertaking ART appears to 'reinforce the idea that one can choose, and that choosing is unconnected to other social constraints and norms' (2015, 113). But she goes on to say that in her study:

> while the choice of donor is clearly articulated within a larger discourse of consumer choice also amongst the patients, it does not follow that the patients internalize this discourse in an unequivocal manner. On the contrary, the interviewees have tended either to downplay the process of choosing, stressing to me how 'strange' the process of choosing had been or in other ways signalling that they did not regard this process as completely unproblematic. (113)

Along similar lines, in a Belgian study, though donor sperm recipients indicated, that familial coherence would be achieved by matching donors with traits that were the same as their own or their partner's personality traits (Ravelingien et al. 2015, 9) they also indicated a preference for a donor with whom they had a rapport 'comparable to what you experience when you make a new friend or fall in love with someone' (9). While users of donated gametes/embryos may initially strive to create sameness or relationships of similarity between themselves and their future progeny when choosing donors, or to eliminate risks of non-normative traits, these desires inevitably bump up against contingent and changing contexts as they engage in their reproductive project of building their families and creating kinship relations. For example, the number of gametes and embryos are limited as are the financial resources to generate additional ones, while in some cases, affective relationships between donors and donees become established that displace the importance of sameness or certain traits. Therefore, the contingency of forming kinship is fluid, diverse and complex unlike the fixity and certainty imagined in testing/screening regulations and policies, and this includes the way that disability is received. In their act of forming kinship relationships, often through constrained choices regarding gametes and gamete donors, ART users may have to, or choose to, discard biomedical models of disability and employ complex, social, embodied, relational concepts of disability and difference transforming disability into a new normal or into something along a continuum of normalcy. Context and contingency are everything in this world of kin-making. As Nordqvist suggests:

> The meaning of genes, similarity … characteristics, aptitudes, physicality … feelings … practices, time, fairness and resemblances [and we would add disability] can be renegotiated, revisited and even transformed, and yet still all be used to signal connectedness. Thereby, we can emphasise the importance of some relations whilst discounting others in a way that fits the family we live with and also cope with an unpredictable future. (280)

This is in contrast to the knowable future as misleadingly assured by prenatal genetic testing/screening.

Choosing fitness or fitting in

Despite a proliferation of policy and screening guidelines from clinics, medical professional organizations and regulatory bodies, the four women interviewed in our studies (see below) fashioned their own ideas of what is normal and acceptable, of what kinds of differences make up the categories of disability and diverse normality. What is normal became an idiosyncratic function of an array of factors including: personal desire, emotional connection, qualities of the embryo that are imagined to have a bearing on the future child, gender preference and a variety of embodied characteristics. Normalcy was crafted as a form of relational fitting in to the partially established and imagined future contours of the life or lives of those seeking to procreate.

The decisions made by donor recipients suggests that the views of disability scholars Rosemary Garland-Thomson and Dan Goodley may find some support among our study participants. Both theorists posit normalcy as a potentially ableist concept and argue, instead, for the positive identification of multiple and varying ways of being. Goodley reminds us that 'a whole host of norms … are, in actuality, limiting and stifling'. Moreover, he recognizes the possibility for non-normative 'exciting, radicalizing and alternative practices of everyday life in counterpoint to the idealized normal citizen of our times' (Goodley 2014, 158). Garland-Thomson, utilizes the concept of 'misfit' which she says 'emphasizes the particularity of varying lived embodiments and avoids a theoretical generic disabled body that can dematerialize if social and architectural barriers no longer disable it' (Garland-Thomson 2011, 592). For Garland-Thomson, disability is not just about functional impairment but rather includes difference that simply does not fit in socially, culturally and materially. She goes on to say:

> When we fit harmoniously and properly into the world, we forget the truth of contingency because the world sustains us. When we experience misfitting and recognise that disjuncture for its political potential, we expose the relational component and the fragility of fitting. Any of us can fit here today and misfit there tomorrow. (597)

This idea of fit as relational insists on the way that normal/cy exists in the interstices of our agreements about what constitutes it as such. It has no objective status outside of our embodied relations with each other and the institutional and environmental contexts within which we are situated. Misfitting too then is relational. It is not that an individual is inherently 'abnormal' but rather that in a network of relations within a social and material context he or she is out of sync or excluded. The concepts of misfitting and fitting require us, as Garland-Thomson states, to 'recognise that bodies are always situated in and dependent upon environments through which they materialise as fitting and misfitting' (598).

In the context of ART use and choosing donor gametes for the purpose of reproduction, applying the concept of mis/fitting illustrates the contingent, relational and situated character of normalcy that operates in the enterprise of kin making. The misfit is not a particular body (or mind), but the mutually constitutive relationship between a body in its temporal, social and material place – one whose embodiment is out of sync with dominant narratives or norms. Those who use donor gametes and embryos themselves already operate outside of the norm. Reproducing with the use of donor gametes, their practice of technological conception as well as their frequent deviation from the creation of the hetero-normative family marks many ART users as misfits. For others, living with embodied difference marked by society as disability, fuels the desire for progeny created from donor gametes that will better fit in an ableist world. Yet, choosing gamete donors, like choosing kin, is complex. As we illustrate below, a gamete donor may be fit, not because of the anticipated genetic qualities he or she will bestow, but because they fit in with the donor recipient's sense of family. Normalcy, in relation to the choice of donor gametes therefore, is sometimes revealed to be a function not of fitness but of fitting in.

Choosing against, between and within normal

In this section, we offer a carefully selected sample of original data from our ongoing and recent research on assisted reproduction.[1] We focus on four participants whose unique set of circumstances have required them to make decisions about testing and screening when reproducing with donor gametes or donating embryos that may have a genetic or chromosomal anomaly. We have chosen these four because they demonstrate a range of responses to the idea of normalcy, the subject of this article. Using a semi-structured interview format, participants were asked to reflect upon why they chose to use donor gametes or to donate embryos.

The examples we draw on demonstrate how the choices made by our participants trouble assumptions about the meaning of and desire for normalcy in relation to one's future child. Where participants were required to make a decision about disability, our case studies uncover how those decisions are taken both within, and in resistance to, the regime of normalcy prescribed by testing protocols. As our analysis reveals, the process of decision-making about the use of donor gametes, for example, suggests a highly textured, contextualized and relational approach. This stands in stark juxtaposition to the apparent normalizing of the decision-making process and the standards it is expected that donor recipients follow in making reproductive decisions as demonstrated by the range of testing/screening guidelines, policies and clinic practices. The act of kin making, as the participant interviews we discuss below demonstrate, seems to displace or elide the assumptions about normalcy that are embedded in policy and screening guideline documents. These guidelines are based on a rationalist model that cannot or will not contemplate affect and contingency. In our research however, we see various users fashion their own ideas of normalcy out of the circumstances with which they are confronted, including information about the actual gametes and embryos before them. 'Normal' becomes contingent on what the technology produces – the number, sex, quality of the embryos in relation to the desires and experiences of those using the technologies and the possibly constrained options they have, given their desire to have a baby. Indeed, Nordqvist, in a study of lesbian parenthood using donor conception, suggests that contingency in family creation should be understood as contributing to the construction of kinship. She notes that:

> [i]t is important to emphasise that … couples experienced a process which was in part shaped by their desires and wishes, and in part by issues beyond their control. As a result, their routes, wishes and options changed with circumstance and with the way their lives and conception journey 'worked out.' This in turn shaped the way in which they perceived and engaged in the process of bringing kinship into existence. Imagining kinship and the future family was a question revisited again and again with every new avenue explored. (Nordqvist 2014, 271)

While Nordqvist's research does not examine donated gamete users' choices about disability in shaping kinship, it is clear from our research (described below) that a similar process of contingency occurs when gamete users confront decisions of possible or likely difference or disability. Moreover, we found that coming up against the contingency of difference does not always result in the rejection of disability but instead can result in a recalibration of what is normal and what might be considered normal kinship. Our case studies demonstrate what happens when the appearance of choice knocks up against the reality of contingency and how this affects the very conceptualization of normalcy. Some of our interviewees actively decided against assumed understandings of 'normal' while others found themselves choosing between different kinds of 'normal'. Their choices gestured towards the possibility of resisting normative/neoliberal expectations and contributing to the realization of non-normative or diverse normative future possibilities.

Consider Dian,[2] who revealed that when choosing an egg donor she went through a complex process that incorporated the donor into the love relationship with her partner. Dian told us:

> We spoke to three egg donors. We fell in love with one of them. Then they're about to sign the contract and we realised that this particular donor apparently has – is a Tay-Sachs carrier. Apparently, that can be quite a fatal situation if both – if William [Dian's husband] was also a carrier. I mean it would be fatal. So at that point we cancelled with this particular donor that we'd fallen in love with, and we went on a major search on egg donors.[3] So I ended up speaking to about seven egg donors over Skype. Then we didn't find anyone. It's like *The Princess and the Pea*. Was it *The Princess and the Pea*? There's a fairy tale like that.
>
> We looked and looked, and there was no-one even close to this particular donor that we really, really fell in love with. William, one day, said 'look, why don't we just consider her again?' So we did, and when we came back we called our agents – the egg donor agency – and said we'd like to go ahead with …

> Interviewer: Because you felt so attached to her?
>
> Dian: Yeah, yeah.
>
> Interviewer: So then how did you handle the Tay-Sachs? Did you get William tested?
>
> Dian: Yeah, William was tested. We just thought, well, we don't fall in love with people based on them being perfect, so I guess it – from that point of view. As a result, here she is [the baby].

The language of love and its association with imperfection is interesting because it returns the clinical and contractual context of the use of ART to the motivation for the kinds of choices that are being made in relation to family formation. Here, Dian expresses an incapacity for satisfaction in relation to other potential donors in the context of love – expressed through the fairy tale of *The Princess and the Pea* – a tale which is both about proving the authenticity of Princesshood (here standing in for motherhood) and the appropriate object of love for the Prince. In our case however, it is the authenticity of the donor as the appropriate object of love for Dian and William, the intending parents, that is established.[4] Dian makes the egg donor the recipient of love and as such normalizes her genetic status – 'we don't fall in love with people based on them being perfect'. In this sense Dian is prepared to accept the donor's carrier status even though it may be passed on to the future child.[5] The development of this love relationship stands in contrast to the moral framework that typically animates bioethicists. They argue that there is a

> morally relevant difference between donor conception and reproduction between partners. Partners want to reproduce together, whereas people needing donor gametes do not (in most cases) want to reproduce only with this donor. And whereas partners cannot be replaced, donors, as providers of gametes are replaceable. (Dondorp et al. 2014, 4)

In Dian's case, the fungibility of donors was absent because of the way she constructed her relationship to the donor inside the love relationship that originally motivated reproduction in the first place. For Goodley, desire 'is a force through which we connect with one another' (165) and disability studies invites us to rethink how and what we desire as we use technological means to create new forms of kin and relationality. Dian's experience with her donor exemplifies the possibility of desiring new non-normative becomings and belongings.

In a second example, Olivia, who initially attempted to use her own eggs but was unsuccessful, was the recipient of both donor oocytes and sperm. Olivia decided to use sex selection because she did not want to have a boy and risk the possibility of having an autistic child.[6] Olivia's brother had two sons she described as 'borderline autistic but highly ADHD.' Olivia sought out an American clinic where she could have genetic testing. By day six when Olivia attended the clinic for the transfer she had six healthy male embryos, one female embryo that tested positive for trisomy 21 (Down syndrome) and four embryos of unknown sex that had been sent for testing without results. Keen to have a girl, she chose not to have one of the six known 'healthy' male embryos transferred but rather to have two of the untested embryos transferred. She did not contemplate transferring the only identified female embryo which she described as 'abnormal'. She went on:

Olivia: Yes, and so I elected to have transfer of two of the four unknown sex embryos.

Interviewer: Oh okay ….

Olivia: Yeah, because they explained to me that if they were abnormal they would not likely work and there was, obviously in my mind there was a higher chance that one of the embryos – because I had two transferred – that one of them or two of them maybe might be female, versus knowing that the other ones are all male. So I received the results the following day and it turned out that the two that they transferred were both healthy male embryos [laughs] and the other two that they didn't transfer were abnormal.

…

> So at that point I spent the following two weeks coming to terms with it and decided that I really wanted a healthy baby more than I wanted a daughter and that having a family is more important to me than anything.

As noted above these kinds of choices and decisions are made in embedded and contingent contexts. In Olivia's case her relationship to her brother and his children had initially driven her quest for a girl. But, her desire for a girl, once established as a choice she might make, appears to have cemented as separate from any disability avoidance strategy. Once, however, that choice bumps up against the contingency and context of her own reproductive options she reframes her desire and normalizes her disappointment. This is evidenced in her interview when Olivia speaks about reading internet forums on 'gender disappointment'. She says:

> There's actually a lot of information about gender disappointment online and so I've read a lot of people's stories and realised that it is unrealistic to expect that you can get what you want all of the time [laughs].

Much later on she says:

> It just emotionally helps you to deal with it all the way through because you're able to then say okay, well there was a girl but it wasn't a healthy embryo.

Goodley argues that '[t]he normal category exists not as a simple fixed position of humanity but as a register, a subject position, a preferred way of living life and a phenomenon of ableist cultures' (118). Thus, while this example might seem more appropriately placed in an article discussing the ethics of gender selection, we have included it here because as Goodley notes 'normals' are each marked by differences associated with gender, class, sexuality, age and ethnicity (118). Therefore though we might accept that '[b]eing normal is one of society's preferred ontological states and moral categories,' (118) we argue that the category of normal is a shifting and flexible signifier. Olivia's imagining of gender disappointment then substantiates Goodley's point that neither normalcy nor disability are simply about having an embodied difference but are inflected by social and cultural readings of difference including how they are gendered.

In contrast to Olivia, Cybil, an interviewee who diagnosed herself with Aspergers, and believes her son born through traditional surrogacy [where the surrogate is also the egg donor] has autism spectrum disorder made it clear that the possibility of ASD from her egg donor was not something that raised concerns. Asked about the kinds of information she received about the medical history of her donor she replies:

Cybil: I think family history of cancer and heart disease, stroke, diabetes and whatever, but either positive or negative. Emmeline [the egg donor and surrogate] disclosed that she had ADHD and there was a history of autism in her family, which we are now seeing probably in Louie. [Cybil's son] He's getting ready to do his ASD assessment.

Interviewer: Okay, so is that Autism Spectrum Disorder?

Cybil: Yeah.

…

Interviewer: Okay … it sounds like it was an expectation that it was not unlikely?

Cybil: Yeah, it was not unlikely and it was a risk we took, so okay, well he could have a chance of having anything. Probably the thing that I was most apprehensive about was if it had a genetic disorder that was compatible with life such as Down syndrome or anything else, … It's hard to know really at the end of the day, but we were pretty convinced that we really didn't want to have a special needs child, because we didn't have any energy left after the end of the whole process that we'd gone through.

Referring to the surrogate, Cybil indicates that she would not have agreed to an abortion and says: 'so we had to roll that dice and it was very nerve-wracking. It was like well, we either choose to take this risk or we don't become parents'. Asked whether she viewed this decision as hard Cybil replies: 'It was just one after the other of massive compromise and letting your values go so that you could get to the end of the journey'. Again we see a clear sense in which desires bump up against contingency and normalcy is reformulated accordingly. Indeed, we see an interesting disconnect between contemporary medical approaches to disability and that of the intending parent. Whereas clinics view their role as limiting the risk of disability, the intending parent appears prepared 'to roll the dice' and deal with contingency.

In this case Cybil viewed ASD as a risk to be taken compared with Down syndrome. This bears out our argument that ideas of normalcy are shifting and flexible and circulate around familial fitting in. Rather than trying to achieve a child with no disabilities or genetic conditions recipients are interested in family coherence and appear to determine normalcy relationally. In Cybil's case, Autism didn't challenge that coherence but Down syndrome did.

This notion is also borne out in the experience of Scarlet (a donor, rather than a donor recipient).[7] She was denied the ability to donate her embryos because they were determined to be genetically affected. Scarlet's genetic condition had a 100 percent transmission rate, but she had identified potential recipients for her embryos who were aware of her genetic condition and wished to receive the embryos notwithstanding. The clinic, however, refused to facilitate the transfer on the basis that it was not in the best interests of the resulting children. Scarlet then put her case (unsuccessfully) before the ethics committee of her clinic. In her interview, she remarked on how confronting it was to be told what amounted to the view that it was not in the best interests of her own children who bore the same condition and were conceived at the same time as the embryos she was seeking to donate, to be born. She said:

my children are immensely loved and showered with everything they need and they're well built up, well cared for and it's hard to say that it was not in their best interests to even exist.

Scarlet's experience, and that of the potential recipients who wanted to transfer her donated embryos, illustrate starkly Davis's argument that disability occupies the 'state of exception'(8) in a regime of normalcy, here enforced by an infertility industry and bioethics regime. But where Davis argues that in conditions of normality construed as diversity, disability falls outside choice (14) and is not chooseable (11), the story of Scarlet suggests otherwise, at least from the point of view of prospective users of ART and recipients of donor gametes and embryos. While Scarlet's aim of donating has been thwarted by ableist policies and practices, by a misfit between the social and cultural devaluation of those who share Scarlet's characteristics and their reproductive aspirations, her expressed desire and that of her potential donor recipients to reproduce that which others regard as unfit to come into being, indicate an active embracing of disability – what we would call diverse normalcy from the point of view of Scarlet and her potential recipients. But what this example makes urgently apparent as well, is that being able to choose against idealized normalcy and embrace diverse normalcy in the creation of one's family, to give material effect to one's choices, is unsurprisingly, contingent and thoroughly political – like the concept of normalcy itself.

Conclusion: who decides who fits?

The idea of the 'normal,' as we have stated in this article, is both a descriptive and prescriptive concept. The prescriptive element in particular is contingent on scientific data coupled with social and cultural explanations to define its content. It follows that the normal is also understood as one side of an oppositional binary, in contrast to the 'abnormal' or disability (Goodley 2014) or, as Davis would state, disability is the exception to the norm of diversity. Thus, normalcy and abnormalcy/disability exist in a relationship of co-constitution. This is not to suggest a permanence to their respective content, but to propose that constructions of normalcy are generally thought to exist against that which an (inferior) Other (disabled/abnormal) is conceptualized. (Goodley 2014, 88).

While agreeing with much of this understanding of normalcy and its relationship to abnormality and disability, in this article, we have offered a more textured and contextual account building on the specific perspectives of interview subjects engaged in choosing gametes or embryos for reproductive purposes. Employing the concept of diverse normality we demonstrate how, in the constrained and contingent context of selecting gamete and embryo donors, some recipients deploy an expansive conception of normalcy, making a reproductive choice that would not otherwise have been contemplated. Moreover, as we have argued, in the context of choosing donor gametes or embryos for purposes of ART, what is normal for some recipients may rely less on assumptions about what it is to be healthy or fit and indeed more on what it means to 'fit in'. Yet for others, the contours of diverse normalcy include an active embracing of disability, apparently breaking down the binary altogether. Garland-Thomson states that 'to fit and be fit, … is to be ensconced in an environment that sustains the particular form, function and needs of one's body' (600). It is clear from our research that for some people fitting in – being normal – is enhanced or delimited not by difference or deviation from some external standard of what is good and right but by love and desire and a matrix of relationships.

Notes

1. The larger project is with Professors Millbank, Stuhmcke and Jackson (ARC DP 15010157: *Regulating Relations*). We refer briefly to earlier research Karpin conducted with Professors Millbank and Stuhmcke (DP ARC DP 986213: *Enhancing Reproductive Opportunity*). Ethics approval was granted by the University of Technology Human Research Ethics Committee for both projects.
2. All interviews use pseudonyms to preserve anonymity and confidentiality.
3. It is worth noting here that the decision to find an unaffected donor is based on the view that donors, unlike intimate partners are fungible and therefore even carrier status is to be avoided. See Dondorp et al. 2014 discussed below.
4. Notably Dian knows the donor only through her communications with her on Yahoo and there are no names exchanged. She is both unknown and known and yet the relationship is characterized in terms of love.

5. While William's test for Tay Sachs is negative, there is still a 25 percent possibility that Dian and William's child will be a carrier of Tay Sachs because the egg donor was a Tay Sachs carrier and the condition is autosomal recessive.
6. It should be noted that there is strong disagreement among the scientific community regarding the association of ASD and maleness. See Karpin 2015.
7. Scarlet was a participant interviewed for the Enhancing Reproductive Opportunity study that preceded the study in which our other case studies were interviewed. Further details of the earlier research can be found in a special issue of the *Journal of Law and Medicine* Volume 20 (4). See specifically Millbank et al. 2013. See also Millbank (2016).

Acknowledgement

The authors wish to thank their co-investigators Professors Jenni Millbank and Anita Stuhmcke from the University of Technology Sydney and Emily Jackson from London School of Economics. We would also like to thank Michaela Stockey-Bridge, Miranda Kaye and Odelia Bay for their research assistance.

Disclosure statement

No potential conflict of interest was reported by the authors.

Funding

This article is funded by ARC DP 15010157 Regulating Relations: Forming Families Inside and Outside Laws Reach.

ORCID

Isabel Karpin (iD) http://orcid.org/0000-0001-9326-3421

References

ACOG (American Congress of Obstetricians and Gynecologists). 2011. Committee Opinion No. 486: Update on Carrier Screening for Cystic Fibrosis. *Obstetrics & Gynecology* 117 (4): 1028–1031. doi:10.1097/AOG.0b013e31821922c2.
ARC DP: *Enhancing Reproductive Opportunity* (ARC DP0986213 Chief Investigators: Professors Jenni Millbank, Anita Stuhmcke, and Isabel Karpin (UTS)).
ARC DP: *Regulating Relations: Forming Families Inside and Outside Laws Reach.* (ARC DP 15010157 Chief Investigators: Professors Jenni Millbank, Isabel Karpin, Anita Stuhmcke (UTS); Partner Investigators: Professors Emily Jackson (LSE) and Roxanne Mykitiuk (Osgoode Hall)) HRC approval UTS reference No. 2015000094.

Commission Directive 2006/17/EC of 8 February 2006 implementing directive 2004/23/EC of the European Parliament and of the Council as regards certain technical requirements for the donation, procurement and testing of human tissues and cells, Annex III, 3.6. http://eur-lex.europa.eu/eli/dir/2006/17/oj.

Daniels, Cynthia R., and Erin Heidt-Forsythe. 2012. "Gendered Eugenics and the Problematic of Free Market Reproductive Technologies: Sperm and Egg Donation in the United States." *Signs: Journal of Women in Culture and Society* 37 (3): 719–747.

Davis, Lennard J. 2013. *The End of Normal – Identity in a Biocultural Era*. Ann Arbour: University of Michigan Press.

Dondorp, W., G. De Wert, G. Pennings, F. Shenfield, P. Devroey, B. Tarlatzis, P. Barri, et al. 2014. "ESHRE Task Force on Ethics and Law 21: Genetic Screening of Gamete Donors: Ethical Issues." *Human Reproduction* 29 (7): 1353–1359. doi:10.1093/humrep/deu111.

Garland-Thomson, Rosemarie. 2011. "Misfits: A Feminist Materialist Disability Concept." *Hypatia* 26 (3): 591–609.

Ginsburg, Faye, and Rayna Rapp. 2015. "Making Disability Count: Demography, Futurity, and the Making of Disability Publics." *Somatosphere*, May 11. http://somatosphere.net/?p=10236.

Goodley, Dan. 2014. *Dis/ability Studies – Theorising Disablism and Ableism*. London: Routledge.

Karpin, I. 2015. "The Regulation of PGD for Medical Sex Selection and the Gendering of Disability in the UK and Australia." In *Revisiting the Regulation of Human Fertilisation and Embryology*, edited by K. Horsey, 185–199. London: Routledge.

McGowan, Michelle L., Deborah Cho, and Richard R. Sharp. 2013. "The Changing Landscape of Carrier Screening: Expanding Technology and Options?" *Health Matrix Clevel* 23 (1): 15–33.

Millbank, Jenni. 2016. "Reflecting the 'Human Nature' of IVF Embryos: Disappearing Women in Ethics, Law and Fertility Practice." *Journal of Law and the Biosciences*. doi:10.1093/jlb/lsw058.

Millbank, Jenni, Eloise Chandler, Isabel Karpin, and Anita Stuhmcke. 2013. "Embryo Donation for Reproductive Use in Australia." *Journal of Law and Medicine* 20 (4): 789–810.

Nordqvist, Petra. 2014. "Bringing Kinship into Being: Connectedness, Donor Conception and Lesbian Parenthood." *Sociology* 48 (2): 268–283.

Payne, Jenny Gunnarsson. 2015. "Reproduction in Transition: Cross-boarder Egg Donation, Biodesirability and New Reproductive Subjectivities on the European Fertility Market." *Gender Place and Culture* 22 (1): 107–122.

Ravelingien, A., V. Provoost, E. Wyverkens, A. Buysse, P. De Sutter, and G. Pennings. 2015. "Lesbian Couples' Views about and Experiences of Not Being Able to Choose Their Sperm Donor." *Culture, Health & Sexuality: An International Journal for Research, Intervention and Care* 17 (5): 592–606. doi:10.1080/13691058.2014.979883.

Reh, Andrea, Alana Amarosa, Frederick Licciardi, Lewis Krey, Alan S. Berkeley, and Lisa Kump. 2010. "Evaluating the Necessity of Universal Screening of Prospective Oocyte Donors Using Enhanced Genetic and Psychological Testing." *Human Reproduction* 25 (9): 2290–2304.

Taylor, K., and R. Mykitiuk. 2001. "Genetics, Normalcy and Disability." *ISUMA: Canadian Journal of Policy Research/Revue Canadienne De Recherche Sur Les Politiques* 2 (3): 65–71.

Wienke, Sara, Kimberly Brown, Meagan Farmer, and Charlie Strange. 2014. "Expanded Carrier Screening Panels – Does Bigger Mean Better?" *Journal of Community Genetics* 5 (2): 191–198.

Eccentricity: the case for undermining legal categories of disability and normalcy

Karen O'Connell

ABSTRACT

Disability discrimination laws are directed at protecting people with disabilities, including people with 'disturbed' behaviour, or behaviour that is a manifestation of a disability, from unfavourable treatment. Yet, in doing so, discrimination laws contribute to the creation of a stigmatized and seemingly static legal category of disability. In response, this paper presents eccentricity as a 'border' region between disability and normalcy, one that can disturb the strict and stigmatizing boundary between these artificially separate categories of identity. Eccentricity, understood as a set of socially unusual or unconventional behaviours and traits, is a heightened version of the quirks and idiosyncrasies we all share, and reveals the interconnection of disability and normalcy. This paper asks whether current legal and biomedical definitions of disability, especially under disability discrimination law, have unnecessarily eradicated this rich and destabilizing category of identity and behaviour. Is law complicit in the narrowing of what it means to be 'normal', the expansion of what it means to be 'disabled' and the destruction of what would otherwise connect those two imagined states of being? This paper examines the way that law deals with eccentricity and argues that it is a concept that can potentially enrich our approach to discrimination law.

Introduction

Bea Miles, 'eccentric' and 'street character' (Allen 1986), famed for tormenting taxi drivers and giving recitations of Shakespeare in the streets of Sydney in the 1930s through to the 1960s, had a complicated and sometimes illuminating relationship to law. Constantly under the scrutiny of police for traffic violations and non-payment of fines, the homeless Bea, in her original writings (Miles 193–), demonstrates a pragmatic fear of law in its punitive aspects.[1] Her account of her travels around Australia is titled 'I leave in a hurry', as she hitches and steals rides out of Sydney to avoid several warrants out for her arrest, easily executed given her notoriety. At the same time, Bea does not submit to legal authority, preferring either to avoid its jurisdiction, or to directly challenge both legal and social rules.[2] One of the many stories about her defiance of convention is that she would sit and smoke outside a Sydney bank – at a time where women did not smoke in public – under a sign that read: 'Gentlemen must refrain from smoking' (Elder 2012).

In this article, I interrogate the place that eccentricity and eccentrics occupy in law, particularly discrimination law. To be eccentric is to be outside of the perceived mainstream of society, not conforming to common rules or standards in a usual or expected way. Eccentricity can include minor social infractions such as dressing in odd ways[3] or not observing rules of etiquette, but it can also include passionate views or interests that are, in their intensity or single-minded focus, outside a perceived norm.[4] Embedded as it is in the social milieu of a specific time and place, eccentricity is a complex, shifting notion, inevitably shaped by co-existing assumptions about class, race and gender. Here, I am focusing on the way that eccentricity, understood as behaviours that are socially unusual or non-conforming, challenges law and categories of disability and normalcy. Eccentricity is not generally thought of, in law or society, as a disability, yet it also is not entirely 'normal' to be eccentric. It is this in-between state – of 'sane whimsy or crazy sanity' ("The sad state of eccentricity" 1969) – that is valuable to rethinking categories in law. Eccentricity demonstrates that the categories of disability and normalcy, treated in popular culture and in law as if they are distinct and opposing, are in fact intertwined. Hard and separate categories of disability and normalcy create material harm by relegating certain people to a stigmatized status of 'disability' and masking the spectrum of abilities and vulnerabilities that exist in all individuals. Rather than retain this definitional commitment to hard categories, we should be softening and expanding all of these categories, so that we have the broadest possible definition of 'disability', the richest and most diverse sense of what might be considered 'normal', and the most expansive grey area in between.

The idea that normalcy and disability are intimately connected may, however, be under threat by an increasingly biomedical approach to challenging behaviour. Bea Miles, who reportedly carried with her a declaration of her sanity written by several prominent doctors (Lewis 1992), could now potentially be protected under disability discrimination laws. In fact, she, along with many other public figures of the past (Kalb 2016), has been retrospectively 'diagnosed' with a disability, in her case with ongoing brain-based behavioural effects from a bout of encephalitis in her youth.[5] With the expansion of neuroscientific and genetic knowledge in particular, combined with psychiatric explanations for various 'disordered' behaviours, biomedical descriptions of behaviour are now commonplace.[6] As more people with unusual behaviours fall under the umbrella of a range of possible 'disorders', they are offered expanded treatment possibilities along with more protective legal and policy measures. For example, discrimination law offers redress to people with unusual behaviours arising from a disability if, for example, they are denied access to public life or goods and services.[7] Pathologizing certain behaviours, therefore, has a recuperative value. However, my contention is that when social and cultural descriptors of identity such as 'eccentricity' are lost there is a corresponding loss of richness and nuance in what we include within the spectrum of 'normal' human behaviour.

Traditionally, law has treated eccentric behaviours as existing within an expansive category of 'normal'. While law is called upon to police and protect innocent others against behaviours that are harmful or threatening, behaviours that are benign or merely odd are in principle outside of the concern of law.[8] Case law distinguishes the 'merely eccentric'[9] from the mentally ill, the incapacitated and the dangerous.[10] Eccentricity can thus be taken as evidence of 'normality'. Nevertheless, it can also be a sign of social or behavioural impairment, and thus evidence of 'disability',[11] and in fact, eccentric behaviour attracts regulation, sometimes even in its most punitive legal forms. Law thus has a fluctuating response to eccentric behaviours, both punitive and protective.

In considering the legal response to eccentric behaviours, I focus in particular on discrimination law, which is directed in part at protecting people with disabilities that manifest behaviourally. What are the anti-discrimination protections, if any, that can be offered people who are eccentric? And what, if anything, might the concept of 'eccentricity' offer disability discrimination law? I use the examples of two discrimination law cases, *Ondrich v Kookaburra Park Eco-Village* [2009] FMCA 260 (*Ondrich*), concerning a woman with an unusual dependence on her pet dog, and *Slattery v Manningham City Council* [2013] VCAT 1869 (*Slattery*), a case involving a man with an overly intense interest in his local community and council affairs. Using these, and other illustrative examples, I put forward two arguments. First, that the definition of disability in discrimination law should be widened so that it is able to encompass eccentricity if people whose behaviour is outside the 'normal' want to take advantage of legal protections. Secondly, that the need for a definition could be removed altogether, with the law focusing on the exclusionary and unreasonable practices of public institutions, rather than concerning itself with the bodily or behavioural attributes of the excluded individual. Claiming back the odd and unusual from a monolithic biomedical account of identity, I also argue that eccentricity can enrich our concept of normalcy while reinstating the normalcy of disability.

Eccentric or unusual behaviour before the law

My interest in unusual or eccentric behaviours arose out of an earlier research project on disability discrimination law,[12] when it became clear that inadequate attention was paid to the situation of people with benign but unusual behaviours that brought them before the law in negative ways.[13] These people were most often impacted by criminal laws, but at times they were also excluded from premises or otherwise discriminated against because of these benign behaviours.

The South Australian Supreme Court wrote in *R v Marafioti* (2014) 118 SASR 511 at [13] that '[b]ehaviours which might appear odd or different to some should not too quickly be associated with illegality. Eccentricities should not be magnets for the exercise of police powers.' Yet, when people with unusual behaviours encounter the criminal law, it often is because acting unusually on its own attracts suspicion, as in the following example of a client of a legal service who had a string collection that he added to as he went about daily life.

> We had one man who, he was in the habit of carrying this huge ball of string around with him. Which was actually something he was working on, just a ball of string. That attracted attention to him and then he was charged, I think, with having scissors in his bag, or having a weapon. (Interview with a disability advocate, 2014)

Having a disability of any sort can also mean that associated behaviours, however harmless, that breach social conventions attract this suspicion. For example, one man told me how his hearing impairment led to negative social judgements:

> I've had people say to me that 'you're very intense'. Because in group situations I tend to stare at faces a lot because if I turn my head away, I can't hear properly … It's embarrassing. I'm an intelligent person … [T]he fact is society has these assumptions and they just assume that if you're staring at somebody … you might have some ulterior motive. (Interview with a disability advocate, 2014)

This same interviewee described a situation where both the criminal law and discrimination law were potentially engaged. He entered a shop, and received a phone call, which he was able to hear and respond to through his hearing aid. Speaking to himself in the back of the shop, the shop worker assumed that he was hearing voices and had a mental disorder. She called the police to escort the man from her shop, and he had to persuade them that he did not have schizophrenia. Legal practitioners who advise or represent people with disabilities that manifest in unusual behaviours report this constant suspicion about their clients and the negative scrutiny of law.

> Lots of our clients – might have an unusual gait or slightly slurred speech that certainly gets them in trouble with the police, they get searched a lot. But often clients get kicked out of premises, discrimination generally I think, excluded from places or services. It's not from assaulting people but it's often perhaps … about how they present, often they get mistaken for being intoxicated. (Interview with a legal practitioner, 2014)

> [I]t's just anyone who is unusual and stands out. Or who other people find scary, they're overly friendly or they're too close. That might also bring negative attention down on them. (Interview with a disability advocate, 2014)

Other examples included a boy who needed to chew gum to stay focused in class (Interview, with a disability advocate, 2014) and a primary school-aged girl excluded from her school swimming carnival in part because of her 'inappropriate' touching of a teacher after tracing the patterns on her skirt with her fingers (Interview, with a legal practitioner, 2014). Since it is often less clear that unusual behaviours constitute or are underpinned by disabilities, they are less likely to fall within the protection of disability discrimination laws, which in theory should prevent people being excluded from premises or denied services on the basis of behaviour that is, or is a symptom or manifestation of, a disability.[14]

Where there is no 'grey' area in social attitudes towards behaviours that fall outside of a norm but could still be seen as part of a spectrum of 'normal', suspicion, undue scrutiny and regulation follow. Thinking of these behaviours as 'eccentric' allows for this grey area. Eccentricity provides a useful tool to break down the hard categories that operate in discrimination law to stigmatize disability and impoverish normalcy.

Eccentricity, disability and normalcy in discrimination law

Eccentricity, as well as being presumptively outside the scope of legal regulation, is often described as a trait that has some social benefit, and must be tolerated by others, despite any attendant difficulties. So, for example, courts and other legal decision-making bodies have pointed out that '[e]ven though it may be upsetting to live next door to an eccentric, that, in itself, does not give a cause of action in nuisance.' (*Bathurst City Council v Saban (No 2)* (1986) 58 LGRA 201 at 208) or that they must 'avoid penalising a practitioner for eccentricity, unorthodoxy, unpopularity, curmudgeonly conduct or even offensive personality traits that may from time to time make life more difficult for colleagues.' (*Coroneos v Medical Board* [2001] QCA 268 at [31]). In *Australian Broadcasting Corporation v Lenah Game Meats Pty Ltd* (2001) 208 CLR 199 at [322] the High Court elevates eccentricity alongside other high social goods, when it quotes with approval an American writer, Rosen, on the contemporary loss of privacy '... we are beginning to learn how much may be lost in a culture of transparency: the capacity for creativity and eccentricity, for the development of self and soul, for understanding, friendship, and even love.'

Eccentricity is thus mourned by commentators who believe that despite its social value, it is in decline. As early as 1969, Time Magazine was lamenting the demise of eccentricity, attributing it to the rise in 'permissiveness'. 'Eccentricity means, literally, to be off-centre. But in the permissive society, where almost anything goes, eccentricity no longer stands out against any dominant "center."' ("The sad state of eccentricity." *Time*, March 14, 1969.).

In this example, from the social upheavals of the 1960s, the perception is that eccentricity has been absorbed into 'normalcy'. Today, eccentricity is further diminishing as a socially significant description of personality and a quality attributed to unusual individuals, but I argue that it is because eccentricity is now being subsumed into an expanding category of disability as more and more traits are seen as biologically determined. As one of my interviewees stated, of children with mild traits from the autism spectrum: 'There are certainly kids who would ten years ago have just been quirky ... [but who] now have an autism diagnosis' (Interview with a disability advocate, 2014).

Eccentric behaviour is thus increasingly seen as more pathological than iconoclastic. Unusual behaviours are associated with a range of disabilities, including schizophrenia, bipolar disorder, conduct disorder, general personality disorder, autism spectrum disorder and Tourette syndrome.[15] As more socially unfavourable or challenging traits are able to be characterized as a disorder or disability, eccentric qualities look more like symptoms than traits (Allen 2014, 33).

The impact of this shift to biomedical descriptions of behaviour on disability discrimination law is potentially profound (Karpin and O'Connell 2015). In social and legal accounts of identity, definitions of 'disability' are contrasted with a (silent) category of 'normalcy', and each of these categories operate to reinforce stigma. A binary way of thinking about identity has been robustly critiqued by feminist and postmodernist philosophers for creating a system that relies on an intrinsic devaluing of one side of the (male/female; black/white; young/old) binary (Cixous 1986; Derrida 1972). In discrimination law, the devalued binary is set against an opposing category that is always the same: 'normal'. With its emphasis on redressing stigmatized harm rather than attending to the privilege that is its natural counterpart (Gaze 2002, 336), in discrimination law the raced body is the black body and the sexed body is a woman's body, leaving white and male bodies unscrutinized, as the 'norm' (O'Connell 2008; Thornton 2002). For example, sexual harassment cases can be a litany of sexualized descriptions of women's bodies, while the male harasser's body remains invisible, thus reinforcing the material conditions of the harassment (Thornton 2002). Similarly, a person with disability is not held in contrast to an 'able-bodied' individual but a 'normal' body. Being defined in contrast to a 'normal' person has a particularly damaging impact, since 'able-bodied' is at least specific in its contestable claim, while 'normal' is diffuse and totalizing. Built into Australia's human rights system[16] was the definition of disability as 'not normal' that came from the UN Declaration of the Rights of Disabled Persons:

> The term "disabled person" means any person unable to ensure by himself or herself, wholly or partly, the necessities of a normal individual and/or social life, as a result of deficiency, either congenital or not, in his or her physical or mental capabilities.[17]

Since the Declaration, the federal *Disability Discrimination Act 1992* (DDA), and the Convention on the Rights of Persons with Disabilities have adopted much more expansive definitions of disability that do not have the same explicit reliance on 'normalcy'.[18] Nevertheless, discrimination law, with its emphasis on the stigmatized body, still indirectly reinforces the creation of a 'normal' identity.

As biomedical descriptions expand what might be defined as a disability, they thus expand what falls within this stigmatized but protected category in discrimination law. This has the benefit of potentially increasing the people who can benefit from discrimination law protections, however, in practice and as I describe below, the existence of these protections are no guarantee that they will be exercised. In addition, any expansion of disability (while the hard categories of disability/normalcy persist) will correspondingly shrink, and thus impoverish, our idea of what counts as 'normal'. When normal is construed as 'normal species functioning', using a statistical average to determine a purportedly acceptable range of human traits, this 'secure[s] the social positioning of the disabled as abnormal and deviant' (Taylor and Mykiyiuk 2001, 67). A robust acceptance of 'eccentricity' can assist in building a richer sense of disability and normalcy by messing with the essentially artificial division between them. Eccentricity can incorporate behaviours that otherwise could fall within an expanded idea of disability but can also be seen as an expanded version of normal.

Case studies: eccentric behaviours in disability discrimination case law

Behaviours that could be characterized as eccentric arise in disability discrimination law under the umbrella of various disabilities, from autism spectrum disorders to anxiety. In the *Ondrich* case, the applicant, Libuse Ondrich, had become intensely attached to a dog she had purchased to alleviate her depression and anxiety. Her reliance on the dog, Punta, to manage her emotional life was such that at times she could only fall asleep sitting in a chair with the dog in her lap. Unfortunately, the by-laws of the community title 'eco-village' where she and her family lived forbade pet cats and dogs. Ms. Ondrich was eventually ordered by the Body Corporate of the eco-village to remove the dog. She was so devastated at the prospect of being separated from Punta that she left her husband and two young children, and went to live with the dog in a women's crisis shelter. She reported that at this time she was suicidal. For almost a year, Ms. Ondrich rented premises away from the eco-village, in order not to be separated from Punta.

Eventually, Ms. Ondrich returned to the eco-village to be with her family, concealing Punta on her lot. She kept the dog hidden for just over two years, when a neighbour heard the dog and reported Ms. Ondrich to the Body Corporate, and she was again asked to remove her. In an attempt not to be separated from Punta, she brought a case against the eco-village, arguing that she had been discriminated against on the grounds of disability.

The DDA protects people with disabilities, as defined in Section 4 of the Act, from being discriminated against in the provision of goods and services and facilities. The definition of disability, as with the Victorian legislation discussed below, includes 'behaviour that is a symptom or manifestation of the disability.' The DDA also, in Section 9, protects people who have an assistance animal from being discriminated against because of that animal.

That Ms. Ondrich had a disability is accepted by the respondent in the case, although the nature of her disability is contested. The respondent disputed Ms. Ondrich's claim that she had Asperger's Syndrome and 'severe' depression, although it accepted that she experienced anxiety and that she had a panic disorder. The medical evidence was inconsistent in part but the magistrate decided that Ms. Ondrich did have anxiety and the panic disorder, as well as a 'low grade' depression. In stating that he was satisfied that Ms. Ondrich was also affected by Asperger's syndrome, the magistrate pointed out that the symptoms would make her 'seem quite awkward and unusual and eccentric', which is 'consistent with my observations of the applicant at trial.'

Although Ms. Ondrich was successful in demonstrating a disability, she was unsuccessful in arguing discrimination, for several reasons. Like many discrimination law cases, hers foundered on technical shortcomings. Although she demonstrated a complete reliance on Punta, Ms. Ondrich had not demonstrated (as required by Section 9 of the DDA) that Punta was *specifically* trained to have this effect on her. Punta had received only obedience training, and thus was not an animal 'trained to assist the aggrieved person to alleviate the effects of the disability' (cf. *Mulligan v Virgin Australia Pty Ltd* [2015] FCAFC 130). Ms. Ondrich lost the case and, in addition, was ordered to pay the eco-village's legal costs.

In this case, Ms. Ondrich's attachment to her dog was only considered in light of her disabilities. If she could not argue that she had a disability, her situation would not attract the potential protection of the DDA. The earlier examples of 'unusual' behaviours, from collecting string to chewing gum, are unlikely to ever make it to court for this reason. Yet, without the disabilities attributed to Ms. Ondrich, it is still imaginable that a person might grow emotionally reliant on her dog in a way that was unusual but not associated with a disability. A harmless obsession with a dog, or a multitude of cats, is a characteristic often associated with eccentrics, as, in fact, are obsessions in general (Marcus 1995, 50). In addition, intense neediness, emotional fragility or dependency are human emotions which most of us, in a life fully lived, will experience at some point. Why, then, must someone meet a definition of 'disability' in order for these experiences to be afforded legal protection? The question of disability seems superfluous in this case. Without the step of proving disability, someone like Ms. Ondrich could, for example, simply argue that she possesses an emotional need for her dog that would be debilitating if not met. This also raises a bigger question, addressed further below, of whether we need definitional hurdles of disability in discrimination law at all.

Ms. Ondrich and her dog did not get a happy ending to their story, but one of the rare 'unusual behaviour' cases that has been sympathetic to the complainant is *Slattery*. If Ms. Ondrich's case demonstrates unusual vulnerability and reliance on an animal, Mr. Slattery's case involves an excess of passion in his dealings with his local community. Mr. Slattery wrote thousands of letters of complaint to his local Council over a period of fifteen years, as well as using 'offensive' and 'inappropriate' language in his dealing with council workers, insulting them and making unsubstantiated allegations of corruption, along with a few acts of aggression. Mr. Slattery was driven by a passionate concern for health and safety issues, and was described by the Tribunal as having 'an ardent desire to be involved in his community, to make a contribution.' He also had a 'compulsion' to monitor health and safety in the community, 'a strong interest in local government, and strong views about local government accountability' ([56]). His constant, compulsive contact with council workers led to Mr. Slattery's indefinite ban from any Council owned, occupied or managed premises. Distressed about his exclusion from community facilities, Mr. Slattery alleged that the ban constituted disability discrimination in goods and services under the Victorian *Equal Opportunity Act* 2010.

Mr. Slattery had multiple diagnosed disabilities: bipolar disorder, attention deficit hyperactive disorder and post-traumatic stress disorder. In addition, he had a hearing impairment and sleep apnoea, and had recently had a stroke, which left him with an acquired brain injury. However, some of his behaviours, particularly his compulsive contact with council members, could not be easily traced to these particular disabilities. This raised the question of whether his behaviour was a manifestation of his disabilities or whether he was a person who behaved in unusual and compulsive ways, and who happened to have unrelated disabilities. Medical evidence was scant because Mr. Slattery was not receiving any treatment for his disabilities. In the end, a doctor who had treated Mr. Slattery in the past, gave additional oral evidence that Mr. Slattery had a compulsive disorder, which was sufficient to show that his behaviour was arising from a disability and therefore fell within the ambit of the legislation ([82]).

Satisfied on the question of disability, the Tribunal found that the ban on Mr. Slattery was 'disproportionately extensive and unspecified', 'blunt, broad and insufficiently tailored', 'indefinite, and … incorporates no transparent process of review' ([131]). The Tribunal found that discrimination had occurred and the parties were sent for compulsory conciliation to find another solution.

There are two issues arising from the *Slattery* case that are important for considering eccentricity in disability discrimination law. While Ms. Ondrich's attachment to her dog did not cause anyone else any harm, the issue being her non-compliance itself, Mr. Slattery is a difficult, offensive and sometimes aggressive man. In evoking the protections of one area of discrimination law, disability discrimination law, Mr. Slattery transgressed others, at least in spirit. He made abusive sexist and racist remarks to council workers, harassed them and inflicted vague threats, making people uncomfortable in their workplace. Yet these very behaviours, that are evocative of sexual harassment and race discrimination case law, constitute Mr. Slattery's disability, as the Tribunal member clearly states: 'I find that the combination of symptoms – compulsion to complain, irrational and anti social behaviours, aggressivity, behaviour that is considered objectionable and unwarranted – constitute the relevant symptoms and manifestations of disability … ([82])

In order to transgress social rules, the eccentric is arguably less sensitive to the impact of his or her variant behaviour on others. In fact, one commentator defines eccentricity in part as a heightened awareness of the role of society in shaping the self, combined with a lack of self-consciousness of one's individual actions (Marcus 1995). In other words, eccentrics are more likely to behave offensively, being less aware of their own foibles and less concerned about their impact on others. A question that needs to be answered more fully, but should at least be raised here, is whether racist and sexist abuse should be accepted as a 'symptom' for the purposes of equality laws. While, as I argue, eccentricity should be accepted within an expanded idea of normalcy, there is nevertheless a question of fairness to those who are impacted by eccentric behaviour, possibly due to vulnerabilities of their own. As the Council noted in *Slattery*, 'it may not assume that all its staff are psychologically robust and capable of absorbing anti-social behaviour.' ([122]) The fact that Mr. Slattery succeeded despite his abusive comments also raises the possibility that another layer of what is considered 'normal' is operating in the case: perhaps sexist or racist behaviour is so ordinary that it is not fundamentally socially challenging.

The second relevant issue in Slattery concerns the issue of biomedical definitions of disability. Mr. Slattery's case makes it clear that unusual behaviours will not be protected if they cannot be traced to a disorder. In this case, precariousness is demonstrated not through the difficulty of proving disability, but in drawing a connection between disability and behaviour, a process which here is revealed to be tenuous and artificial. For a person, such as Mr. Slattery, who chose not to receive medical treatment, the lack of interaction with medical experts made it more difficult to establish a connection between his behaviour and his disabilities. As with *Ondrich*, the medical evidence, in this case of the connection between Mr. Slatterly's difficult behaviour and a disability, take us further from the important project of inclusion that underpins discrimination law. Rather than focusing on the medical or biological underpinnings of individual behaviour, a better question is whether the Council's exclusion of Mr. Slattery unfairly or unreasonably 'disabled' him from accessing public life. I turn now to whether a return to the social or institutional over the individual in discrimination law would be more inclusive of eccentric or unusual behaviours, or whether the hurdle of defining disability could be bypassed altogether.

Bringing eccentricity within the protection of disability discrimination laws

What counts as disability or normalcy in law does not have to follow biomedical definitions. Discrimination laws, and in particular the human rights principles that underpin them,[19] are anchored in social rather than scientific understandings of identity. What if, inspired by the cases on eccentricity and unusual behaviours, we considered ways of expanding the definition of disability that would more clearly include diverse behaviour? Given the breadth of the current legislative definition of disability in discrimination law, there is no reason that a more expansive legal definition of disability could not operate alongside biomedical understandings of disability.[20] The definition of disability in the DDA does not explicitly require a diagnosis. Disability, and normalcy, are always socially constructed categories of identity, and as a social institution that creates and enforces definitional boundaries, law has a role to play in that construction. Similarly, the way that we choose to understand eccentricity will impact medical, social and legal definitions of disability, as Farias, Underwood, and Claridge (2013, 365) point out: 'The way we perceive unusual ideas and experiences has implications for the diagnosis of mental illness'.

One reason to support a legal definition of disability that is not overly reliant on medical evidence is in order to actively craft a definition that can be guided to particular social goals, such as equality. Such a definition can be as expansive and inclusive as the outcome requires. Biomedical understandings of identity can work to undermine an equality project, especially if they unwittingly import social stigma in the guise of objectivity. A classic example lies in the past classification of homosexuality as a psychiatric disorder, but equally, there are many current examples of biomedical accounts of identity that are contested on gendered, raced or ableist grounds.[21] This is not to say that social accounts are unfettered by bias, only that there are no inherently pure descriptors of identity, so that reliance on any one source of 'knowledge' about disability and normalcy risks an overly simple approach to both.

The definition of disability in the federal DDA was intended to be broad, and its wording is wide enough to extend to aspects of identity that would already go beyond any popular understanding of disability. For example, the definition covers a person, currently well, who could be imputed to have a risk of a future disability, such as the risk of developing certain types of cancer due to a 'faulty' gene. Disability advocate and former Disability Discrimination Commissioner Graeme Innes argues that the 'definition' section of disability discrimination laws should be broad, since there are other limitations in the DDA that prevent someone opportunistically benefitting from a generous definition. He believes that the first 'gate', the definitional gate, to accessing a legal remedy, should not be the point at which a claim unnecessarily founders (Graeme Innes interview with author, August 28, 2014).

Despite this, the broad definition of disability narrows substantially when coupled with a biomedical approach to proving that disability exists. Both *Ondrich* and *Slattery* are evidence of the precariousness of proving both the existence of disability, and that unusual behaviours arise from that disability. The disability discrimination law case of *Mariani v NSW Police Force State of NSW* [2013] NSWADT 35 (11 February 2013) (*Mariani*) is a further example where a biomedical approach negated the existence of a disability. *Mariani* involved a young man who claimed that he was discriminated against in the provision of services by police in relation to his treatment in custody. It was claimed that although the young man's parents told police at the station following his arrest that he had Asperger's Syndrome and depression, he was not treated as a vulnerable person. In this case, the NSW Administrative Decisions Tribunal held that the man did not meet the requirement of a 'disability' because there was no recent diagnosis, assessment or treatment of Asperger's syndrome or depression. In relation to the Asperger's syndrome, Mr. Mariani had been accepted by his family as having the condition since an original diagnosis in the course of his schooling in the United States ten years before but had not received any treatment. The lack of medical involvement was fatal to the man's case, even though the criminal charges against him, for assaulting his brother, had already been dismissed in court under the *Mental Health (Forensics Procedures) Act* 1990 (NSW), on the basis of his Asperger's Syndrome.

While the *Mariani* case exemplifies the way that a broad legislative definition of disability can operate narrowly when coupled with a biomedical approach to proving its existence, it also suggests another possible approach to defining 'disability'. As with the definition of 'aboriginality' in Australian law (O'Connell 2007), beneficial legislation such as anti-discrimination statutes could have a component of defining disability that is based in acceptance in a family group or community. If someone defines themselves as having a disability, and is treated, by their family and community, as having that disability, a court or tribunal could not then find that they do not have access to beneficial legislation on the basis that they do not have a diagnosis or treatment regime. This would go some way to acknowledging the social component of disability, the component that is shaped by what is believed to be 'disabling' in society. It would mean for someone like Mr. Mariani, if he is treated as someone with Asperger's syndrome, his disability could be presumed and the absence of recent medical interaction would be irrelevant.

A further possibility is to remove the requirement of defining disability at all. Fineman (2008, 2012) has critiqued the foundations of anti-discrimination law in categories of identity and suggests that a better way forward is to ground legal protections in a single shared human experience of 'vulnerability'. Australian discrimination law is currently founded on identity categories, 'attributes' of race, sex, age and disability that form the scaffolding of the anti-discrimination acts. Removing 'disability' as a definitional hurdle altogether could work if the legislation was based, as in the Fineman model, on an alternative concept such as 'vulnerability', or if it simply protected anyone who is unreasonably excluded from public life, regardless of their identity attributes. How such legislation would be framed needs much more discussion (see O'Connell 2016), but as part of that consideration, it is important to remember that existing disability discrimination laws already contain other limitations that prevent the scope of the legislation being too broad (such as the 'reasonable' limitations in Sections 5 and 6 of the DDA). The gains from expanding, or indeed losing, the definition of disability are the increased inclusion of people with unusual behaviours and the breaking down of the hard categories of disability and normalcy. Discrimination law would no longer play its unwitting role in reinforcing stigma, since it is the definition of disability itself that creates the 'difference' on which this stigma is based.

Conclusion: enriching normalcy

Current disability discrimination law does not deal generously with eccentric behaviours. People without a diagnosis are unlikely to either define themselves, or be seen in law, as having a disability, so those who are simply a bit odd or unusual will not have a remedy if this forms the basis of less favourable treatment in public life. Expanding the definition of disability to explicitly include these behaviours is one way forward. However, there is a lot at stake when people claim disability before the law. People are required to take on a stigmatized status they do not necessarily welcome or identify with, all for the tentative promise of protection that may not be realized (O'Connell 2015). Even the most expansive definitions of disability can operate narrowly in an unsympathetic judicial environment, and Australian courts and tribunals have been overwhelmingly unsympathetic to challenging behaviours as the foundation of equality claims.[22] Mr. Slattery's claim narrowly succeeded. For Ms. Ondrich and others, their public claim of vulnerability and need is not only unmet, but further burdened by the punitive impact of paying legal costs and the stress of engagement with legal processes.

While an expansive disability discrimination law should remain, legal responses to discrimination can never substitute for greater social acceptance of odd and unusual behaviours. This returns to the traditional principle that eccentric behaviours should be outside the purview of law because they are indicators of an expansive normalcy rather than a deviation: strange but benign, unusual but sound, they evidence mental and legal capacity, not impairment. For those people referenced earlier in this paper, those with the unusual gaits, unfashionable hats, strange habits, tics and obsessions, their public lives will be protected by expanding a social sense of normal human behaviour more than by any legal or medical definition of disability. While at times, and as Mr. Slattery evidenced, this inclusion has a corresponding social and sometimes individual cost, at other times there is little or no cost attached. As one of my interviewees said of the school child with autism spectrum disorder who had to chew to stay calm: 'That's all it is, is a piece of gum!' (Interview with a disability advocate, 2014). However, expanding a social sense of normalcy to encompass unusual behaviours is an aspiration that cannot replace legal responses to discrimination. Discrimination laws were enacted, in part, because social inequality is pervasive and difficult to change. They must persist in some form to provide legal redress, compensate for the material harms arising from inequality and to help to shift social perceptions of inequality over time.

The way that categories of disability and normalcy tend to work in law is that stigma resides in one category, privilege in the other, and if you expand one category, you shrink the other. The beauty of eccentricity is that it is a concrete demonstration that disability and normalcy exist side by side, and in the same person, depending how we choose to define each. Instead of simply expanding the category of disability, eccentricity invites us to recognize the coexistence of disability and normalcy. Where a category of 'disability' may be required for pragmatic reasons (to decide who can access certain welfare payments, for example), the eccentric is a reminder to retain a foundational sense of disability and normalcy as essentially intertwined.

Bea Miles, towards the end of her life, after spending almost all of her adult life on the streets, was taken in by the Sisters of the Poor in Randwick in 1964. When asked by the Sisters about her health, she reportedly said: 'I have no allergies that I know of, one complex, no delusions, two inhibitions, no neuroses, three phobias, no superstitions and no frustrations' (Miles as quoted in Allen 1986).

We all have our lists of idiosyncratic mental and bodily states that fluctuate throughout our lives. Disability theorists have long critiqued a deficit model of identity that places human flaws and vulnerability in the body of the disabled person. Yet in both popular and legal understandings of disability, this fundamental injustice remains. The eccentric is not presumptively normal or disabled, but then again, may be either, and so is a potential mechanism for disrupting the artificial distinction of disability and normalcy. Eccentricity reinstates a sense that the many variations of human behaviour are in themselves not pathological, and that embracing this can enrich our concept of normalcy while reinstating the normalcy of disability.

Notes

1. The spelling of Bea Miles' first name differs in public records. Almost all public references use the more conventional 'Bea', but her own writings and the corresponding archival references use 'Bee Miles'. I have also used the variant spelling 'Bee' to reference these.
2. 'Pack a bag and clear out;' Bea Miles' account of her travels starts, 'tired of going to jail, or perhaps, not in the mood', but she leaves by train, without a ticket, and writes about the first train guard she encounters: 'And he says "well, be a good girl and get off next stop"/And I say "righto" but don't' (Miles 193–, 1–2).
3. See *Howroyd* v *Howroyd* [2011] TASSC 73: 'Mr. Howroyd was described as "his own person". By that I gather it was meant that he was an independent thinker and did things his own way, to the point of eccentricity. By way of example, he continued wearing a gentleman's hat, a pork pie hat or similar, long after it was out of fashion.'
4. David Weeks, in his psychological study of eccentrics (1995), developed 15 characteristics of eccentrics, which he places in descending order of frequency, with these first five, he claims, applying to virtually every eccentric: Non-conformity; Creative; Strongly motivated by curiosity; Idealistic; Happily obsessed with one or more hobby horses.
5. Many popular contemporary articles now reference this encephalitis, saying that it either caused or amplified her lack of conventionality: e.g. 'Whether Bea was an eccentric made or born is still debated today, but a bout of encephalitis (a disease that can cause brain damage), seemed to amplify her most outlandish tendencies' ("Colourful Sydney Identity: Bea Miles." *TimeOut Sydney*, updated April 1, 2015. http://www.au.timeout.com/sydney/art/features/1251/bea-miles). Bea Miles was confined to Gladesville Mental Hospital by her father in her 20s, however, it was questionable that she was ever considered insane, or whether it was her father's inability to control her that led to her hospitalisation. Bea's own fascinating account of her father's obsession with her and her admission to hospital is contained in an interview with her shortly before her death (Bea Miles interviewed by James Ricketson, 25 August 1973, State Library, MLOH 535).
6. For example, in the Diagnostic and Statistical Manual of Psychiatric Disorders (APA 2013), Personality Disorders include a class designated as Cluster A (odd or eccentric disorders). United States based prevalence rates are 5.7 per cent for Cluster A, and 9.1 per cent for any PD (Lenzenweger et al. 2007). Prevalence rates are much lower for people of Asian origin, showing, that '[p]ersonality and culture are deeply intertwined' (Ryder et al. 2014). Pickersgill (2013) has traced how recent changes in the pathology of personality disorders in the UK were 'mutually constituted' by law, policy and clinical practice. Conduct disorders include Intermittent Explosive Disorder (APA 2013, 466) and Oppositional Defiant Disorder (APA 3013, 462).
7. Australian disability discrimination laws protect people with disabilities from both direct and indirect discrimination in designated areas of public life (such as employment, education and the provision of goods and services). As well as the federal Disability Discrimination Act 1992 (DDA) (Cth), disability discrimination is covered by separate legislation in every State and Territory of Australia; *Discrimination Act 1991* (ACT); *Anti-Discrimination Act 1977* (NSW); *Anti-Discrimination Act 1996* (NT); *Anti-Discrimination Act 1991* (Qld); *Equal Opportunity Act 1984* (SA); *Anti-Discrimination Act 1998* (Tas); *Equal Opportunity Act 2010* (Vic); *Equal Opportunity Act 1984* (WA). In the absence of any Constitutional guarantee of equality, these laws play a crucial role in a legislative framework of rights. Disability discrimination laws in Australia, particularly in how they define disability, are written broadly and explicitly include 'behaviour' in the definition.
8. For example, in *Coare v Firearms Appeals Committee* (2006) VCAT 21 the licencing tribunal had to decide whether a man's behaviour in response to children in his street screaming while they played – which was, in part, to stand and scream outside their houses in response – constituted harmless eccentric behaviour or was threatening enough to warrant denying him a gun licence.
9. See e.g. the succession cases, *Grynberg v* Muller [2001] NSWSC 532 [47] in which the Court referred to 'whether particular conduct or speech bespeak merely eccentricity on the one hand or lack of capacity on the other'; and *Borebor v Keane* (2013) 11 ASTLR 96 at [45]: 'Alex's emails between December 2004 and October 2006 are consistent with more than mere eccentricity. They reveal a continuing decline in his thinking, consistent with him developing dementia.'
10. *R v Islam* [2011] ACTSC 32 (unfair to draw adverse conclusions from eccentric behaviour in criminal case); *Tsagouris v Bellairs* [2010] SASC 147 (testamentary capacity not reserved for those with conformist values); *Nicholson v Knaggs* [2009] VSC 64 (necessary to separate eccentric habits from cognitive decline).

11. While eccentricity is used in succession cases as indicating capacity, it can also be used to argue incapacity: *Aspland v Tsakalakis* (2012) 7 ASTLR 1 at [16] 'Mr. Aspland felt that Mr. Rendle was no longer capable of looking after himself properly. He gives some examples of eccentricities and obsessions, the details of which need not be mentioned.'

12. My research for this article comes from two projects, my postdoctoral project on 'Equality Laws in the Biotechnological Age' (2010–2015) (UTS HREC REF NO. 2014000013), and a current ARC Discovery Project with Prof. Isabel Karpin on 'The Legal Regulation of Behaviour as a Disability' (Project number DP150102935). In the first, I conducted a case study of discrimination against school students with challenging behaviour, including the interviews quoted in this article, and in the second, Prof. Karpin and I are researching the way that social stigma and inequalities manifest in the body as biological effects and disabilities, and how law responds to those inequalities. As part of this research, we gathered case law since 2000 that referenced 'eccentric' behaviour. The empirical work from these projects has been presented and written about elsewhere (See e.g. Karen O'Connell 'Should we take the 'disability' out of disability discrimination laws? The case of challenging behaviour in schools' (2016, under submission)). This paper references both interviews and case law that was gathered as part of these projects, but is not primarily empirical, rather it is a conceptual paper inspired by this research.

13. For the project 'Equality Laws in the Biotechnological Age' I interviewed 23 professionals and advocates directly or indirectly involved in disability discrimination work. The purpose of these interviews was to gather data from experts in a field of law that is largely shielded from public, including academic, scrutiny. Interviewees were selected from personal contacts, recommendations and publicly known experts, and included equal opportunity complaints staff, current and past equal opportunity commissioners, disability advocates and service providers, staff from government departments and non-government organizations, community legal staff and teachers with direct experience of students with challenging behaviour. These professionals came from around Australia, including New South Wales, Victoria, Queensland, Tasmania, South Australia and Western Australia. Ethics approval was based on keeping the identity of my interviewees confidential but I have grouped them into general categories of disability advocate, legal practitioner or education practitioner.

14. The federal legislation includes in its definition of disability people whose disabilities include disturbed behaviour, and/or whose challenging behaviours are a symptom or manifestation of a disability: *DDA 1992* (Cth) s 4; the Victorian legislation refers to behaviour as a symptom or manifestation of a disability: *Equal Opportunity Act 2010* (Vic) s 4; the other State and Territory acts refer to disturbed behaviour: *Anti-Discrimination Act 1977* (NSW) s 4; *Equal Opportunity Act 1984* (SA) s 5; *Anti-Discrimination Act 1998* (Tas) s 3; *Discrimination Act 1991* (ACT) s 5AA; Northern Territory *Anti-Discrimination Act 1996* (NT) s 4; Queensland *Anti-Discrimination Act 1991* (QLD) Schedule – Dictionary; Western Australia *Equal Opportunity Act 1984* (WA) s 4.

15. These have unusual behaviour components included in their definitions in the American Pyschiatric Association. 2013. *Diagnostic and Statistical Manual of Mental Disorders (DSM-5)*.

16. The Declaration is included in Schedule 5 to the *Australian Human Rights Commission Act 1986* (Cth).

17. Proclaimed by General Assembly resolution 3447 (XXX) of 9 December 1975. http://www.ohchr.org/EN/ProfessionalInterest/Pages/RightsOfDisabledPersons.aspx.

18. Section 4 of the DDA defines 'disability' broadly, as '(a) total or partial loss of the person's bodily or mental functions; or (b) total or partial loss of a part of the body; or (c) the presence in the body of organisms causing disease or illness; or (d) the presence in the body of organisms capable of causing disease or illness; or (e) the malfunction, malformation or disfigurement of a part of the person's body; or (f) a disorder or malfunction that results in the person learning differently from a person without the disorder or malfunction; or (g) a disorder, illness or disease that affects a person's thought process, perception of reality, emotions or judgement or that results in disturbed behaviour; and includes a disability that: (h) presently exists or (i) previously existed but no longer exists; or (j) may exist in the future (including because of a genetic predisposition to that disability); or (k) is imputed to a person.' It adds: 'To avoid doubt, a *disability* that is otherwise covered by this definition includes behaviour that is a symptom or manifestation of the disability'.

19. All of Australia's federal anti-discrimination laws reference human rights conventions and principles.

20. Above n 17.

21. For e.g. see Karpin 2016, Constantino and Charman 2015 and Gillis-Buck and Richardson 2014.

22. For example, a spate of cases in the education field involved students with challenging behaviours claiming that they did not receive equal treatment at school because of their disabilities. All of these cases were unsuccessful. See, from the period 2010–2015, the disability discrimination cases *RW v State of Victoria (Human Rights) [2015] VCAT 266 (3 March 2015); Lambert v State of Victoria [2014] FCA 1064 (3 October 2014); USL obo her son v Ballarat Christian College (Human Rights) [2014] VCAT 623 (2 June 2014); Kiefel v State of Victoria [2013] FCA 1398 (20 December 2013); AB v Ballarat Christian College (Human Rights) [2013] VCAT 1790 (21 October 2013); Sievwright v State of Victoria [2013] FCA 964 (24 September 2013); Abela v State of Victoria [2013] FCA 832 (16 August 2013); Walker v State of Victoria [2012] FCAFC 38 (22 March 2012); Walker v State of Victoria (2011) 279 ALR 284; Phu v NSW Department of Education and Training [2010] NSWADT 152 (17 June 2010).*

Acknowledgements

I thank Professor Isabel Karpin (University of Technology Sydney) and the anonymous reviewers of this article for helpful comments, and Valerie Gutenev Hale for excellent research assistance. The views expressed herein are those of the author and are not necessarily those of the Australian Research Council.

Disclosure statement

No potential conflict of interest was reported by the author.

Funding

This research was supported under Australian Research Council's Discovery Projects funding scheme [project DP150102935] and a University of Technology Sydney Chancellor's Postdoctoral Research Fellowship.

References

Allen, Frances. 2014. *Saving Normal: An Insider's Revolt against Out-of-control Psychiatric Diagnosis, DSM-5, Big Pharma, and the Medicalization of Ordinary Life*. New York: William Morrow.

Allen, Judith. 1986. "Beatrice (Bea) Miles, (1902–1973)." *Australian Dictionary of Biography*, http://adb.anu.edu.au/biography/miles-beatrice-bea-7573.

Cixous, Hélène. 1986. "Sorties: Out and out: Attacks/Ways out/Forays." In *The Newly Born Woman, by Hélène Cixous and Catherine Clement*, 63–129. Translated by Betsy Wing. Minneapolis: University of Minnesota Press. Originally published as Cixous, Hélène and Catherine Clement. 1975. La jeune nee. Paris: Union Generaled'Editions.

Constantino, John N., and Tony Charman. 2015. "Diagnosis of Autism Spectrum Disorder: Reconciling the Syndrome, Its Diverse Origins, and Variation in Expression." *The Lancet Neurology*. Online publication. doi: 10.1016/S1474-4422(15)00151-9.

Derrida, Jacques. 1972. *Positions*. Translated by Alan Bass. Chicago: University of Chicago Press.

Elder, Bruce. 2012. "Eccentric City: Bea Miles." *Sydney Morning Herald*, January 13. http://www.smh.com.au/entertainment/eccentric-city-bea-miles-20120112-1pxba.html.

Farias, Miguel, Raphael Underwood, and Gordon Claridge. 2013. "Unusual but Sound Minds: Mental Health Indicators in Spiritual Individuals." *British Journal of Psychology* 104: 364–381.

Fineman, Martha Albertson. 2008. "The Vulnerable Subject: Anchoring Equality in the Human Condition." *Yale Journal of Law & Feminism* 20 (1): 1–23.

Fineman, Martha Albertson. 2012. "Beyond Identities: The Limits of an Antidiscrimination Approach to Equality." *Boston University Law Review* 92 (6): 1713–1770.

Gaze, Beth. 2002. "Context and Interpretation in Anti-discrimination Law." *Melbourne University Law Review* 26 (2): 325–354.

Gillis-Buck, Eva M., and Sarah S. Richardson. 2014. "Autism as a Biomedical Platform for Sex Differences Research." *BioSocieties* 9: 262–283.

Kalb, Claudia. 2016. *Andy Warhol Was a Hoarder: Inside the Minds of History's Great Personalities*. Washington: National Geographic Society.

Karpin, Isabel. 2016. "Regulatory Responses to the Gendering of Transgenerational Harm." *Australian Feminist Studies* 31 (88): 139–153.

Karpin, Isabel, and Karen O'Connell. 2015. "Stigmatising the 'Normal': The Legal Regulation of Behaviour as a Disability." *UNSW Law Journal* 38 (4): 1461–1483.

Lenzenweger, Mark F., Michael C. Lane, Armand W. Loranger, and Ronald C. Kessler. 2007. "DSM-IV Personality Disorders in the National Comorbidity Survey Replication." *Biological Psychiatry* 62 (6): 553–564.

Lewis, Berwyn. 1992. "The Incredible Lightness of Bea." *Sydney Morning Herald*, April 23, 16.

Marcus, George E. 1995. "On Eccentricity." In *Rhetorics of Self-making*, edited by Debborra Battaglia, 43–58. Berkeley: University of California Press.

Miles, Bee (in this source spelt as Bee but also known as Bea). c. 1930. *I Leave in a Hurry and I Go on a Wild-goose Chase, Being Accounts of Trips to Queensland, Northern Territory and Bourke, New South Wales.* Available on microfilm at the State Library of NSW.

O'Connell, Karen. 2007. "'We Who Are Not Here': Law, Whiteness, Indigenous Peoples and the Promise of Genetic Identification." *International Journal of Law in Context* 3 (1): 5–58.

O'Connell, Karen. 2008. "Pinned like a Butterfly: Whiteness and Racial Hatred Laws." *ACRAWSA e-Journal* 4 (2). http://www.acrawsa.org.au/files/ejournalfiles/49OConnellPinnedLikeaButterflyFINAL.pdf.

O'Connell, Karen. 2016 "Should We Take the 'Disability' out of Disability Discrimination Laws? The Case of Challenging Behaviour in Schools." (Under submission).

Pickersgill, M. 2013. "How Personality Became Treatable: The Mutual Constitution of Clinical Knowledge and Mental Health Law." *Social Studies of Science* 43 (1): 30–53.

Ryder, A. G., et al. 2014. "Personality Disorders in Asians: Summary, and a Call for Cultural Research." *Asian Journal of Psychiatry* 7 (1): 86–88.

"The Sad State of Eccentricity." 1969. *Time*, March 14.

Taylor, Kerry, and Roxanne Mykiyiuk. 2001. "Genetics, Normalcy and Disability." *Isuma* 65–71.

Thornton, Margaret. 2002. "Sexual Harassment Losing Sight of Sex Discrimination." *Melbourne University Law Review* 26 (2): 422–444.

Weeks, David, and Jamie James. 1995. *Eccentrics: A Study of Sanity and Strangeness.* New York: Kodansha America.

Eugenics and the normal body: the role of visual images and intelligence testing in framing the treatment of people with disabilities in the early twentieth century

Elizabeth Stephens and Peter Cryle

ABSTRACT

This article examines how the emergence of a statistical concept of the normal at the end of the nineteenth century led to the development of a theory of eugenics, and examines the cultural pathways by which this theory came to shape both the public perception and institutional treatment of people now understood as disabled. The statistical idea of the normal and the theory of eugenics were developed simultaneously in the work of one man: Francis Galton, cousin of Charles Darwin and often identified as the first 'social Darwinist.' Beginning with an analysis of the role of composite photography in Galton's research, this article traces the historical co-emergence of normality and eugenics along two key lines of development: the use of new visual imagining techniques in the public sphere as a means by which to popularize these ideas amongst a general audience, and their application in the institutional and legal treatment of disabled people in the first three decades of the twentieth century. In so doing, the article intends to provide a careful history of the development and application of eugenical thinking and practice in the Anglophone world over this period of emergence and influence.

In the late 1870s, the statistician and inventor of eugenics Francis Galton began a series of experiments in a photographic procedure he termed 'composite portraiture'. Composite portraits were made by layering a number of individual photographic portraits onto a single plate, through the partial exposure of each image.[1] The result was a sort of photographic palimpsest: the ghostly impression of a composite face that retained the hazy outline of each of its originals. (See Figure 1.) Strange as they may appear to contemporary eyes, composite portraits were one of Galton's most important research tools, and they were a central part of his studies in anthropology, statistics and eugenics. The purpose of composite portraits, Galton explained, was not to represent 'any man in particular,' but rather to 'portray an imaginary figure possessing the average features of any group of men. These ideal faces have a surprising air of reality', Galton continued. 'Nobody who glanced at them for the first time would doubt its being the likeness of any living person, yet … it is no such thing; it is the portrait of a type and not an individual' (1878, 97). Where the composite image was most distinct, it represented those features held in common by the greatest number of that group; where it was most hazy, it represented the trace of those features that deviated most from the average. In this respect, composite portraits were best understood as a form

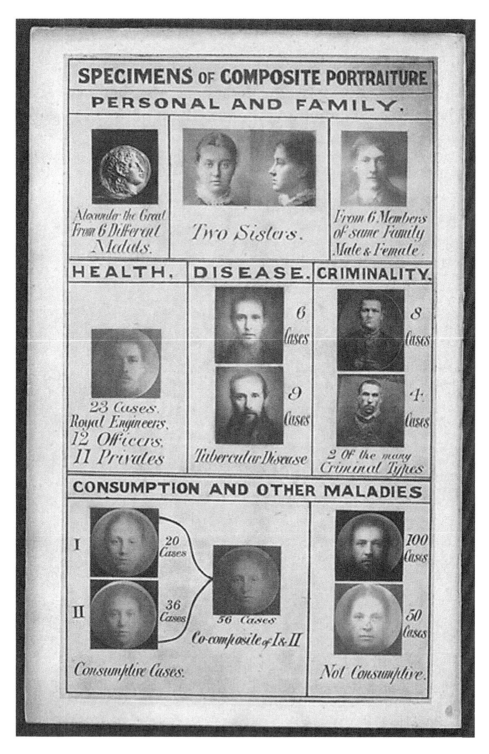

Figure 1. Frontispiece of Galton's Inquiries into Human Faculty, 1883. Courtesy of the Wellcome Library.

of 'pictorial statistics', Galton argued (1878, 97). Unlike 'ordinary numerical statistics', which 'concerned themselves solely with Averages', composite portraits had the advantage of including range of variation, or 'the features of every individual of whom they are composed' (1879, 163).

The significance of composites portraits, within the context of this special issue of *Continuum* on normality and disability, is that Galton was the first person to understand this relationship between the average and individual variation as one of 'normal distribution' and, in so doing, to elaborate a fully developed statistical concept of the normal. Prior to this, the normal had been primarily understood as a medical concept – in which it signified a dynamic state of functional health – rather than a mathematical one – in which it represented a fixed standard.[2] In this way, Galton's composite portraits cast new light on the cultural and historical intersections between normality and disability that emerged at the end of the nineteenth century. They allow us to recover the conditions in which his theories of eugenics emerged, and the means by which these moved into the public sphere and then into institutional practice during the first decades of the twentieth century. In the first instance, composite portraiture draws attention to the prominent role played by visualization practices and public display in the development and popularization of a quantitative understanding of the normal at this time. Secondly, they are representative of the complex network of institutions and discourses in which the theory of eugenics emerged and this time, and demonstrate how these came to shape the medical and legal treatment of people now understood to be disabled. As Alan Sekula has memorably argued, in Galton's composite portraits, 'the bell curve wore a human face' (1986, 33). Yet, it is a blurry and uncertain face we see in Galton's composites, representative of the novelty and instability of the idea of the normal at this point of emergence at the turn of the century.

Visualizing eugenics: normality and the logic of numbers

Composite portraits played a key role in Galton's research on biological inheritance, which he would eventually come to term eugenics. To understand the development of eugenics in Galton's thinking, we need to recall that Galton's work found its broad scientific purpose in engagement with the evolutionary theory of his cousin Charles Darwin. Indeed, Galton was the first person to consider what Darwin's theories of natural selection meant for contemporary human society, claimed the biometrician Karl Pearson, making him the first 'social Darwinist' (1914, 109). Because 'the whole course of modern social evolution has served to suspend the action of natural selection', Pearson argued, it was imperative for science to intervene to ensure the health and future of the race (1914, 79). Pearson praised the boldness of Galton's vision in addressing this issue: 'If it is given to few men to name a new branch of science and lay down the broad lines of its development, it is the lot of fewer still to forecast its future as a creed of social conduct' (1914, 217). It was to this field of research Galton gave the name eugenics.

He coined the term eugenics in *Inquiries into Human Faculty and its Development* (1883), noting that its purpose was to examine 'the practicability of supplanting inefficient human stock by better strains, and to consider whether it might not be our duty to do so' (1883, 1). He provided a more detailed account in *Essays in Eugenics* (1909), in which he explained:

> The creed of eugenics is founded upon the idea of evolution; not on a passive form of it, but on one that can to some extent direct its own course. Purely passive, or what may be styled mechanical evolution, displays the awe-inspiring spectacle of a vast eddy of organic turmoil. ... But it is molded by blind and wasteful processes, namely, by an extravagant production of raw material and the ruthless rejection of all that is superfluous. (1909, 68–69)

Where evolution and natural selection were tumultuous and unruly processes, characterized by extravagant waste, the benevolent and improving hands of science could bring order and efficiency to racial development, ensuring its progress and betterment: 'Eugenics co-operates with the workings of Nature by securing that humanity shall be represented by the fittest races', Galton argued. 'What Nature does blindly, slowly, and ruthlessly, man may do providently, quickly, and kindly'. (1909, 42)

Galton's elaboration of a theory of eugenics was directly enabled by the quantitative theory of the normal as a principle of mathematical regularity, or normal distribution. Heredity, Galton claimed: 'now admits of exact definition and of being treated mathematically, like birth and death rates, and other topics with which actuaries are concerned' (1909, 38). The significance of this for Galton's later work on eugenics resides in his claim that quantitative forms of knowledge ensured both scientific precision and political neutrality: 'Eugenics seeks quantitative results. It is not contented with such vague words as "much" or "little," but endeavours to determine "how much" or "how little" in precise and trustworthy figures' (1909, 81). Statistics, Galton was claiming, would support the scientific rationale of eugenics. This argument was a direct parallel to the claim that drove his research on composite portraiture: that these were verifiably objective scientific images because they were produced by the mechanical precision of the camera. In this way, composite portraits were 'independent of the fancy of the operator, just as numerical averages are' (1882, 478–479). Like photography and with it, Galton was arguing, statistical analysis could scientifically prove that biological inheritance conformed to knowable laws whose range and variation could be identified and calculated in advance: 'the statistical effects [of the laws of biological inheritance] are no longer vague, for they are measured and expressed in formulae', he claimed in *Essays in Eugenics* (1909, 33). As a result, heredity 'now admits of exact definition and of being treated mathematically' (1909, 38). This is the context in which the idea of normality enters the quantitative and social sciences at the end of the nineteenth century, then: by claiming a dispassionate objectivity based on 'precise and trustworthy figures' that enabled the development of a theory of programmatic racial and social discrimination (1909, 81). It is this central proposition that enabled the development of eugenics, and which shaped its application in the first decades of the twentieth century.

Central to this theorization of eugenics, and underpinning its claims to scientific objectivity and accuracy, was the law of normal distribution, again understood to be made visible through composite portraiture:

> It is the essential notion of a race that there should be some ideal typical form from which the individuals may deviate in all directions, but about which they chiefly cluster, and towards which their descendants will continue to cluster. The easiest direction in which a race can be improved is towards that central type, because nothing new has to be sought out. It is only necessary to encourage as far as practicable the breed of those who conform most nearly to the central type, and to restrain as far as may be the breed of those who deviate widely from it. Now there can hardly be a more appropriate method of discovering the central physiognomical type of any race or group than that of composite portraiture. (1883, 9)

Here, we see how the law of normal distribution was used by Galton to form the statistical basis of eugenic theory. The normal curve and the normal law of frequency enabled him to calculate the patterns of biological inheritance as well as the hereditary basis of various traits. The law of normal distribution, which decreed that variance would inevitably regress towards the mean, could thus be used to predict directions of biological evolution: the 'filial center falls back further towards mediocrity in a constant proportion to the distance to which the parental center has deviated from it, whether the direction of the deviation be in excess or in deficiency' (1869, xviii). In this way, Galton used a mathematical law as the basis of a proposed social law: mathematics, like evolution, was understood as a readily available intellectual practice that the benevolent and rational hands of science could use to improve the race. Eugenics, as it was conceived by Galton, was thus not only shaped by a quantitative understanding of the normal, but could also be understood in quite narrowly mathematical terms as a policy of normalization.

For Galton, the eugenical improvement of a race or type was both a naturally occurring dynamic, one that could and should be harnessed by scientists to increase the rate of progress and racial improvement with greater efficiency. 'The most merciful form of what I ventured to call "eugenics"', wrote Galton, 'would consist in watching for the indications of superior strains or races, and in so favoring them that their progeny shall outnumber and gradually replace that of the old one' (1883, 33). Galton equivocated in his account of how eugenicist processes could be expected to work. 'The aim of eugenics', he wrote, 'is to represent each class or sect by its best specimens; that done, to leave them to work out their common civilisation in their own way' (1909, 36–37). But what exactly was the relation between Darwinian survival of the fittest and the notion of a common civilization? The gap between the two could only be closed by action of a kind Galton was disinclined to consider. As Pearson noted, Galton's own ambitions were largely restricted to the application of positive eugenics: 'Galton would have been content to grade physically and mentally mankind, and to have urged that marriage within your own grade was a religious duty for those of high grades and castes' (1914, 111).

The subsequent history of eugenics – from its application as a programme of biological normalization in 1920s USA to that of biological extinction in Nazi Germany in the 1930s – suggests that there was in eugenicist thinking a logic that led almost inevitably to the imposition of a governmental practice of normality in the first decades of the twentieth century. Yet, as Daniel Kevles has shown in *In The Name of Eugenics: Genetics and the Uses of Human Heredity*, eugenics was far from persuasive in Britain in the early 1900s: the members of the Eugenics Society numbered only in the hundreds, it did not enjoy broad institutional support, and few of its policies were implemented (1985, 3–19). Nancy Stepan, too, observes of eugenics in *The Idea of Race in Science: Great Britain 1800–1960*: 'From the beginning, its critics labeled its claims as at best naive, at worst exaggerated and dangerous' (1982, 112). And yet eugenic thinking and the quantitative concept of the normal on which this rested would come to inform the legislation and treatment of people identified as mentally or physically disabled in the early decades of the twentieth century in a range of important ways. One of the most influential of these was in the study of intelligence that grew out of Galton's work on biological inheritance. Although programs of either positive or negative eugenics found little uptake in the institutional practice or government policy of the late nineteenth and early twentieth century in Britain, Europe or America, the study of intelligence provided the means by which these would come to move into the public sphere in the decades to come. Thus, it is to these we must turn if we are to understand the complex cultural networks by which these emergent ideas of the normal and eugenics came to shape the treatment of people now understood to be disabled in the first half of the twentieth century.

The emergence of 'intelligence' as an object of study

Galton was one of the first to argue for the scientific feasibility of studying intelligence as a set of hereditary qualities. To set about the task, Galton first needed to defend the very idea of studying 'genius' – or, to use the term that tended to displace it in the decades that followed, 'intelligence' – as a hereditary phenomenon. He began his 1869 essay, *Hereditary Genius*, by conceding that the notion had hitherto been derided by many and advocated as an object of study by only a few (1869, vi). Scepticism of that kind needed to be answered scientifically, and he now proposed to do just that by the application of statistical method: 'I may claim to be the first to treat the subject in a statistical manner, to arrive at numerical results, and to introduce the "law of deviation from an average" into discussions on heredity' (1869, vi). The pertinence of this law to any study of heredity, he noted, had already been demonstrated through tabulations of 'form and physical features', which were clearly 'derived by inheritance' (1869, 1). The way was open to study hereditary intelligence on the assumption that the physical features he had named would not be just inherited characters, but also the physiological vehicles, the literal incarnation of intellectual ability. If appropriate data were to hand, an inquiry based in statistics would then make it possible to ascertain 'the laws of heredity with respect to genius' (1869, 2).

The most convenient way to set about studying hereditary genius, Galton asserted in his 1869 essay of that title, was to study families. He had begun with questions of race, a more general concern of anthropology at the time, but had come to the view that he did not need to range far afield in order to find exemplary patterns of hereditary intellectual ability:

> The idea of investigating the subject of hereditary genius occurred to me during the course of a purely ethnological inquiry, into the mental peculiarities of different races; when the fact that characteristics cling to families, was so frequently forced on my notice as to induce me to pay especial attention to that branch of the subject. (1869, v)

It was only when Galton returned in the same essay to claims about racially inherited intelligence that his statements took on disquieting political overtones. He rehearsed the standard anthropological proposition of the time about degrees of civilization found in the various races, but then went on to make a narrower claim about differential intellectual ability within his own national group:

> To conclude, the range of mental power between – I will not say the highest Caucasian and the lowest savage – but between the greatest and least of English intellects, is enormous. There is a continuity of natural ability reaching from one knows not what height, and descending to one can hardly say what depth. (1869, 26)

It mattered little in Galton's political terms whether a notional English race was superior to others on the anthropometric scales generally favoured by anthropologists. What mattered far more to him were perceived hereditary disparities in natural ability within his own nation. The politics implicit in eugenics were potentially more acute and more local than those of a global racism. In that figurative sense, eugenics was for Galton a family affair.

While earlier work in fields such as craniometry had established a rigorous set of procedures, no one had done comparable work for the measurement of intelligence. There was no agreed mensurative technique, and no agreed scale. Without those things, there could be no data for statistical analysis, and no standardization of knowledge. A method of testing was urgently required. As Nancy Stepan points out, eugenics helped to shape scientific inquiry at this point. It established intelligence as a topic for psychology, and in so doing helped create a requirement for intelligence testing in Britain:

> It was of course 'genius', 'talent', or 'intelligence' (as it came to be called) that was of first importance to the eugenists. It was they who placed the subject of intelligence at the centre of psychological science and made the word so potent in the English language and in English education. Intelligence tests underwent explosive growth between 1900 and 1930, exactly the period that eugenics enjoyed its greatest popularity. (1982, 131)

The pioneers of intelligence testing were not British, however, and they were not eugenicists. During the early years of the twentieth century, Alfred Binet and Théodore Simon, working mainly in France, developed a series of tests and a corresponding scale for use on children between the ages of 3 and 13.[3] Their research did indeed answer a requirement of eugenicist thinking and was widely taken up in England and elsewhere, but its history ought to be read with care.

Binet and Simon began their study of the development of intelligence in children by observing that there had been controversy in recent years about whether intelligence could effectively be measured at all. Their approach in the face of such controversy was not to enter into 'theoretical discussions' of the matter, but to attempt to resolve it as a 'factual problem' (Binet and Simon 1907, 1). The key difficulty as they saw it from the outset was that the formal analogy between physical anthropometry and their own anthropometric interest was inadequate and misleading. Once Binet and Simon's set of tests had been developed, they were available to serve the purposes and policies of eugenics, even though they appear to have done so casually rather than systematically. In an essay published in 1907, *Les Enfants anormaux* (Abnormal children), Binet made it clear just what was at stake for the practice of intelligence testing in France. In the first decade of the twentieth century, the children deemed to be missing out were referred to in official generic terms as 'abnormal'. 'Abnormal' was a catch-all category. Binet himself called it a 'heterogeneous' group, offering this indicative list: 'deaf-mute children, blind ones, epileptics, idiots, imbeciles, feeble-minded children, unstable ones, etc' (Binet 1907, 6–7). Every kind of 'abnormality' that might have a systematic effect on a child's success at school seemed to be included.

So what confronted Binet and Simon was a disparate set of pupils identified by teachers as needing expert attention. The teachers were asking, in fact, whether ostensibly abnormal children really were abnormal in some psychological sense yet to be defined with authority (Binet and Simon 1907, 47). In order to answer that question systematically, Binet first had to sort out the cases and types that had been lumped together. The first critical move he made was to question the applicability here of the term 'abnormal', precisely because the term owed so much to medical discourse. 'Medical language applies the term "abnormal" to any individual who is clearly at a sufficient distance from the average to constitute a pathological anomaly', said Binet, pointing out as he did so that there might well be anomalies that ought not to be considered pathological insofar as they posed no threat to the individual's health or that of their descendants (Binet 1907, 6; 6n1). In any case, the category of 'abnormal children' needed to be broken down into better defined sub-groups. Given the terms in which the question was being put by teachers and school principals, it was possible to exclude some kinds of children from the present problematic. Deaf mutes and blind children had long been recognized as needing special kinds of teaching: they did not require expertise about intelligence to explain in principle why they might be having difficulties with their schooling (Binet 1907, 7). In much the same way, 'idiots' could be excluded from the group identified for analytical attention because they were known to require continuous medical treatment (Binet 1907, 7). These methodical exclusions left a residual group of pupils who were behind with their schooling for reasons that were still to be explained.

The problem, put trenchantly, was that abnormality was taken to be a manifest phenomenon, while the normal condition which might have defined it contrastively was not: 'everyone is ignorant of how much intelligence a child needs in order to be normal' (Binet and Simon 1907, 85). So there were in fact two possible standards, and two kinds of normalization possible within the school system. The obvious difficulties that had so far been taken to define abnormality had to do with pupils being behind in their schooling. That allowed Binet and Simon to produce a working definition of the abnormal child defined by performance:

> we have defined abnormal children at school purely and simply by the weakness of their schooling faculty [*faculté scolaire*]. Any child who is three years behind in their studies should be considered abnormal unless the delay can be excused by a lack of time at school.' (Binet and Simon 1907, 75)

But that did not establish of itself whether such pupils were behind with their schooling because of inferior intelligence. Binet and Simon's working assumption, and something their tests tended to confirm, was that many children who were behaviourally 'abnormal' were in fact of normal intelligence (Binet and Simon 1907, 77).

American eugenics exhibitions: legislating the normal

Such work on intelligence testing makes clear the complex ways in which a quantitative understanding of the normal as a standard of measurement infiltrated institutional practice and scientific knowledge in the first decades of the twentieth century. While intelligence testing demonstrates the institutional purpose to which ideas about normality shaped by eugenic principles affected the treatment of people understood as mentally 'feeble' (in the terminology of the time), neither eugenics nor normality had yet become embedded in law. This would change in the following decades, and to understand the conditions in which it did so we need to turn again to the sphere of public exhibitions and visualization practices.

One of the most important exhibitions on eugenics was staged as part of the Second International Congress of Eugenics, held at the American Museum of Natural History in New York in September and October 1921. The Congress included an exhibition whose purpose was to explain eugenics to a general public. An introductory poster placed near the entrance, titled *What is Eugenics?*, defined it as:

> that science which studies the inborn qualities – physical, mental, and spiritual – in man, with a view to their improvement. Nothing is more evident in the history of families, communities and nations than that, in the change of individuals from generation to generation, some families, some races, and the people of some nations, improve greatly in physical soundness, in intelligence and in character, industry, leadership, and other qualities which make for human breed improvement; while other racial, national, and family stocks die out – they decline in physical stamina, in intellectual capacity and in moral force. (Laughlin 1934, 13)

This point was illustrated by a pair of composite statues, which, like Galton's composite portraiture, was intended to demonstrate the effects of biological inheritance on character and physiology. The first of these, visible at the entrance of the exhibition, was the figure of 'the Composite Athlete, 30 Strongest Men of Harvard' (Laughlin 1923, 12). Opposite this, at the far end of the hall, was a second figure: 'the Average Young American Male, 100 000 White Veterans 1919' (Laughlin 1923, 12). (See Figure 2.) This display was intended to be a comparative one, and to prove a eugenic point. Where the statue of the Harvard 'Composite Athlete' was presented as an aspirational figure, the idealized embodiment of the physical and mental elite of young white American masculinity, the 'Average Young American Male' was presented as proof of the racial decline of the white American male population.

Despite – or perhaps because of – this, it was 'the Average Young American Male' statue that attracted all the attention during the exhibition. Very little was recorded about the design and manufacture of 'the Composite Athlete', and no known images of this piece survive.[4] The 'Average Young American Male', on the other hand, was the focus of a great deal of commentary in its own time, and has recently been the subject of a number of scholarly studies (see for instance, Coffey 2006). This statue was modelled using

69

Figure 2. "The Average Young American Male," Jane Davenport, 1921. In Harry Laughlin's The Second International Exhibition of Eugenics, 1923. Courtesy of the Wellcome Library.

the averages of the vast collection of anthropometric records of drafted and demobilized American soldiers undertaken during the First World War by Charles Davenport and Albert G. Love, commissioned by the Office of the Surgeon General.

The 'Average Young American Male' statue was produced by Davenport's daughter, Jane Davenport, and widely seen as proof of a worrying decline in white American masculinity: 'Contrasted with the vigorous and idealised body of the composite Harvard athlete', Mary Coffey notes, 'the average male's slight shoulders, distended belly, and lack of firm musculature implied that the national (white) body was degenerating as a result of an improvident mixing with inferior European stocks' (2006, 198).

Although the data used to model the statue was drawn from enlisted and decommissioned soldiers, the influence of the Great War on the state of the average young American masculinity was never mentioned. Rather, the focus of discussions by the leading figures in eugenics gathered at the Congress, many of whom presented public lectures as part of the proceedings, was the perilous effect of immigration on the racial health of white Americans. The opening address by Henry Fairfield Osborn (co-founder of the Galton society) exemplified this, exhorting the mostly affluent and professional men in the room to recognize they were 'engaged in a serious struggle to maintain our historic republican institutions through barring the entrance of those who are unfit to share the duties and responsibilities of our well-founded government' (Davenport 1923, 2). While such sentiments had been expressed in the closed spaces of learned societies and academic journals for some time, in the 1920s they were increasingly disseminated to a general public through public lectures and exhibitions like that of the Eugenics Congress, continuing an expansion into the public sphere that had begun earlier with Galton's public lectures and participation in international exhibitions. Charles Davenport's Eugenics Record Office, for instance, compiled and exhibited photographs as well as anthropological data, and ran popular competitions like the Fittest Families contests held in the 1920s.

Despite this, eugenics continued to find limited applications in the USA in the 1920s, experiencing resistance on a number of institutional and social fronts. In a series of legal challenges, for instance, programs of involuntary sterilization had been ruled unconstitutional in a number of states. In non-totalitarian contexts, unlike those in which eugenic principles would later flourish in 1930s Germany, institutions and professional figures did not necessarily concur on the status and best treatment of individuals, nor was it always easy to demonstrate that subjects were sufficiently 'mentally feeble' or physical degenerate to a point that would warrant involuntary state intervention. In response, Harry Laughlin, Charles Davenport's Assistant Director at the Eugenic Records Office at Cold Springs Harbor, wrote the 'Model Eugenical Sterilization Law' designed provide a legal template that could be adapted and applied in eugenic policy and programs, especially with regards to the involuntary sterilization of those deemed mentally or physically unfit. The model law targeted anyone who 'regardless of etiology or prognosis, fails chronically in comparison with normal persons, to maintain himself or herself as a useful member of the organized social life of the state' (Laughlin 1922, 446). It is significant to note that this document, whose application depended on a legal assessment and ruling on normality, never defined the word normal, even as it enshrined the term in law for the first time. This is representative of the way the idea of normality moved into the legal sphere and came to shape the treatment of people identified as 'abnormal': the idea of the normal remained blurry and undefined even as its effects gained cultural authority and power. Nonetheless, Laughlin's legal template was widely utilized: using this, the first sterilization law was passed in Virginia in 1924, and eventually such laws were in effect in thirty states in the USA. Some 65 000 involuntary sterilization procedures were undertaken in America between 1927 and the mid-1960s.[5]

It should also be recognized that Laughlin's work, and that of other American eugenicists, directly influenced the development and implementation of German eugenic policy at this time. Indeed, Laughlin would receive an honorary degree from the University of Heidelberg in 1936 for his work behalf of the 'science of racial cleansing' (Black 2012, 185). The popularization and uptake of eugenics in the USA was closely related to the culture of public exhibitions in which figures like Laughlin and Davenport were so immersed. Eugenic exhibitions would remain popular throughout the USA during the 1930s, some of which were imported directed from Germany. For instance, a number of American health workers, including representatives of the American Public Health Association, visited the Second International Hygiene Exhibition in Dresden in 1930, which featured the famous Transparent Man and Transparent Woman exhibits: these were large plastic anatomical models that allowed the internal organs to be illuminated with the press of a switch. The American delegation arranged for this exhibition to come to the USA, and Transparent Man was exhibited at the 1933 World's Fair in Chicago.[6] In 1934, an exhibition titled 'Eugenics in New Germany' toured the US in 1934 before finding an eventual permanent home at the Buffalo Museum of Science.[7] These exhibitions were representative of the changes in public health policy underway at this time. In the following decades, in the USA, Europe and Anglophone world, an increasing number of medical interventions would practiced on the bodies seen to deviate from normal, even as the term normal itself remained problematically imprecise: surgeries to assign a binary gender to intersex children, or separate conjoined twins or to correct physical anomalies such as cleft palate, began to be much more widely practiced from the early decades of the twentieth century (see, for instance, Davis 1995; Spade 2011; Dreger 2004; and Garland-Thomson 1997).

Conclusion

The history of eugenics as practiced and implemented in the first decades of the twentieth century both informed, and was informed by, an emergent culture visual culture of which Galton's composite portraits and eugenic exhibitions are key examples. Such images and exhibitions were an important part of the new sites in which public health discourses were not only popularized but also produced. Galton's composite portraits and Davenport's composite statue were seen to provide impartial and objective images of bodies because they were the visualization of statistically averages. In this way, they exemplify the way a new idea of the normal as a law of numerical regularity enabled the development of eugenics, and facilitated its eventual application in practice during the first half of the twentieth century. The means by which this new quantitative idea of the normal came to determine the legal and medical treatment of those seen to be mentally or physically unfit are more complex than often recognized, as we have seen, finding points of application in such practices as intelligence testing, whose legacy has been much more enduring and widespread than that of eugenics itself, especially in Anglophone contexts. Both, however, have played a key role in the history of normality and normalization. As this paper has shown, the co-emergence of normality and eugenics can be seen in, and was enabled by, the culture of visual images and public exhibitions whose impact would be evident in the public policy and legal treatment of those now identified as disabled, even as these images themselves would largely be forgotten in the decades to come.

Notes

1. Galton described the technical process by which composite portraits were produced in an early article on the topic: 'Suppose that there are eight portraits in the pack, and that under existing circumstances it would require an exposure of eighty seconds to give an exact photographic copy of any one of them', Galton explained. 'We throw the image of each of the eight portraits in turn upon the same part of the sensitised plate for ten seconds ... The sensitised plate will now have had its total exposure of eighty seconds; it is then developed, and the print taken from it is the generalised picture of which I speak' (Galton 1878, 97).
2. On the rise of a quantified concept of the normal, and its relation to medical understandings of the term, see Ernst (2006); Lock (2000); and Hacking (1990).
3. Binet and Simon discuss the age range (1907): 59–60.
4. Although there is no information about who produced this statue, there is a good likelihood that it was one made some decades earlier by Robert Tait McKenzie. McKenzie was the first medical Director of Physical Education at McGill University, and from 1900 he began to produce 'sports statues' based on the anthropometric data of college students he had collected over the previous years.
5. For a detailed account of the application of eugenic policies in the USA during the first half of the twentieth century, see Black (2012).
6. An account of the manufacture and exhibition of the Transparent Man can be found in Currell and Cogdell (2006).
7. The exhibition was re-curated in 1943, and all the displays relating to Nazi eugenic programmes were destroyed. A detailed account of this exhibition is provided in Rydell, Cogdell, and Largent (2006).

Disclosure statement

No potential conflict of interest was reported by the authors.

Funding

This work was supported by funding from the Australian Research Council [grant number DP 1093542].

References

Binet, A. 1907. *Les Enfants anormaux. Guide pour l'admission des enfants anormaux dans les classes de perfectionnement* [Abnormal Children. Guide for the Admission of Abnormal Children into Advanced Classes]. Paris: Colin.

Binet, A., and T. Simon. 1907. "Le développement de l'intelligence chez les enfants." [The Development of Intellingence in Chidlren.] *L'année psychologique* 14: 1–94.

Black, E. 2012. *War Against The Weak: Eugenics and America's Campaign to Create a Master Race*. New York: Dialog Press.

Coffey, M. 2006. "The American Adonis: A Natural History of the Average American (Man), 1921–1932." In *Popular Eugenics: National Efficiency and American Mass Culture in the 1930s*, edited by Susan Currell and Christina Cogdell, 185–216. Athens, OH: Ohio University Press.

Currell, S., and C. Cogdell, eds. 2006. *Popular Eugenics: National Efficiency and American Mass Culture in the 1930s*. Athens, Ohio: Ohio University Press.

Davenport, C., ed. 1923. *Scientific Papers of the Second International Congress of Eugenics*. Baltimore, MD: Williams and Wilkins.

Davis, L. 1995. *Enforcing Normalcy: Disability, Deafness and the Body*. London: Verso.

Dreger, A. D. 2004. *One of Us: Conjoined Twins and the Future of the Normal*. Cambridge, MA: Harvard University Press.

Ernst, W., ed. 2006. *Histories of the Normal and the Abnormal: Social and Cultural Histories of Norms and Normativity*. London: Routledge.

Galton, F. 1869. *Hereditary Genius: An Inquiry into its Laws and Consequences*. London: Macmillan.

Galton, F. 1878. "Composite Portraits Made by Combining Those of Many Different Persons Into a Single Figure." *Nature* 18: 97–100.

Galton, F. 1879. *Generic Images*. London: Clowes.

Galton, F. 1882. "An Inquiry into the Physiognomy of Phthisis by the Method of 'Composite Portraiture.'" *Guy's Hospital Reports* 25: 475–493.

Galton, F. 1883. *Inquiries into Human Faculty and Its Development*. London: Macmillan.

Galton, F. 1909. *Essays in Eugenics*. London: Eugenics Education Society.

Hacking, I. 1990. *The Taming of Chance*. Cambridge: Cambridge University Press.

Kevles, D. 1985. *In The Name of Eugenics: Genetics and the Uses of Human Heredity*. Berkeley: University of California Press.

Laughlin, H. 1922. *Eugenical Sterilization in the United States*. Chicago, IL: Psychopathic Laboratory of the Municipal Court of Chicago.

Laughlin, H. 1923. *The Second International Exhibition of Eugenics held September 22 to October 22, 1921, in Connection with the Second International Congress of Eugenics in the American Museum of Natural History, New York; an Account of the Organization of the Exhibition, the Classification of the Exhibits, the list of Exhibitors, and a Catalog and Description of the Exhibits*. Baltimore, MD: Williams and Wilkins.

Laughlin, H. 1934. "What Eugenics Is All About." In *A Decade of Progress in Eugenics: Scientific Papers of the Third International Congress if Eugenics*, edited by H. F. Perkins, 11, Plate 3. Baltimore: Williams Wilkins.

Lock, M. 2000. "Accounting for Disease and Distress: Morals of the Normal and Abnormal." In *The Handbook of Social Studies in Health and Medicine*, edited by Gary L. Albrecht, Ray Fitzpatrick, and Susan C. Scrimshaw, 259–276. London: Sage.

Pearson, K. 1914. *The Life, Letters and Labours of Sir Francis Galton:*. vol. 1. Cambridge: Cambridge University Press.

Rydell, R., C. Cogdell, and M. Largent. 2006. "The Nazi Eugenics Exhibition in the United States, 1934–1943." In *Popular Eugenics: National Efficiency and American Mass Culture in the 1930s*, edited by Susan Currell and Christina Cogdell, 359–384. Athens, Ohio: Ohio University Press.

Sekula, A. 1986. "The Body and the Archive." *October* 39: 3–64.

Spade, D. 2011. *Normal Life: Administrative Violence, Critical Trans Politics, and the Limits of Law*. Brooklyn, NY: South End Press.

Stepan, N. 1982. *The Idea of Race in Science: Great Britain 1800–1960*. London: Macmillan.

Thomson, R. G. 1997. *Extraordinary Bodies: Figuring Physical Disability in American Culture and Literature*. New York: Columbia University Press.

The construction of access: the eugenic precedent of the Americans with Disabilities Act

Stephanie K. Wheeler

ABSTRACT

This paper interrogates the language of the legal precedents of the Americans with Disabilities Act (ADA) and their function, including the 1891 Immigration Law and the series of 'ugly laws' that spanned from the late nineteenth century until the early twentieth century. Legislative language is used to construct and deploy static definitions of normalcy and disability, relying on 'objective' evidence couched in medical and scientific discourse. The purpose of this paper is to uncover the legislative precedents of the Americans with Disabilities Act Amendments Act (ADAAA) that were motivated by the eugenicist imperative to strengthen the image of a productive and robust nation. I begin by outlining eugenicist logic and demonstrate how it functions within a semiotic system. Then, I will introduce the process by which eugenicist logic works within legal semiotics. Lastly, I will provide three examples of how this process functions in the legislative language and implementation of the 1891 Immigration Act, the 'ugly laws' and the ADAAA. Ultimately, I will demonstrate how all three provide evidence of a pattern of semiotic systems that pathologize human difference and manages these differences so as to segregate and disenfranchise in the name of nationalism.

With the current American election cycle upon us, the disdain for weakness, failure and outsiders has come to characterize the nativism that is driving the political divides. These appeals to strength and victory make it impossible not to hear echoes of the eugenics movement of the early twentieth century: DenHoed (2016) succinctly points out that 'fears of procreation and infiltration still have force, although they're directed not at "hopelessly vicious protoplasm" but at "anchor babies"; instead of the pure blood of the Nordic races, we hear invocations of that other superior species, the Winners'. The imagined future of American identity is bound up in tirades against the unfit, often deploying scientific terminology to justify the hegemonic construction of spaces of belonging. In *Disabled Upon Arrival: The Rhetorical Construction of Disability and Race at Ellis Island*, Dolmage (2011, 55) argues that 'we see not just the ways that spaces and discourses work together to impose social order, creating spaces in which deviation is sequestered; we also see how spaces and discourses in part create deviation and difference'. This attention to deviation and difference reflects how much the foundational concepts regarding the legal usage of space has historically been bound up in medical and scientific discourse. Snyder and Mitchell's (2006, 3) examination of what they call the 'cultural locations of disability' demonstrate how spaces are characterized by the demarcation between normative and undesirable bodies. Consequently, they argue, disabled bodies in these spaces are often understood as undesirable and deviant within medical, legal and social contexts. As a result, they are deposited in physical and cultural locations shaped by a eugenic ideology, where they are subject to objectification and scrutiny under the guise of goodwill, betterment or knowledge-building. They argue that the origins of these 'goodwill' practices are eugenic and 'a primary source of disabled people's oppression today' (28–29), given the emphasis on the disabled body as 'a wellspring of medical knowledge of all bodies' (28). As a result, shaping locations – particularly through legal language – in the name of improvement for people with disabilities often do just the opposite.

The purpose of this paper is to uncover the legislative precedents of the Americans with Disabilities Act Amendments Act (ADAAA) that were motivated by the eugenicist imperative to strengthen the image of a productive and robust nation by limiting the existence and participation of people with disabilities in the name of goodwill or betterment. First, I will outline what I mean by 'eugenicist logic' and demonstrate how it functions within a semiotic system. Then, I will introduce the process by which eugenicist logic works within legal semiotics. Lastly, I will provide three examples of how this process functions in the legislative language and implementation of the 1891 Immigration Act, the 'ugly laws' and the ADAAA. Ultimately, I will demonstrate how all three provide evidence of a pattern of semiotic systems that pathologize human difference and manages these differences so as to segregate and disenfranchise in the name of national improvement.

Signs of deviance: semiotic constructions of space and law

Dolmage's assertion relies on Michel De Certeau's ([1984] 2002) distinction between space and place, wherein 'a place is the order (of whatever kind) in accord with which elements are distributed in relationships of coexistence,' and thus is 'an instantaneous configuration of positions. It implies an indication of stability'. Alternatively, De Certeau (117) explains that a 'space is composed of intersections of mobile elements' and should thus be considered a practiced place. In other words, where place is considered static, defined by its material conditions, space is malleable, defined through the practices that occur within those conditions. Cities, for example, are constantly changing, moving and creating; as a result, Wagner argues (2011, 231), mobility and malleability are central to the success of a space, especially an urban one.

Yet, the laws regarding public space often regard that space as a *place,* a static, geographical site that can be controlled through language. As a consequence, the language used to create those laws carries the assumption with it that the 'static' and 'neutral' nature of legislative language – that is, the nature of the 'official' language will not be misconstrued. Maley (1994, 22) clarifies this reliance on the notion of fixed meaning in legislative language: 'Technical language in the sense of words with fixed and definite meaning is generally considered to be one of the most distinctive features of legal discourse in general'. Yet, as Kevelson (1988) notes, finding a fixed meaning in legislative language is impossible because it works within a semiotic system of movement and differences, and is enforced via semiotic processes of the same nature. Thus, as Wagner (2011) argues, if we are to understand the legal language that conditions the usage of space, we must treat space as also part of a semiotic system. Space, for Wagner, is a form of non-verbal communication that enables law, language and audience access to the complex signification that it communicates. Despite the fact that visual signs are not considered language, they do belong to and form a system with elements of language (Mitchell 2005, 21); thus, the visual space of urban locations and the laws that condition their use and functions are governed by the same, larger semiotic system (Marusek 2005, 2009; Wagner 2006; Summerfield and McHoul 2009). Foucault's (1975) insistence that space functions as displays of power and control inform the analysis Wagner (2011) offers, demonstrating how urban space does not display 'an innocent control. This is the case of public urban planning whose reshaping is supposed to dissuade and also make repression easier in a non-transparent and invisible way'. Accordingly, regarding space as a semiotic system provides an opportunity to engage spaces of access – those that provide limit and create access – within the semiotic power structures in which they were conceived.

Constructions of deviance: eugenics and biosemiotics

Cobley (2010, 234) observes that in the field of biosemiotics – the study of biological processes as a semiotic systems – language is regarded as a complex modelling device that is foundational to communication because of 'semiotic freedom' that is, the symbol's ability to grow. This growth, Favareau (2010, 32) reminds us, is not a random process, but one of the 'enacted accomplishment[s]' that will have to be understood as accomplishments of intent 'if we are ever to understand the bio-logical side of living organisms' material interactions'. The implication of Cobley's observation in light of Faverau's argument is that biology and biological functioning are subject to the same kinds of dynamic interplays within and between semiotic systems. Put another way, if we are to accept biology as a semiotic system (as we accept law as a semiotic system), we must also accept that functions of the body – like functions of space – produce signs that rehearse cultural narratives the same way that laws produce spaces that rehearse the same narratives. Significantly, understandings of biological functions are subject to the same influences of power and control that law has on space.

Perhaps, there is no greater example of power and control over biological functions and bodies than that of eugenics. Although scholars such as Baker (2002, 665) concur that 'primarily [eugenics] refers at the broadest level to a belief in the necessity of "racial" or "national" improvement through the control of populational reproduction' taking a semiotic – and in this case, a biosemiotic approach allows inviting an extension of this understanding of eugenics to include the discursive practices of eugenics itself. In doing so, understandings of eugenics can move towards recognizing its function as a semiotic practice that seeks to maintain power structures over unwanted bodies and practices in the name of improvement. Fuchs-Kittowski and Rosenthal (2007, 99) maintain that:

> Living systems are semiotic systems: They respond to their surroundings in selective ways specified by their own organization. Living systems, as self organizing, actional systems, present also the creative power to generate new structures and functions and thus new properties, new signs and meanings, new information during their evolution.

In this view, eugenics is an intervention into the self-organizing, actional semiotic systems of biology in the attempt to improve the human species. It is an attempt to direct the growth of symbols and signs, or in some cases, to prevent the growth altogether. This attempt to control the biological organization, action and contexts of living systems is an attempt to edit the text of life itself (Baer 1992). Consequently, any intervention into a biological system is a semiotic one that manipulates the structure of reproductive processes regarding certain genetic structures while simultaneously preventing those deemed undesirable. Fuchs-Kittowski and Rosenthal (2007, 89) write that the 'connection between structure and function is mediated by meanings which are formed only in this interaction process'. In other words, the meaning or outcome that arises from the interaction between the structure and the biological elements and processes can be profoundly impacted by any kind of intervention. Wachbroit (1987, 6) notes that eugenics, like any medical therapy, is an interruptive procedure that runs the risk of undesired consequences, despite the intention of avoiding disadvantages: 'what we regard as shortcomings may be no more than local prejudices' (7). Thus while scholars such as Gillham (2001), Ballif (2004) and Gould (1981) have situated eugenics as discourse that enforces power structures, this project extends that work by specifically demonstrating the operation of eugenics as a practice that promotes the manipulation of semiotic structures regarding human variation. In doing so, eugenics transforms from an intervention to its own semiotic system.

This semiotic system of eugenics transforms signs into markers of difference to designate the boundaries between normal and abnormal, desirable and undesirable. And because of its biological implications, it worries the line between intention (an aim) and agency (the capacity to act). Furthermore, Wagner and Broekman (2010, x) assert that any semiotic activity is responsible for creating meaning in culture, and as a result, because law is semiotic, it is not just 'a discourse of norms, commands, or related social signs but rather an all-embracing language to conceive such entities, which leads to the construction of social institutions'. Ultimately, if we understand eugenics, biology, law and language as semiotic systems, the varying manifestations of power and control can be revealed; specific to this project, then, if we consider the language of the 1891 Immigration Act, the 'ugly laws,' and the Americans with Disabilities Act (ADA) as semiotic, then we can trace a pattern of eugenic power and control that continues to shape our understandings of disability: it manipulates the biological aim of reproduction (intention) into an act of nativism (the illusion of agency). In what follows, I will demonstrate that differences are pathologized – that is, regarded as semiotic – in order to gain access to sign systems with the purposes of intervening and manipulating the process of semiosis under the guise of nativism, that is, taking control of biology for the strength and health of the nation. Thus, we can understand eugenics *as an intervention into semiotic system for the purposes of improvement;* what distinguishes eugenics from any other kind of intervention into a semiotic system is that system's impact on and appeals to the body, particularly as it functions as a biosemiotic system. This intervention manifests in three ways: naming, categorizing and conditioning.

Ellis Island and the 1891 Immigration Act

The nineteenth-century disciplinary concerns for transforming human diversity into quantifiable data promoted the systematic segregation of unworthy, irresponsible citizens from the worthy and responsible ones, rendering disability as a sign of conflict in the growing narrative of American culture and body politic. This narrative was constructed via the juxtaposition of the material body of the citizenry against the idealized body of the nation. 'For the national body to become increasingly "coherent,"' Snyder and Mitchell (23) argue, 'citizens must begin to recognize themselves as either contributors to or detractors from the overall health of the body politic'. Placing this in the terms of biosemiotics, the nation was a body, dependent on a labouring system designed to keep it healthy. Disability was a disease and a hindrance to that health. Eugenics provided the tools necessary to 'edit the text of the disease' (Baer 1992) out of the system.

During this time, anthropometrics became the tool that determined the need for this editing. Anthropometry is the science of quantifiable measurements of the human body. To distinguish between the worthy and unworthy citizens, anthropometric data were collected, analyzed and deployed in an effort to create designated norms, the standard by which all bodies were held against. Tremain (2010, 4) observes that the anthropometric research data yielded inspired 'a new type of medicine … whose main function was public hygiene, and whose institutions centralized the power of the new medicine, normalized its knowledge, and coordinate the care that is distributed under its auspices'. She continues: 'Regulatory mechanisms are put into place that prescribe norms, adjust to an equilibrium, maintain an average, and compensate for variations within the "general population"'. Thus in the attempt to create and maintain a normality that fostered notions of public hygiene, anthropometrics provided a way to situate difference through the enforcement of designated norms sustained by scientific and medical data. In his acquisition of anthropometric data, Francis Galton, 'father of eugenics', appealed to the cultural investment in normalization and invited the public to document their own physical and mental characteristics. By taking this approach, Galton provided the public a crucial cultural technique by which to standardize their bodies, effectively positioning 'quantification as a universal cultural value' (Lundgren 2011, 14) that established an imagined, ideal citizen based on ability, genetics and ideology. Immigrants and other undesirable people threatened this imaginary citizen, and from the standpoint of eugenicist logic and semiotics, threatened the future of the nation by multiplying that which halted the progress and future of the United States.

Thus legislations such as the 1891 Immigration Act were written in service of protecting what was believed to be the existence of an ideal American citizen and identifying who was not. While it was certainly not the first legislation that governed immigration, it was, however, the first that approached immigration in a comprehensive, exclusionary way that could be administered through a federal government agency and policy. Officials were granted permission by the federal government to deny entry of persons appearing to be a convict, disabled or unlikely to, 'take care of himself or herself without becoming a public charge' (Chap. 551, Section 1), marking the beginning of the medical exclusion of immigrants into the United States. Bodies that did not meet the medical standards of 'imagined authenticity' – or those who refused to be quantified through this process – were not permitted access into the nation and by extension, citizenship. This law is a legal intervention into a semiotic system of citizenship, reflecting the relationship between the perceived weakness of a nation and its ability to control immigration Ong (1999, 9). Similarly, Snyder and Mitchell's (2006, 23) contention that 'if a national body was made up of a multitude of individual bodies, then each "person" was recognized as a microcosm of the state,' meaning that the Immigration Act and the processes of admittance into the United States served as a preventative measure to improve the strength and health of the nation.

Hence the restriction of 'all idiots, insane persons, paupers, or persons likely to become a public charge, [and] persons suffering from a loathsome or dangerous contagious disease' ('Immigration Act' 1891, Chap. 551, Section 1). This discrimination of persons with disabilities is coded in medical language: *idiots, insane, disease*. The context of this medical language suggests that people with disabilities are people who are, and should be, feared: loathsome, dangerous and contagious – all signal the fear of disability, and relate it directly to the health of the nation and its people. To code ableism in 'objective,' medical language is to say that the fear of people with disabilities is a legitimate response to 'worthy' citizens, since the static definition of disability emphasizes the threat of the evolutionary progress of both the nation, but of the people themselves. Moreover, the act denies entrance to those whose ticket was paid for by another – suggesting that they could not care for themselves, or depended on the assistance of others to survive. To associate disability and disease within the context of immigration is to also put those same labels onto the bodies of the immigrants themselves. Because the Immigration Act describes what is not wanted and what is considered unhealthy to the nation, it is not insignificant that it opens up with a description of disabled bodies. By situating what is unhealthy to the nation within the context of immigration, this act is very clearly implying that the bodies of immigrants are diseased and unhealthy. Situating these bodies in the context of medical language is legitimizing the nation's place as part of a semiotic system that appeals to biosemiotic and legal semiotic framings of language, namely the attempt to control and limit the movement of signs of disability as always 'diseased', 'unhealthy' and 'threatening'.

Identifying the bodies of those who defied the statistic averages, however, was not just limited to the languaging of deviance. While the practices designed to uphold the law, and by extension, the definitions of normal and abnormal that the law implied, reflected this language around disability, the practice of anthropometry, however, was the tool by which bodies were held accountable to these ideas of 'normal'. After the passage of the Act, Ellis Island became the hub of immigration processing and anthropometric practices. Dolmage (2011) argues that 'the social processing that Ellis Island engendered was all about identifying and sometimes manufacturing abnormal bodies: these elements are out of place; these bodies are disordered'. Ellis Island served as a type of designating station, wherein bodies were subjected to a normalizing gaze that determined their level of difference and its relationship to the development of 'the norm' in the United States. Safford (1925, 246), a medical doctor stationed at Ellis Island, describes in his memoir, the motivation behind the medical inspection:

> The scheme as it was maintained in actual operation at Ellis Island during my time there provided an opportunity for an observer to inspect an immigrant systematically both at rest and in motion at a distance of about twenty or twenty-five feet; for an observer to inspect or scrutinize the immigrant as he approached the observer, and finally after the immigrant came close at hand. Somewhere in this inspection process provision was to be made for the close examination of hands, eyes, and, if deemed advisable, of throat. No attempt was to be made on such an inspection to determine what was wrong. Suspicion that something might be wrong was alone sufficient justification for turning a person aside.

Part of this 'scheme' of identifying 'deficiencies' that Safford describes is dependent on the measurement and quantification of bodily ability. Anthropometrics operates here in the interest of eugenicist logic to determine the acceptability of bodies within the context of American nationalism and productivity. The notion of disability and practices of disabling are often linked to the restriction of productivity and participation; as Snyder and Mitchell (2006, 39) write, because disability 'extracted individuals from productive membership in a capitalist economy, people with physical and cognitive differences found themselves controlled by new terms'. This shift to new terms is an example of a shift and intervention in semiotic systems. Within a capitalist system that privileges labour as a key to development and improvement, a shift to new terms means that bodies are not just pathologized, but also subject to a scientific and medical measure of worth. Eugenic logic intervenes in the system of citizenship, capitalism and labour – indeed, prior to the 1882 Act, immigration was largely welcomed so as to build a strong labour force – by pathologizing difference and restricting definitions of participation. In doing so, the nation became regarded in a biosemiotic sense, wherein disabled, non-labouring bodies represented a threat to the 'natural' sustainability of the country. Accordingly, this eugenic intervention manifested through language (legislative language meant to invoke scientific and medical rationales for restriction), statistical cataloguing of bodily averages (anthropometrics at Ellis Island) and the conditioning of participation based on language and cataloguing (participation is only granted once someone can evade the language and statistics of 'deviance').

The ugly laws

'[T]his person is made out of words,' writes Susan Schweik (2009, 85) in a discussion of the legislative language of the 'ugly laws.' Contemporary to the Immigration Act and the social processing at Ellis Island, what came to be known as the 'ugly laws' were created in the United States that barred people with 'unsightly or disgusting' disabilities from public spaces on the grounds that their appearance was offensive and a legal liability.[1] These laws were intended to prevent street begging, but also served to emphasize the idea of the imagined America and American citizen by removing all offenders from sight. Schweick contextualizes this relationship between legislative language and offending bodies (2009, 85):

> If there is some comfort in remembering that this is a legal and therefore entirely 'insubstantial' person, perhaps a person with rights, there is discomfort in noticing how quickly *this* person is bound back into a body and an identity: not a person *with*, for instance (as in 'person with a disability') but 'any person *who is*' (diseased, maimed, or what have you).

'Personhood' functions as a semiotic system here, whereby a person is defined only by the relationship their bodies have to this legislative language. The semiotic system that creates the meaning of 'personhood' is interrupted by eugenic logic that serves to distinguish between the bodies of those who *are* valuable verses those *with* value. The first ugly law on record is an 1867 law passed by the city of San Francisco, and opens up with the express restriction against any kind of practice of or related to begging in public places, but also:

> any person who is diseased, maimed, mutilated, or in any way deformed so as to be an unsightly or disgusting object, or an improper person to be allowed in or on the streets, highways, thoroughfares or public places in the City or County of San Francisco, shall not therein or thereon expose himself or herself to public view. (San Francisco 1869)

It is important to remark that these terms – *diseased, maimed, mutilated, deformed, disgusting* – were highly subjective and indicative of the desired outcome of these laws. Unlike the Immigration Act, where individuals had to prove their worth under the umbrella terms of *normal* and *able-bodied*, the ugly laws required the enforcers to default to 'static' language in order to argue against the participation of abnormal bodies. There was no room for interpretation or disagreement once enforcers languaged these unwanted bodies.

Interestingly, each word used to describe the unwanted body in public spaces hold multiple meanings (as language does), but they all serve the illusion of unchanging meaning: human difference is largely undesirable. *Diseased* is a particularly interesting word choice, given that the conditions these laws attempted to prevent were often understood in terms of the body, rendering these undesirable bodies as the disease of the nation, not simply a symptom or consequence of a larger 'disease', namely the harmful conditions crafted by the systems of power against aberrant bodies. *Maimed* is also an interesting choice of word, since 'maimed' is used to refer to the deprivation of the use of a part of the body, invoking impairment, disability and more significantly, disablement. When that impairment occurred as a result of a wartime injury, however, that impairment was esteemed because it was risked in the name of nationalism and patriotism (Schweik 2009, 150). Any other body designated as 'useless' consequently becomes maimed by systems of disablement. *Mutilated* also invokes a similar use, making imperfect by damaging parts of the body. *Deformed* threatens to alter a form, specifically with regard to aesthetics and *disgusting* refers to the offence of moral sense or good taste. Putting these words together achieved a constructed, unchanging context that did not define the unwanted body, but rather created it. The body that must be removed from public view and participation is the body that is abnormal and harmful, deprived of usefulness, damaged, aesthetically abnormal and repulsive. Significantly, these words and concepts can also be understood as manifestations of the fears of the nation i.e. becoming abnormal, useless, diseased, etc. But by putting this language onto bodies, language – such as the law – can control and remove them if so desired. Medical and legal languages create the standard upon which normality is held against, but it also conditions that normality within medical and scientific discourses. The standard of normalcy is never fully elaborated, but is instead determined differentially against medical understandings of disability. Therefore, no matter how unsteady the meaning of 'normal' is, it will always depend on the semiotic functioning of language to exist. And from this process of differentiation, that is, in the context of abnormal, harmful, useless and repulsive, the able body emerges – one that is normal, safe, useful and appealing.

Thus one of the many ways language was used in the ugly laws was to determine what was wanted by laying out what was feared: the fears of what the nation might become were turned into metaphors that relied on the metaphor of the nation as a body. Legal discourse created unwanted bodies that became refigured as 'diseases' that threatened the health of the nation and its biosemiotic system; the 'medicine' that would cure society of what ailed it would similarly be refigured in a legal semiotic system. The context of the ugly law is driven by the eugenicist intervention into language, which guides the multiplicity of meanings by discouraging the production of those meanings that would be deemed undesirable: diseased, maimed, mutilated, deformed, disgusting bodies cannot ever be healthy, beautiful, appealing, or useful. Schweik's (2009) invaluable analysis of the language of the ugly laws has firmly situated this language as hygienic, functioning as its own biosemiotic system: 'The law seems to have its own kind of raw shuddering body: law as gag reflex, a law with guts. *Disgusting* adds a biological force to the ordinance, framing it as the legal concomitant of nausea' (94). The eugenic motivation of improvement creates what Schweik (2009) calls 'legalized disgust'. Bodies become managed through language and naming based on medical standards of 'normal', thereby conditioning participation of 'abnormal' bodies to cleanse and create ideological and material spaces.

Americans with Disabilities Act

Similarly, the ADA, like all legislation, employs regulatory language with the aim of giving the veneer of static meaning in the name of consistency. Just as in the case of the ugly laws, a recognition of the failure of regulatory language's attempt to control the dynamic interplay of signs and meanings provides an entry point into understanding the ways that power is deployed in the attempt to limit those meanings. The ADA opens with a definition of disability, borrowed from Section 504 of the 1973 Rehabilitation Act (20.b.i): an individual with a disability 'has a physical or mental impairment which substantially limits one or more of such person's major life activities'. A person with a significant disability 'has a severe physical or mental impairment which seriously limits one or more functional capacities' and has physical or mental disabilities resulting from a number of causes (21.a.iii). With the passage of the Americans with Disabilities Act Amendments Act (ADAAA, 2008), a third prong of disability qualification was added, referred to as the 'regarding as'. Here, people are protected from discrimination based on stereotypes of assumptions based on disability, a move that Befort (2010) notes is a move that reflects the function of the medical and social models of disability. What these definitions suggest is that once a body becomes languaged with sign systems, it becomes legally and/or medically disabled, and available to the access the ADAAA lays out. Contradictorily, legal language is in service of public protection, yet these definitions only apply to the private management of disability (Essig 2005). Thus, the degree to which a condition is disabling is subjective, but only legitimate once corroborated and framed by public, medical discourse and visible conduct. Disability must be at once both private (managed) and public (stated) for the ADAAA to apply.

Thus the fixed language attached to the experience of disability is only described differentially when addressing access. What this means – and what Essig (2005) has effectively demonstrated – is that the ADA is only applicable when disability is languaged, not necessarily embodied. Therefore, disability becomes defined largely in terms of access. Yet, much like the writers of the ugly laws, the writers of the ADA and the ADAAA (Americans with Disabilities Amendments Act) do not define what accessibility is, but rather rely on language in order to provide an idea of what accessibility is not. In this way, the ADAAA expects disability to come in a specific form, one that will give the veneer of inclusion, but one that does not threaten the ideological structure of the institutions subject to the law. This is best seen in the ways in which accommodation are handled under the ADAAA. Accommodations and 'reasonable accommodations' largely do not disrupt or threaten the structures already in place. The term 'reasonable accommodation' is a modification or adjustment that enables access to the available benefits and privileges of a programme or employment opportunity. The ADAAA cites three aspects that are subject to reasonable accommodation: (1) equal opportunity in the application process, (2) to enable a qualified individual with a disability to perform the essential functions required of him or her in the programme or job and (3) to enable a person with disabilities access to equal benefits and privileges of employment or enrolment in a programme (1211.9). What results from this language is the expectation that disability is experienced in private but must be hidden in public: in US Airways, Inc v. Barnett, for example, Essig (2005) observes that:

> the Court expressed the expectation (both its own and that of other employees) that individuals with disabilities 'cover' by refraining from engaging in conduct (such as requesting reasonable accommodations) that would require others to confront their disability status. By thus narrowing the scope of the ADA's reasonable accommodations provision, the Court broadened the scope of expected covering by people with disabilities.

In this way, the redesign of structures to accommodate persons with disabilities is not in service of accommodation for all, but rather in service of a different version (or performance) of an able body.

What emerges in this analysis is the ADAAA's dependence on and creation of binaries: private and public, conduct ('acting' disabled) and status (languaged as disabled), closeting (Essig 2005; not disclosing a disability) and covering (Yoshino 2006; disclosing a disability but not 'performing' it). These binaries should not be surprising, however, if we are to understand the ADAAA as both a part of a semiotic system and its own semiotic system. Again, meaning can only arise through differences and the play of contradictions. The ADAAA's intent to free persons with disabilities from discrimination and open avenues of access and participation is conditioned by the eugenic logic of betterment via semiosis: the ADAAA seeks to redefine disability through language, medical statistics and participation in the name of access and civil rights. Essig (2005) argues that the Court has consistently gone:

> beyond expressing a preference that people with disabilities remain closeted and held, ironically, that if they do so through the use of medications or other devices that alleviate disabling symptoms, they no longer have disabilities and are not entitled to the ADAAA's protection.

Cole's observation reflects the contradictory implications of the legislation I have outlined here, and indeed, the contradictory stances the Courts have taken in upholding ADAAA legislation.[2] And because this improvement for the lives of people with disabilities relies on semiotics – the pathologizing of bodies and sign systems as a way to re-assign meaning (Linton 1998) to them and from them – the appeals to language, statistics and participation inevitably rehearse eugenic intervention in the name of national improvement (via civil rights legislation).

Conclusions

Identity – who has control over assigning it and what can be done with it – emerges as a focal point in the legislation. I have analyzed above: the Immigration Act identifies who is (or is capable of becoming) a citizen and the ugly laws identify who is a *person*. The ADAAA, I argue, follows this same line of thought and attempts to combine the two: it provides previously inaccessible opportunities to participate and contribute to the larger citizenry (through work, education and the like), while simultaneously outlining what that contribution may look like (through protections and reasonable accommodations). It does this by intervening in the semiotic systems that have come to define disability, participation and personhood so as to provide more opportunities to foster the growth of a healthy, thriving and progressive nation.

Of course this is not exactly a bad thing. Under my definition of eugenics, however – that is, eugenics as an intervention into a semiotic system for the purposes of improvement, manifested in attempts to name, categorize and condition – it would follow that the ADAAA's intervention into semiotic systems is a eugenic one. via an appeal to biology and science, it creates a biosemiotic system and deploys it as a legal system. As a consequence, bodies are subjected to legal and medical language in the name of betterment – for their own lives and the lives of their fellow citizens. Yet the freedom gained from access is just another form of hegemonic control, often at the cost of those bodies who do not fit the biological or legal category of 'disabled'.[3] While I in no way intend to suggest that the ADAAA has had direct, material consequences on the bodies of those who have been, and continue to be, subjected to eugenic medical practices, I do want to highlight the lineage that from which the logical functioning of the ADAAA works. The earliest appeals to eugenic practices in the work of Plato and Aristotle were couched in improving language and lessons of good men speaking well. The so-called 'origin story' of eugenics – the one with Francis Galton naming the science of race betterment – always begins with a word: eu (meaning better, or good) genics (meaning birth). Thus, while I am not arguing that the ADAAA is a eugenic legislation – nor the Immigration Act or the ugly laws – its appeal to semiotic functioning and reliance on languaging existence and personhood should not be taken lightly. In Snyder and Mitchell's (2006) terms, I suggest that the ADAAA is a cultural location of disability.

Eugenics is in and of itself a binary system: define one as desirable or undesirable, Reproduce or sterilize, Cultivate or repress. Herein lies the crux of my argument: I am not arguing that every system that is sustained by removal and reproduction is a eugenic project. I am, however, arguing that those patterns of languaging, cataloguing and conditioning that are central to the workings of eugenic systems are the same that structure our basic notions of how language and meaning making works. Very often, appeals to improvement are languaged and made into metaphors that implicate the body. Consequently, it behoves us to take note of the modes of meaning making around embodied difference, as I have done here, and to take responsibility for interrogating those meanings, intended or not. Doing so provides us a tool that reminds us that despite the consistent attempts to remove or hide unwanted bodies, these bodies never fully disappear and will not disappear as long as we continue to look for the additions that grow from the subtractions, and the subtractions that grow from the additions. For every absence there is a presence; for every removal there is an addition.

I opened this article up with a reference to the 2016 American Presidential election and I will conclude it with a quote that is deeply relevant here: in 1927, the United States Supreme Court ruled that compulsory sterilization of the 'unfit' – including those with cognitive, intellectual and physical disabilities – was constitutional on the grounds that it was 'for the protection and health of the state' (xxx 1927).[4] Justice Oliver Wendell Holmes, Jr, spoke of his pleasure in writing the decision, noting that 'sooner or later one gets a chance to say what one thinks' (as quoted. in Cohen 2016, 277). In an age where politicians and the justice system systematically favours the strong over the weak, the winners over the losers and the haves over the have-nots, Holmes' pleasure and entitlement of using language to dehumanize, disenfranchise and manipulate the bodies of an entire citizenry should feel distressingly familiar to all who are following the American election campaign. At its core, eugenicist logic posits the removal of unneeded or unwanted elements as an integral part of development, yet this idea of always moving towards something larger, that something can in fact be fully achieved or completed, runs counter to the ways in which meaning is made within semiotic systems. If we continue to overlook how eugenicist logic has the capacity to thrive at the foundations of social justice legislation, bodies will continue to become effaced and forgotten, allowing language and communication based on eugenicist logic to construct our ideas about difference, human variation and disability.

Notes

1. Most states' ugly laws were not repealed until the mid-1970s. (Chicago was the last to repeal in 1974).
2. See, for instance, Bragdon v. Abbot, Cleveland v. Policy Management Systems Corporation, Toyota Motor Manufacturing, Kentucky, Inc. v. Williams for examples of the Court insisting on closeting; alternatively, Sutton v. United, Murphy v. United Postal Service, Albertstons v. Kirkinburg, and Raytheon Company v. Hernandez have all demonstrated a preference for covering. (Essig 2005).
3. Here I refer to the medical model of defining disability vs. the social model; in other words, it is the difference between those persons told that their impairments are not disabling, or in the case of chronic illnesses like fibromyalgia, are told that these illnesses or impairments do not exist, vs. those whose disabilities are not covered under the legal definitions of disability in the ADAA, especially the 'regarded as' prong.
4. The Supreme Court has never explicitly overturned Buck v. Bell.

Disclosure statement

No potential conflict of interest was reported by the author.

References

Americans with Disabilities Amendments Act (ADAAA). 2008. http://www.ada.gov/pubs/ada.htm.

Baer, Eugen. 1992. "Editing the Text of a Disease: Semiotic and Ethical Aspects of Therapeutic Genetic Engineering." In *Biosemiotics: The Semiotic Web 1991*, edited by T. Sebok and J. Umiker-Sbeok, 15–25. New York: Mouton de Gruyter.

Baker, Bernadette. 2002. "The Hunt for Disability: The New Eugenics and the Normalization of School Children." *Teachers College Record* 104 (4): 663–703.

Ballif, Michelle. 2004. "Reproducing Rhetoric, Eugenically." *Rhetoric Society Quarterly* 34 (4): 5–31.

Befort, Stephen F. 2010. "Let's Try This Again: The ADA Amendments Act of 2008 Attempts to Reinvigorate the 'Regarded As' Prong of the Statutory Definition of Disability." *Utah Law Review* 4: 993–1028. doi:10.2139/ssrn.1576503.

Buck v. Bell. 1927. 274 U.S. 200.

Cobley, Paul. 2010. "The Cultural Implications of Biosemiotics." *Biosemiotics* 3 (2): 225–244.

Cohen, Adam. 2016. *Imbeciles: The Supreme Court, American Eugenics, and the Sterilization of Carrie Buck*. New York: Penguin.

De Certeau, Michel. (1984) 2002. *The Practice of Everyday Life*. Translated by Steven F. Rendall. Berkeley: University of California Press.

DenHoed, Andrea. (2016). "The Forgotten Lessons of the American Eugenics Movement." *New Yorker*, April 27. http://www.newyorker.com/books/page-turner/the-forgotten-lessons-of-the-american-eugenics-movement.

Dolmage, Jay. 2011. "Disabled upon Arrival: The Rhetorical Construction of Disability and Race at Ellis Island." *Cultural Critique* 77 (1): 24–69. doi:10.1353/cul.2011.0000.

Essig, Melissa Cole. 2005. "Gimp Theory and the ADA's 'Feedback Loop.'" *Saint Louis University Law Journal* 4: 1047–1075.

Favareau, Donald. 2010. "Introduction: An Evolutionary History of Biosemiotics." In *Essential Readings in Biosemiotics: Anthology and Commentary*, edited by Donald Favareau, 1–77. Amsterdam: Springer Netherlands.

Foucault, Michel. (1975) 1995. *Discipline and Punish: The Birth of the Prison*. Translated by Alan Sheridan 1977. Second VintageBooks ed. New York: Random House.

Fuchs-Kittowski, Klaus, and Hans-Alfred Rosenthal. 2007. "Biosemiotics, Bioinformatics, and Responsibility: Ambivalent Consequences of the Deciphering of the Human Genome for Society and Science." *TripleC: Cognition, Communication, Co-Operation* 5 (2): 87–100.

Gillham, Nicholas W. 2001. "Sir Francis Galton and the Birth of Eugenics." *Annual Review of Genetics* 35: 83–101.

Gould, Stephen Jay. 1981. *The Mismeasure of Man*. New York: Norton.

Immigration Act, 1891, 26 Stat. 1084, 51st Cong., 2nd. Sess. (March 3, 1891) LexisNexis Academic.

Kevelson, Roberta. 1988. *The Law as a System of Signs*. New York: Plenum Press.

Linton, Simi. 1998. *Claiming Disability: Knowledge and Identity*. New York: New York University Press.

Lundgren, Frans. 2011. "The Politics of Participation: Francis Galton's Anthropometric Laboratory and the Making of Civic Selves." *The British Journal for the History of Science* 46 (3): 445–466. doi:10.1017/S0007087411000859.

Maley, Yon. 1994. "The Language and the Law." In *Language and the Law*, edited by John Gibbons, 11–50. London: Routledge.

Marusek, Sarah. 2005. "Wheelchair as Semiotic: Space Governance of the American Handicapped Parking Space." *Law, Text and Culture* 9: 177–188.

Marusek, Sarah. 2009. "Legality beyond the Scope of Policy." In *Images in Law*, edited by Anne Wagner and Vijay K. Bhatia, 137–148. Aldershot: Ashgate.

Mitchell, William J. Thomas. 2005. *What Do Pictures Want?* Chicago, IL: University of Chicago Press.

Ong, Aihwa. 1999. *Flexible Citizenship: The Cultural Logics of Transnationality*. Durham, NC: Duke University Press.

Rehabilitation Act of 1973, PL 93-112, 93rd Cong., (September 26, 1973).

Safford, Victor. 1925. *Immigration Problems: Personal Experiences of an Official*. New York: Dodd, Mead.

San Francisco. 1869. *The General Orders of the Board of Supervisors*. San Francisco: Cosmopolitan Printing Company. Order No. 783 (Approved July 9, 1867).

Schweik, Susan M. 2009. *The Ugly Laws: Disability in Public*. New York: New York University Press.

Snyder, Sharon L., and David T. Mitchell. 2006. *Cultural Locations of Disability*. Chicago, IL: University of Chicago Press.

Summerfield, Tracey, and Alec McHoul. 2009. "On Sight/on Site: Visuality in Native Title Claims: Can We Even Speak?" In *Images in Law*, edited by Anne Wagner and Vijay K. Bhatia, 149–166. Aldershot: Ashgate.

Tremain, Shelley. 2010. "Foucault, Governmentality, and Critical Disability Theory: An Introduction." In *Foucault and the Government of Disability*, edited by Shelley Tremain, 1–26. Ann Arbor: University of Michigan Press.

Wachbroit, Robert. 1987. "What's Wrong with Eugenics?" *Philosophy & Public Policy Quarterly* 7 (2/3): 1–8.

Wagner, Anne. 2006. "The Rules of the Road, a Universal Visual Semiotics." *International Journal for the Semiotics of Law* 19 (3): 311–324.

Wagner, Anne. 2011. "French Urban Space Management: A Visual Semiotic Approach behind Power and Control." *International Journal For The Semiotics Of Law* 24 (2): 227–241. doi:10.1007/s11196-010-9206-5.

Wagner, Anne, and Jan M. Broekman. 2010. "Promises and Prospects of Legal Semiotics – An Introduction." In *Prospects of Legal Semiotics*, edited by Anne Wagner and Jan M. Broekman, v–xvii. New York: Springer.

Yoshino, Kenji. 2006. *Covering: The Hidden Assault on Our Civil Rights*. New York: Random House.

Disability and torture: exception, epistemology and 'black sites'

Dinesh Wadiwel

ABSTRACT

Taking into consideration the November 2015 Australian Government Senate Standing Committees on Community Affairs final report on violence towards people with disability in institutional and residential settings, this paper explores the framing and epistemology of torture as practised against people with disability in sites of incarceration. Examining Giorgio Agamben's account of biopolitical sovereignty, this paper considers torture against people with disability as facilitated by legal exception. Extending this perspective further, and drawing on scholarship which examines anti-black violence in the context of policing and mass incarceration, it is argued that torture against people with disability constitutes an epistemic problem, where people with disability are framed as available for excessive violence without recourse to justice systems. This essay argues for more attention to the links between the torture experienced by people with disability in different sites of incarceration and systemic violence against racialized populations, particularly in the context of mass imprisonment.

In November 2015 the Australian Government Senate Standing Committees on Community Affairs released its final report on violence towards people with disability in institutional and residential settings (Senate Standing Committees on Community Affairs 2015). The report found evidence of 'widespread violence, abuse and neglect of people with disability' (267), providing case studies involving people subject to forcible restraint (59; see also 91–102); electroshock (48, 219); beatings and other physical violence (e.g. 50, 60); periods of seclusion or solitary confinement (see 101–103) and in judicial settings, the use of civil orders to effect indefinite detention (see 100). The Community Affairs Committees report the repeated use of cages to incarcerate adults and children with disability. In one case study, an outdoor cage was utilized by a group home small residential facility to incarcerate an adult:

> … a grandmother arrives to see her grandson on a freezing Tasmania winter's day. She finds him locked out of his own home in a courtyard that is used as a cage. No staff are present and she cannot get to him. Staff are located at the rear of the property smoking and laughing. The courtyard was a regular punishment and lockdown space, no amount of family requests or demands or reporting this to the senior practitioner ceased this restrictive practice in three years. But as expected the provider made it clear we the family were the problem and the service decides to stop family visits and drop in and time for Nan to visit him in his own home. (Joyce Langmaid as quoted in Senate Standing Committees on Community Affairs 2015, 50; see Doran 2015)

In another context, any of these practices could be understood as constituting torture.[1] But while the Community Affairs Committees came close to this finding ('Under the guise of "therapeutic treatment", people with disability can be subjected to forcible actions that could be considered assault in any other context' [xxvi]), it remained cautious about naming these acts of violence 'torture.' Indeed, it is remarkable how little discussion is devoted to the problem of torture in the final report.[2] On face value, it is difficult to explain this absence. Why is it that there is a reluctance to name torture in this instance? And how might this relate to the epistemological construction of disability?

'Torture' is a powerful word describing a violence that fundamentally offends the dignity of its target. Because the word 'torture' describes an egregious, illegitimate violence (it is understood as 'exceptional'), it has immense potency as a method of identifying injustice and mobilizing political action.[3] But, the economy of what constitutes torture and what does not is fraught. Not so long ago Catharine A. Mackinnon, in her frank critique of the gendered nature of the construction of torture within the international system, argued that for men 'suffering has the dignity of politics and is called torture' (MacKinnon 2006, 22). In MacKinnon's view, the definition of torture under international law,[4] constrained to acts of violence conducted by public officials, fails to draw attention to the systematic violence experienced by women (for example, domestic and sexual violence), violence that might be torture by another name. MacKinnon's critique highlighted an epistemological problem in relation to torture; or at least highlighted the way that relations of truth and power produce the visibility of torture. If naming as torture assumes that the torture victim has an inherent dignity which is being violated through specific acts of violence, what can we say about forms of inflicted suffering that are not regarded as violating inherent dignities (forms of violence that are not granted signification as torture by social or legal institutions, including for example, organized State violence in the context of mass incarceration)? And simultaneously, what can we say about subjects of violence who are rendered as not having a dignity to violate? That is, as I shall discuss, what happens if torture is naturalized as a form of imperceptible violence? Does this epistemological violence constitute a different kind of torture 'by stealth'?

There has arguably been strong progress internationally towards recognizing forms of treatment experienced by people with disability as torture; in particular, forms of forced restraint and seclusion practised against at least some people with disability have been identified as being at odds with international norms (see Nowak 2008; Méndez 2013). This paper does not seek to challenge or unsettle this work: it remains vital. However, in this paper I am interested in trying to understand the practice of torture against people with disability as not simply an aberrant feature of care and support regimes; but on the contrary, as a systemic form of practice that is aided and abetted by State and other legalized institutions, is central to the social and political practice of exclusion, hierarchization and segregation of people with disability, and also interacts with a broader racialized politics of mass incarceration. This paper has two parts. Firstly, I consider torture through the lens of 'exception', as articulated through Giorgio Agamben's description of sovereign biopolitics. Secondly, I explore torture as an epistemological problem. Through a discussion of routine anti-black violence in the context of policing and mass incarceration, I argue that systemic violence against people with disability resonates strongly with systemic State violence against racialized populations, at least in so far as this violence is routine, and is rendered 'invisible' in so far as it is naturalized.

Torture as 'exception'?

Within recent political theory, there has been a lot of interest in the Italian philosopher Giorgio Agamben and his work on sovereign exception and biopolitics (1998; see also 2004). Drawing from Carl Schmitt (1988), Michel Foucault (1998, 2004), Hannah Arendt (1976) and Walter Benjamin (1996), Agamben puts forward the view that political sovereignty is based upon the capacity to place life within a zone of legal exception. Agamben's prominent example for understanding this relationship is the European concentration camp, in particular Auschwitz, which he argues represents a defining moment within the twentieth century in the development of biopolitical sovereignty (1998, 166–180; see also 1999).[5] State sovereignty here rests on the power to generate spaces where the law is suspended and life within this zone of exception is subject to extraordinary forms of violence: 'the original political relation is the ban (the state of exception as a zone of indistinction between outside and inside, exclusion and inclusion)' (1998, 181).

A range of scholars have been usefully applying a biopolitical perspective and the work of Agamben to understanding disability over the last decade. This includes Fiona Kumari Campbell's linking of exception and biopolitics to understanding the operation of ableism (2009; see also Jordan 2013); Donna Reeve's examination of Agamben's concept of 'homo sacer' and its relationship to the lives of people with disability, including compulsory detention of people with psychosocial disability (2009); Bernadette Baker's discussion of exception and learning disability (2010); Joanne Maddern and Emma Stewart on geographies of exclusion and accessibility (2010); and Bill Hughes on eugenics and disability (2012; see also Mitchell and Snyder 2003; Sirnes 2005; and Overboe 2007). Recently, David T. Mitchell with Sharon L. Snyder have intertwined Agamben's notion of biopolitics with citizenship under neoliberalism which they suggest has been 'fashioned on the basis of systems of oversight specific to disability and others occupying peripheral embodiments' (2015, 7).

There is certainly scope to extend Agamben's analysis directly to understand the way torture against people with disability has operated as a rolling and unquestioned form of legal exception, what Linda Steele has described as a 'lawful violence' (2014). Examining one site for systemic violence against people with disability – the large segregated residential 'care' institution[6] – we might observe a resonance between the perspective advanced by Agamben on the camp, and the reality of confinement for many people with disability within institutional environments. For Agamben, the camp is a space for the exercise of a concentrated biopolitics. This is a space where nutrition, sleep, movement, sexuality and work may be ruthlessly surveyed (see Chapman, Carey, and Ben-Moshe 2014, 14, 15). Legal exception is crucial here. The law appears as suspended, because the camp is a physical space of pure exception; where decisions over the life of its inmates may be made quickly, without reference to regular legal convention (courts, defence, evidence etc.), or more accurately, because the law and everyday norm lose any distinction: everything in the camps is 'truly possible' (Agamben 1998, 170).

This characterization of the legal exception of the camp does not seem far from the practice of torture against people with disability in institutional settings; on contrary, it is disturbing to understand how close the resemblance is between Agamben's classic model of exception and the kinds of practices that some people with disability are routinely subject to in care institutions. Firstly, the context of institutionalization is precisely one where extreme biopolitical controls are exerted over movement, nutrition, reproduction, sexuality and sleep (see for example Sullivan 2008). These deep controls form a background to the complete materialization of the world of the person with disability in a way that refuses home and sociality; on the contrary, just as Elaine Scarry describes in her classic work on torture, the objects associated with home – the bed, the chair – are reconstructed as weapons (Scarry 1985, 42–45). Secondly, routine violence against people with disability – such as the use of restriction (such as physical and chemical restraints) and solitary confinement – occur without attracting legal scrutiny or sanction (see Erevelles 2014, 83). Indeed, the social, legal and political void which surrounds the violence experienced by people with disability renders torture as *not* torture, producing zones where truly everything is truly possible. Where allegations are made, they are ignored or inverted in such a way as to make people with disability themselves culpable.[7] As a number of policy reports have documented, including People with Disability Australia's important 2009 study *Rights Denied*, this includes the tendency to 'naturalise' this violence or treat it as merely an aberration (rather than systemic) within care regimes; failures to deal adequately with complaints during investigation and prosecution, and the conspiracy of legal systems which have not enabled support for people with disability to make decisions and realize rights (French, Dardel, and Price-Kelly 2009, 54–58).

However, this also highlights a problem of meaning. If torture against people with disability is routine, if it is naturalized as everyday within prevailing institutions, then in what sense is it marked out as an exception, or an aberration, to otherwise routine legalized violence? This is, in a sense, an epistemological problem, in so far as the subject of violence is rendered by knowledge systems as open to force without this registering as an injustice. How can we make sense of this epistemic problem? How does it alter the way we might think about exception and the practice of torture?

'Black sites': the epistemological of torture

Recent media and scholarly discussion have referred to secret torture facilities as 'black sites', particularly in reference to the alleged global network of secret intelligence prisons operated and/or supported by the United States Central Intelligence Agency in the context of the war against terror (see Sadat 2006; Mayer 2007; Danner 2009; Pugliese 2013). The 'black site' as a concept offers an imaginary for a space of social, political and juridical exception that hides extensive and intense violence against those who are captured within this zone of confinement. Certainly, the phrase 'black site' has proved to possess a degree of purchase in capturing a public imagination, and fostering opposition to torture. In particular, the public documentation of torture practice at Abu Ghraib and the subsequent release of the so-called 'Torture Memos' documenting the United States administration approved interrogation methods between 2002 and 2004 (see Greenberg and Dratel 2005; also Bybee 2002, 2005; Yoo 2005) have drawn international attention to the routine practices used by military and paramilitary organizations worldwide, and the immense power of contemporary state sovereignty to disappear people into spheres of social, political, legal and administrative non existence. Here the 'black site' is marked by its extraordinary character: it captures the public imagination because it is understood to be an aberration within the landscape of legal penality.

But, the 'black site' need not be exceptional with respect to the functioning of domestic law; it may also be so unremarkably fused with everyday policing that it almost escapes attention. In February 2015, an exposé by *The Guardian* unveiled a secret police operated interrogation facility located in 'a nondescript warehouse on Chicago's west side known as Homan Square' (Ackerman 2015a). The Chicago facility was dubbed by media a 'black site': a nod to the alleged US operated global network of secret intelligence facilities discussed above. But this phrase in this context is also revealing of the racialized targets of the violence enacted in this site, since black people constituted some 82% of the detainees at Homan Square (Ackerman 2015a). Inside the facility detainees were held for long periods of time by police without charge or legal counsel. Family and friends were not notified where suspects were detained. Detainees were subject to beatings and prolonged shackling; there are reports that some detainees were placed in a cage (Batta, Ryan, and Ackerman 2015). The expose has so far revealed records of over 7000 people taken to Homan Square over the period 2004 to 2015 (Ackerman 2015b). Importantly, this was a 'domestic' rather than extra-territorial example of exception: this 'black site' was not located outside of the borders of the nation state, nor operated in the formal context of the declared national emergency of the 'War Against Terror', but instead operated by stealth internally, as a routine institution within the landscape of policing.

Homan Square points to a different history of biopolitics, one that more overtly situates the genealogy of biopolitics with the history of colonial power, imperialism, slavery and conquest. Indeed, while Agamben's thesis (described above) is that the European concentration camp is the most refined example of biopolitical violence (see 1998, 166–168), other scholars have actively questioned Agamben's exclusive focus on the experience of Europe.[8] This concern over the Eurocentrism of the understanding of biopolitics is amplified by recent work examining the history and persistence of systematic anti-black violence within modernity and what this means for understanding the logic of biopolitical violence (see Sexton 2010 and Wilderson 2010; see also James 1996 and Weheliye 2014, 53–73). Jared Sexton, in particular, contests Agamben's view that the rise of biopolitics might be located in the policies of denaturalization that accompanied European nationalist terror, positing instead racialized slavery as a foundational moment:

> The general failure of the inscription of nativity in the order of the nation-state and the state's management of the biological life of the nation is predated and prepared by the strict prohibition of nativity under the regime of racial slavery and the state's management of the biological life of the enslaved throughout the Atlantic world, most pointedly through the sexual regulation of race in the British North American colonies and the United States. And the racial circumscription of political life (*bios*) under slavery predates and prepares the rise of the modern democratic state, providing the central counterpoint and condition of possibility for the symbolic and material articulation of its form and function. (Sexton 2010, 40)

This foundational political positionality of slavery and the production of the black subject – or in Frank Wilderson's rendering, as an 'ontological' political status (see Wilderson 2010, 22, 23) – suggests that anti-black violence informs other violence in modernity. Here, the extraordinary, 'exceptional' space of the 'black site' is deeply informed by historical modalities of colonial violence, including prominently the history of racial slavery, and is continually reiterated in the ordinary, routine, anti-black violence that occurs as part of everyday domestic policing operations and mass incarceration. As Sexton and Elizabeth Lee argue, Abu Ghraib is a production of a military superpower that is founded on systematic anti-black violence, including through 'domestic' techniques of torture exported for use within the externally located military prison: 'the "peacetime" assault finds it *raison d'être* and its most compelling rationalization in the persistence of the domestic black population, and the frontline of this carceral regime obtains in the ever-increasing powers of the police exercised particularly over the lives of black women and men' (Sexton and Lee 2006, 1014; see also Smith 2013; Richter-Montpetit 2014, 51–54; Richter-Montpetit 2015).

Sexton and Lee's perspective is useful for situating and understanding the practice of torture against people with disability for at least two reasons. *Firstly*, the 'black sites' of torture are not merely those which attain media attention as exceptional; instead, they are simply a reminder of a continuing 'gratuitous' violence, including systemic State anti-black violence, in the context of policing and mass incarceration.[9] This perspective allows us to shift focus from not merely systematic violence against people with disability in care institutions, but also to understand how this violence (for example, restriction and seclusion)[10] is routinely imposed against *all* people who are incarcerated. In drawing attention to this history, we should not forget that the genealogy of torture against people with disability is not confined to the residential 'care' institution, but is also contained within the history of penal detention and policing; as Chris Chapman, Allison C. Carey and Liat Ben-Moshe propose, an 'interlocking' analysis is required to understand both the differences, and the profound connections between 'care' institutions and prisons (Chapman, Carey, and Ben-Moshe 2014). Given the over-representation of people with disability within criminal justice systems (see for example Hayes et al. 2007; Holland and Persson 2011; Baldry 2014; Chapman, Carey, and Ben-Moshe 2014) or in other sites of imprisonment such as immigration detention (Soldatic and Fiske 2009), it might be usefully observed that these 'black sites' also serve particular functions in terrorizing people with disability. This alerts us to the need to think broadly about the rationalities that underpin the exercise of torture, wherever they may happen (prison, institution, the group home, immigration camp), and their relationship to the biopolitical construction of disability as a 'naturalised' target of violence in itself.[11] As a political project then, a broad politics of opposition to sites of mass incarceration that produce situations of torture for a range of bodies (rather than only opposition to specific acts of violence which we decide to call 'torture') provides an alternative focus of action. This means, for example, that the common link between the use of restraint and seclusion in residential institutions, and coercion and solitary confinement in police detention and prisons, is the rationality of incarceration, which holds the body and subjects it to repeated excessive violence:

> sites of incarceration, such as medical institutions, nursing homes, and prisons, emerge and take shape in interaction with each other as various populations are sorted, identified, and treated according to rationalities and practices which, while different in many ways, all mark certain people as deviant and thus justify controlling what they can and cannot do. (Carey, Ben-Moshe, and Chapman 2014, x; see also Chapman, Carey, and Ben-Moshe 2014 and Erevelles 2014)

There is a connection here with a broader problematic on how systems of violence materially produce disability. This is not simply a politics of creating 'impairment' through injury, but understanding the way in which manifold relations of power, including physical force effects, mould social and political landscapes to materialize ability and disability, often as ways to politically demobilize the resistive force of those who are the target of violence. Jasbir Puar has recently observed, for example, that Israeli 'shoot to maim' policies against Palestinians in Gaza effect a debilitation: 'the practice of breaking the arms of stone-throwers in the first Intifada, shoot to cripple attempts to pre-emptively debilitate the resistant capacities of another Intifada, the next Intifada' (Puar 2015, 3). Sites of incarceration focus violence in order to debilitate: this violence is understood as productively necessary for the functioning of systems, to maintain order; 'bodies are employed in the production processes precisely because they are deemed available for injury' (Puar 2009, 168).

Secondly, Sexton and Lee's analysis suggests the need to pay attention to torture as an epistemic problem. The 'black site' only comes into view when it is rendered visible by available knowledge systems. Violence that is routine, is 'unexceptional', is everyday, fails to be rendered as torture and becomes unremarkable; barely anyone seems to notice or treat it as a problem of justice. A body that is subject to excessive violence, that carries the trace of this force, is rendered unavailable to justice since this violation is not coded as being 'torture': either the violence this body experiences is not of a magnitude or intensity for it be recognized by knowledge systems as 'torture', or alternatively this body is not coded by knowledge systems as having a dignity that can be infringed. This, I believe, resonates with Sexton's articulation of the social death of blackness as a kind of non-existence (see Sexton 2011): a space of being subject to 'that structure of gratuitous violence in which a body is rendered as flesh to be accumulated and exchanged' (Sexton 2010, 38; see also Patterson 1982, 2–13), an arrangement of force and knowledge that establishes a subject that is perpetually open to violence, but this violence is explicitly not subject to justice or remedy. There is at least a resonance here in understanding the person with disability, who is potentially subject to high rates of routine violence without access to justice systems (see Erevelles 2014, 82, 83), a violence that is frequently explicitly racialized: a recent US report on police violence finds that between a third and half of people killed by police are people with disability (Perry and Carter-Long 2016, 1; see also Cockley 2015).

This dynamic of torture, which does not need to conceal the body of the tortured out of reach of the public gaze, but instead relies on knowledge systems to construct the body as non-torturable and thus veil the material practice of violence in plain view, resonates with the 'stealth' history of contemporary torture which emerges in the twentieth century. One of the central arguments that Darius Rejali makes in the landmark volume *Torture and Democracy* is that torture in the twentieth century has undergone a number of shifts in practice, in part reflective of a transition towards so called 'clean torture' (see 2007, 405–445). While it is true that many forms of torture in military and paramilitary contexts reflect older styles of physical violence towards bodies which injure in visibly perceptible ways, leaving evidence of scars (4), the twentieth century saw the proliferation of new techniques – such as electrocution, positional torture, environmental torture (such as perpetual loud music, bright lights), sleep deprivation, chemical torture and waterboarding – which are deployed because they leave little evidence of their use. Rejali makes the argument that these practices are created specifically in a context of emerging global norms which absolutely prohibit torture, and the simultaneous development of democratic forms of rule which place an emphasis on transparency and visibility: 'The history of modern democratic torture is part of the history of stealth torture' (405). However, how torture may be rendered visible is complicated by political status: Rejali notes that the question of visibility is in part shaped by the demands of a civic order to decide who belongs and can exercise freedoms within the civil political space (see also Rejali 2003). In a discussion of the use of police violence against African American and Latino people, Rejali stresses that the torture that is seen as a problem will be the violence that is seen as exceptional rather than uncomfortable but necessary: '"torture" is often an "informal arrangement" among police men in tough neighbourhoods. Appreciative residents and businesses aid them by not thinking too hard about why the streets are safe again' (2007, 58). Here, torture is made 'clean' through a failure of signification: 'Clean torture, in particular, encourages misrecognition. Its effects are demobilizing and depoliticizing' (58).

Combining these perspectives would suggest that in the case of the torture of people with disability, the non-detectability of torture is a combination of both clean practices that defy detection and a prevailing epistemic order which crafts violence as a beneficent or 'good' care (see Steele 2014), or excuses violence in the name of protection. Here torture is rendered as not an exception to the prevailing order, but instead becomes a non-negotiable requirement: institutions make the demand that people with disability need to be tortured, it is violence that is naturalized as necessary to the functioning of institutions, and is therefore rendered as non-violence. Here violence is as epistemic as it is material. In a sense this is a version of the concept of 'epistemic violence' described by Gayatri Chakrovarti Spivak

(1988) as the operation of systems of knowledge which remove the possibility of some to speak or be listened to (see Couldry 2009). Importantly for Spivak, epistemic violence produces the object of force as available for this violence in a way that is non-challengeable by prevailing knowledge systems: 'The women actually wanted to die' (1988, 93). Sexton's analysis suggests that the 'black site' of violence is also a meeting point of epistemological hostility: the 'black' site defies detection because of an order of knowledge which demands a violence be visited on those within, and for this violence to be rendered as non-violence.[12] In this context, the challenge isn't so much paying attention to the 'black sites' that are registered as legible and visible to prevailing orders of knowledge, but comprehending and organizing against the ongoing sites of violence that are treated as unremarkable, that resist signification as sites of injustice.

Conclusion

The Australian Federal Government is currently exploring the 'safeguards' for its new lifetime care and support entitlement, the National Disability Insurance Scheme (NDIS). The preliminary discussion paper released in 2015 reinforced previous calls to develop a nationally consistent framework for dealing with the use of restriction and seclusion (Australian Government 2015). In the discussion of all of the four possible options proposed by the Australian Government, it is disturbing that none proposed an absolute prohibition on the use of restrictive practices, and none specifically committed to testing current practices against international norms around torture (79–83). Instead, all options proposed monitoring regimes for the use of restrictive practices, at best suggesting that the use of restrictive practices could be authorized by an independent decision-maker, such as a guardianship tribunal (82). This outcome is perverse in many respects. Immediately after 11 September 2001, prominent US lawyer Alan Dershowitz controversially called for the legal regulation of torture: in his view, if torture was to be justified in the context of interrogations in the war against terror, it was better to expose existing practices to public scrutiny and consistency principles than to allow then to occur out of public oversight (Dershowitz 2002). In some respects the options proposed by the Australian Government in relation to restrictive practices and seclusion under the NDIS appear disturbingly similar, particularly in their fatalistic commitment to the continuation of the practice of torture against people with disability, except authorized by regulation.[13]

There is another danger here, and this relates to the epistemic dimension of torture. The persistent failure to name specific acts of force as torture simply assumes that some people with disability are epistemologically constructed as requiring systemic violence as part of their 'care'. In regulating practices of restriction and seclusion against people with disability, the Federal Government uses a new care regime – the NDIS – to reiterate that some people with disability remain available to be tortured; but this torture will happen with transparency, rendered as not torture. The epistemic goal here is to make it appear as if torture is not torture, merely responsible care: in other words, this is the perfect clean torture. Are we on the verge of a new regulatory order in the torture of people with disability in Australia within newly configured 'black sites' under the NDIS? Will this newly regulated order create torture that is legal, undetectable and perfectly 'clean'? How might this violence interact with the broader problem of torture in the context of racialized policing and mass incarceration, and what exactly does 'restriction' and 'seclusion' mean in this context? And will our materialized understanding of disability shift with this landscape, and not necessarily in ways that offer people respite from authorized violence?

Notes

1. Or cruel, inhuman or degrading treatment. One definition of torture is provided by Article 1.1 of the United Nations' *Convention Against Torture and Other Cruel, Inhuman or Degrading Treatment or Punishment*:
   any act by which severe pain or suffering, whether physical or mental, is intentionally inflicted on a person for such purposes as obtaining from him or a third person information or a confession, punishing him for an act he or a third person has committed or is suspected of having committed, or intimidating or coercing him or a third person, or for any reason based on discrimination of any kind, when such pain or suffering is inflicted by or at the

instigation of or with the consent or acquiescence of a public official or other person acting in an official capacity. It does not include pain or suffering arising only from, inherent in or incidental to lawful sanctions' (1984).

2. My own count in the report reveals a mere six instances where the word 'torture' is used, most frequently quoting stakeholder submissions (see Senate Standing Committees on Community Affairs 2015, 20, 21, 77 and 80).

3. Note that the political purchase of the word 'torture' relies on its potential ability to mobilize social, political and legal institutions. While we live in a world where torture is systematically carried out, we also know that forms of violence which are understood to conform to a definition of torture will attract a level of public condemnation. The potential for public condemnation and system change makes appeal to the word 'torture' as a mode of addressing injustice useful for political actors.

4. See n1.

5. The formulation of biopolitics by Agamben, which extends the work of Foucault, has excluded vital perspectives that may have allowed for a stronger theorization of exactly what biopolitics is, where its origins may stem from, and the coordinates of how biopolitical violence emerges today. For example, I will discuss below Jared Sexton's suggestion that Agamben's argument excludes an understanding of racial slavery and its continuing 'afterlife' in anti-black violence (Sexton 2010; see also Weheliye 2014). There are other perspectives on biopolitics worth noting. For example, focusing on the gendered dynamics of biopolitics, Anna Marie Smith (2010) has observed the relationship between State control of reproduction through welfare policies as a form of biopolitical exception; Dean Spade has explored how biopolitical population management through administrative categorization, gendered / racialized policing and incarceration work to produce 'harmful practices that shorten trans lives' (Spade 2011, 124; see also Bassichis and Spade 2014). There is also work occurring within animal studies and posthumanism exploring how exception might work in relation to animals. Cary Wolfe (2012) argues that the separation between human and animal is foundational for other forms of inter-human violence such as racism; I have argued previously that the modern industrial slaughterhouse might count as an important example for understanding the nature of sovereign exception, biopolitics and its importance to law (Wadiwel 2002). Alexander G. Weheliye utilizes black feminist perspectives to offer a critique of the construction of human within the Western enlightenment project and explore the project of ushering 'different genres of the human' (2014, 2, 3).

6. This sort of institution has been a primary focus for much advocacy, at least in the Global North, and has to an extent framed a human rights conceptualization of what torture against people with disability might look like (see for example Nowak 2008; Méndez 2013). This model of control is declining in many countries as a result of policies of de-institutionalization (see Beadle-Brown, Mansell, and Kozma 2007). However, large residential institutions remain a reality for many people with disability: for example the large number of institutions for adults and children in Central and Eastern Europe and the Former Soviet Union (Tobis 2000) and the current continuing battle to close institutions in Australia (see for example Fisher et al. 2015).

7. The Senate Community Affairs report concedes that 'in most cases, victims and allegations are forgotten; victims are blamed for the crimes perpetuated against them; and the violence, neglect and abuse continues' (2015, 49). Indeed, the structurally perceived personal characteristics of the person with disability (such as a 'lack of inhibition' or unquestioning compliance with authority figures) can become the focus of legal and social interventions, as systems that reproduce violence against disability displace the culpability for this violence onto people with disability themselves (see French, Dardel, and Price-Kelly 2009, 20).

8. For example Achille Mbembe has argued that it is not the concentration camp but the colony that has always been Europe's primary site of violent exception (2003); while Suvendrini Perera has argued along similar lines that we find the camp present in Australia's history as a penal colony, in segregation policies against Indigenous people, and contemporary policies of mandatory detention of stateless people (2002; see also Perera 2010).

9. The United States houses over 20% of the world's prisoners (Walmsley 2016) and 37% of this prison population is African American, with black males up to 10 times more likely to go to prison than white males (Carson 2015, 15) It is worth noting in this context that Australia also practises overtly racialized imprisonment: Aboriginal and Torres Strait Islander people comprise 27% of the prison population, while only making up 2% of the general population (Australian Bureau of Statistics 2015).

10. It is perhaps no accident that some of the techniques that belong to the repertoire of torture practice in the context of military and paramilitary detention also resonate with practices applied to people with disability in the context of institutional care regimes. Forced restraint (which might extend to positional torture), chemical restraint, electrocution, extended seclusion and environmental controls are all practices that occur in both paramilitary and military detention, and in sites of institutional internment of people with disability. Indeed, there is probably a strong case to argue that the innovation in the development of some techniques, such as electrocution and chemical restraint, share intertwined histories between the contexts of medicine and military and policing. Rejali for example notes that this inter-twined history applies to the development of electroshock (2007, 138); note, as the controversy surrounding the Judge Rotenburg Centre revealed, electroshock is still being pursued as a form of 'therapy' against people with disability (see Rosenthal and Ahern 2012, 16, 17). We might similarly observe that 'positional devices', such as straightjackets, which aim to hold individuals in restrictive positions in order to restrain movement and enable forced interventions, have their origins within institutions designed to exert violence on

people with disability (Soreff and Bazemore 2006, 17), yet are also present in the history of torture in military and paramilitary operations (e.g. see Rejali 2007, 81 and 310).

11. This would, in some contexts, suggest the development of technologies of violence that are deployed with a rationality of explicitly targeting people with disability. As Rejali observes, with reference to the use of the taser: 'American police used Tasers just as they had used stun guns, mainly on inarticulate subjects, with criminal or institutional histories' (2007, 245).

12. This might suggest a project of achieving epistemic justice, as described by Miranda Fricker (2007) as either comprising campaigns to combat prejudice (or 'testimonial injustice') and/or the provision of adequate knowledge resources to allow a subject to be recognized ('hermeneutic injustice'). Caution should be exercised here though, since deep epistemic oppression may not be resolvable within the terms of an existing knowledge system, particularly one that structurally reproduces racialized hierarchies, gender difference and or ableism. On epistemic oppression and the limits of Fricker's approach, see Kristie Dotson (2012).

13. Similarly disturbing is the commitment expressed towards achieving legislated protection for workers who use these practices, rather than the more pressing need to protect people with disability from violence. Former US President George W. Bush publicly argued in 2004, in a veiled defence of the infamous torture memos, that the aim was to protect US interrogation personal who were putting themselves on the line in the war against terror: 'We'll make sure professionals have the tools necessary to do their job within the law' (Bush as quoted in McAskill 2008).

Acknowledgements

I thank Linda Steele, Jessica Robyn Cadwallader and Gerard Goggin for their encouragement and support to publish this essay. I also thank the invaluable comments made by the anonymous reviewers. Finally, I thank Lori Gruen, Claire Jean Kim and Timothy Pachirat for involving me in the Race and Animals Institute at Wesleyan University in June 2016, which has profoundly influenced the shape of this essay.

Disclosure statement

No potential conflict of interest was reported by the author.

References

Ackerman, Spencer. 2015a. "The Disappeared: Chicago Police Detain Americans at Abuse-Laden 'Black Site.'" *The Guardian*, February 25. http://www.theguardian.com/us-news/2015/feb/24/chicago-police-detain-americans-black-site.

Ackerman, Spencer. 2015b. "Homan Square Revealed: How Chicago police 'Disappeared' 7,000 People." *The Guardian*, October 19. https://www.theguardian.com/us-news/2015/oct/19/homan-square-chicago-police-disappeared-thousands.

Agamben, Giorgio. 1998. *Homo Sacer: Sovereign Power and Bare Life*. Stanford, CA: Stanford University Press.

Agamben, Giorgio. 1999. *Remnants of Auschwitz: The Witness and The Archive*. New York: Zone Books.

Agamben, Giorgio. 2004. *The Open: Man and Animal*. Stanford, CA: Stanford University Press.

Arendt, Hannah. 1976. *The Origins of Totalitarianism*. Orlando, FL: Harvest.

Australian Bureau of Statistics. 2015. *Prisoners in Australia*. 4517.0. Canberra: Australian Bureau of Statistics. http://www.abs.gov.au/ausstats/abs@.nsf/Lookup/by%20Subject/4517.0~2015~Main%20Features~Aboriginal%20and%20Torres%20Strait%20Islander%20prisoner%20characteristics~7.

Australian Government. 2015. *Proposal for a National Disability Insurance Scheme Quality and Safeguarding Framework: Consultation Paper*. Canberra: Australian Government Disability Reform Council.

Baker, Bernadette. 2010. "States of Exception: Learning Disability and Democracy in New Times." *Disability Studies Quarterly* 30 (2). http://dsq-sds.org/article/view/1232/1279.

Baldry, Eileen. 2014. "Disability at the Margins: Limits of the Law." *Griffith Law Review* 23 (3): 370–388.

Bassichis, Morgan, and Dean Spade. 2014. "Queer Politics and Anti-Blackness." In *Queer Necropolitics*, edited by Jin Haritaworn, Adi Kuntsman, and Silvia Posocco, 191–210. Abingdon: Routledge.

Batta, Philipp, Mae Ryan, and Spencer Ackerman. 2015. "Chicago's Homan Square 'Black Site': Surveillance, Military-style Vehicles and a Metal Cage." *The Guardian*, 25 February. http://www.theguardian.com/us-news/2015/feb/24/chicago-homan-square-black-site.

Beadle-Brown, J., J. Mansell, and A. Kozma. 2007. "Deinstitutionalization in Intellectual Disabilities." *Current Opinion in Psychiatry* 20: 437–442. doi:10.1097/YCO.0b013e32827b14ab.

Benjamin, Walter. 1996. "Critique of Violence." In *Selected Writings Volume 1, 1913–1926*, edited by M. Bullock and M. W. Jennings, 236–252. Cambridge: The Belknap Press of Harvard University Press.

Bybee, J. S. 2002. *Memorandum for John Rizzo Acting General Counsel of the Central Intelligence Agency*. Washington, DC: Office of the Assistant Attorney General, U.S. Department of Justice.

Bybee, J. S. 2005. "Standards of Conduct for Interrogation under 18 U.S.C. §§2340-2340A." In *The Torture Papers: The Road to Abu Ghraib*, edited by Karen Greenberg and Joshua Dratel, 172–217. New York: Cambridge University Press.

Campbell, Fiona Kumari. 2009. *Contours of Ableism: The Production of Disability and Ableness*. New York: Palgrave Macmillan.

Carey, Allison C., Liat Ben-Moshe, and Chris Chapman. 2014. "Preface." In *Disability Incarcerated: Imprisonment and Disability in the United States and Canada*, edited by Liat Ben-Moshe, Chris Chapman, and Allison C. Carey, ix–xiv. New York: Palgrave Macmillan.

Carson, Anne E. 2015. *Prisoners in 2014*. Washington, DC: Bureau of Justice Statistics, U.S. Department of Justice. http://www.bjs.gov/content/pub/pdf/p14.pdf.

Chapman, Chris, Allison C. Carey, and Liat Ben-Moshe. 2014. "Reconsidering Confinement: Interlocking Locations and Logics of Incarceration." In *Disability Incarcerated: Imprisonment and Disability in the United States and Canada*, edited by Liat Ben-Moshe, Chris Chapman, and Allison C. Carey, 3–24. New York: Palgrave Macmillan.

Cockley, Rebecca. 2015. "Police Violence Against People with Disabilities." *Black Star News*, July 6. http://www.blackstarnews.com/us-politics/justice/police-violence-against-people-with-disabilities.html.

Couldry, Nick. 2009. "Rethinking the Politics of Voice." *Continuum* 23 (4): 579–582. doi:10.1080/10304310903026594.

Danner, Mark. 2009. "US Torture: Voices from the Black Sites." *The New York Review of Books*, April 9. http://www.nybooks.com/articles/2009/04/09/us-torture-voices-from-the-black-sites/.

Dershowitz, Alan M. 2002. "Want to Torture? Get a Warrant." *SFGate*, January 22. http://www.sfgate.com/opinion/openforum/article/Want-to-torture-Get-a-warrant-2880547.php.

Doran, Matthew. 2015. "Use of Cage for Boy with Autism at Canberra School Prompts Call for National Education Standard." *ABC News*, April 3. http://www.abc.net.au/news/2015-04-03/experts-slam-need-to-cage-boy-wth-autism-at-canberra-school/6369470.

Dotson, Kristie. 2012. "A Cautionary Tale: On Limiting Epistemic Oppression." *Frontiers: A Journal of Women Studies* 33 (1): 24–47.

Erevelles, Nirmala. 2014. "Crippin' Jim Crow: Disability, Dis-location, and the School-to-prison Pipeline." In *Disability Incarcerated: Imprisonment and Disability in the United States and Canada*, edited by Liat Ben-Moshe, Chris Chapman, and Allison C. Carey, 81–99. New York: Palgrave Macmillan.

Fisher, Karen R., Deborah Lutz, Friederike Gadow, Sally Robinson, and Sandra Gendera. 2015. "A Transformative Framework for Deinstitutionalisation." *Research and Practice in Intellectual and Developmental Disabilities* 2 (1): 60–72. doi:10.1080/23297018.2015.1028089.

Foucault, Michel. 1998. *The Will to Knowledge: The History of Sexuality 1*. London: Penguin Books.

Foucault, Michel. 2004. *Society Must Be Defended: Lectures at the Collège de France, 1975–76*. London: Penguin Books.

French, Phillip, Julie Dardel, and Sonya Price-Kelly. 2009. *Rights Denied: Towards a National Policy Agenda about Abuse, Neglect and Exploitation of Persons with Cognitive Impairment*. Redfern: People with Disability Australia.

Fricker, Miranda. 2007. *Epistemic Injustice: Power and the Ethics of Knowing*. Oxford: Oxford University Press.

Greenberg, Karen, and Joshua Dratel, eds. 2005. *The Torture Papers: The Road to Abu Ghraib*. New York: Cambridge University Press.

Hayes, Susan, Phil Shackell, Pat Mottram, and Rachel Lancaster. 2007. "The Prevalence of Intellectual Disability in a Major UK Prison." *British Journal of Learning Disabilities* 35: 162–167.

Holland, Shasta, and Peter Persson. 2011. "Intellectual Disability in the Victorian Prison System: Characteristics of Prisoners with an Intellectual Disability Released from Prison in 2003–2006." *Psychology, Crime & Law* 17 (1): 25–41.

Hughes, Bill. 2012. "Civilizing Modernity and the Ontological Invalidation of Disabled People." In *Disability and Social Theory: New Developments and Directions*, edited by D. Goodley, B. Hughes, and L. Davis, 17–32. Basingstoke: Palgrave Macmillan.

James, Joy. 1996. *Resisting State Violence: Radicalism, Gender and Race in U.S. Culture*. Minneapolis: University of Minnesota Press.

Jordan, Thomas. 2013. "Disability, Able-bodiedness, and the Biopolitical Imagination." *Review of Disability Studies: An International Journal* 9 (1). http://www.rds.hawaii.edu/ojs/index.php/journal/article/view/70.

MacKinnon, Catharine. 2006. *Are Women Human?: And Other International Dialogues*. Cambridge: Harvard University Press.

Maddern, Joanne, and Emma Stewart. 2010. "Biometric Geographies, Mobility and Disability: Biologies of Culpability and the Biologised Spaces of (Post)modernity." In *Towards Enabling Geographies*, edited by Vera Chouinard, Edward Hall, and Robert Wilton, 237–253. Farnham: Ashgate.

Mayer, Jane. 2007. "The Black Sites: A Rare Look Inside the C.I.A.'s Secret Interrogation Program." *The New Yorker*, August 13. http://www.newyorker.com/magazine/2007/08/13/the-black-sites.

Mbembe, Achille. 2003. "Necropolitics." *Public Culture* 15 (1): 11–40.

McAskill, Ewen. 2008. "London Bombs Justify 'Torture,' Says Bush." *The Guardian*, February 15. http://www.theguardian.com/world/2008/feb/15/terrorism.usa1.

Méndez, Juan. 2013. "Report of the Special Rapporteur on Torture and Other Cruel, Inhuman or Degrading Treatment or Punishment." New York: United Nations, General Assembly, A/HRC/22/53.

Mitchell, David, and Sharon Snyder. 2003. "The Eugenic Atlantic: Race, Disability, and the Making of an International Eugenic Science, 1800–1945." *Disability & Society* 18 (7): 843–864.

Mitchell, David T., and Sharon L. Snyder. 2015. *The Biopolitics of Disability: Neoliberalism, Ablenationalism, and Peripheral Embodiment.* Ann Arbor: University of Michigan Press.

Nowak, M. 2008. *Interim Report of the Special Rapporteur on Torture and Other Cruel, Inhuman or Degrading Treatment or Punishment.* New York: United Nations, General Assembly, A/63/175.

Overboe, James. 2007. "Disability and Genetics: Affirming the Bare Life (The State of Exception)." *The Canadian Review of Sociology and Anthropology* 44 (2): 219–235.

Patterson, Orlando. 1982. *Slavery and Social Death.* Cambridge, MA: Harvard University Press.

Perera, Suvendrini. 2002. "What is a Camp…?" *Borderlands e-Journal* 1 (1): 1–12.

Perera, Suvendrini. 2010. "Torturous Dialogues: Geographies of Trauma and Spaces of Exception." *Continuum: Journal of Media and Cultural Studies* 24 (1): 31–45.

Perry, David M., and Lawrence Carter-Long. 2016. *The Ruderman White Paper on Media Coverage of Law Enforcement Use of Force and Disability: A Media Study (2013–2015) and Overview.* Ruderman Family Foundation. http://www.rudermanfoundation.org/wp-content/uploads/2016/03/MediaStudy-PoliceDisability_final-final1.pdf.

Puar, Jasbir K. 2009. "Prognosis Time: Towards a Geopolitics of Affect, Debility and Capacity." *Women & Performance: A Journal of Feminist Theory* 19 (2): 161–172.

Puar, Jasbir K. 2015. "The 'Right' to Maim: Disablement and Inhumanist Biopolitics in Palestine." *Borderlands e-Journal* 14 (1): 1–27.

Pugliese, Joseph. 2013. *State Violence and the Execution of Law: Biopolitical Caesurae of Torture, Black Sites, Drones.* London: Routledge.

Reeve, Donna. 2009. "Biopolitics and Bare Life: Does the Impaired Body Provide Contemporary Examples of Homo Sacer?" In *Arguing about Disability: Philosophical Perspectives*, edited by K. Kristiansen, S. Vehmas, and T. Shakespeare, 203–217. London: Routledge.

Rejali, Darius. 2003. "Torture as a Civic Marker: Solving a Global Anxiety with a New Political." *Journal of Human Rights* 2 (2): 153–171.

Rejali, Darius. 2007. *Torture and Democracy.* Princeton, NJ: Princeton University Press.

Richter-Montpetit, Melanie. 2014. "Beyond the Erotics of Orientalism: Lawfare, Torture and the Racial-sexual Grammars of Legitimate Suffering." *Security Dialogue* 45 (1): 43–62.

Richter-Montpetit, Melanie. 2015. "Why Torture When Torture Does Not Work? Orientalism, Anti-blackness and the Persistence of White Terror." *The Disorder of Things, Blog Post.* January 21. https://thedisorderofthings.com/2015/01/21/why-torture-when-torture-does-not-work-orientalism-anti-blackness-and-the-persistence-of-white-terror/.

Rosenthal, Eric, and Laurie Ahern. 2012. "When Treatment is Torture: Protecting People with Disabilities Detained in Institutions." *Human Rights Brief* 19 (2): 13–17.

Sadat, Leila Nadya. 2006. "Ghost Prisoners and Black Sites: Extraordinary Rendition under International Law." *Case Western Reserve Journal of International Law* 37: 309–342.

Scarry, Elaine. 1985. *The Body in Pain: The Making and Unmaking of the World.* New York: Oxford University Press.

Schmitt, Carl. 1988. *Political Theology: Four Chapters on the Concept of Sovereignty.* Cambridge: The MIT Press.

Senate Standing Committees on Community Affairs. 2015. *Violence, Abuse and Neglect Against People with Disability in Institutional and Residential Settings, Including the Gender and Age Related Dimensions, and the Particular Situation of Aboriginal and Torres Strait Islander People with Disability, and Culturally and Linguistically Diverse People with Disability.* Canberra: Commonwealth of Australia.

Sexton, Jared. 2010. "People-of-color-blindness: Notes on the Afterlife of Slavery." *Social Text* 28 (2 103): 31–56. doi:10.1215/01642472-2009-066.

Sexton, Jared. 2011. "The Social Life of Social Death: On Afro-Pessimism and Black Optimism." In *Tensions Journal* 5 (Fall/Winter). http://www.yorku.ca/intent/issue5/articles/jaredsexton.php.

Sexton, Jared, and Elizabeth Lee. 2006. "Figuring the Prison: Prerequisites of Torture at Abu Ghraib." *Antipode* 38: 1005–1022. doi:10.1111/j.1467-8330.2006.00490.x.

Sirnes, Thorvald. 2005. "Deviance or Homo sacer? Foucault, Agamben, and Foetal Diagnostics." *Scandinavian Journal of Disability Research* 7 (3–4): 206–219.

Smith, Anne Marie. 2010. "Neo-eugenics: A Feminist Critique of Agamben." *Occasion: Interdisciplinary Studies in the Humanities* 20 (2): 1–12. http://arcade.stanford.edu/sites/default/files/article_pdfs/Occasion_v02_Smith_122010_0.pdf.

Smith, Christen A. 2013. "Strange Fruit: Brazil, Necropolitics, and the Transnational Resonance of Torture and Death." *Souls* 15 (3): 177–198. doi:10.1080/10999949.2013.838858.

Soldatic, Karen, and Lucy Fiske. 2009. "Bodies 'Locked Up': Intersections of Disability and Race in Australian Immigration." *Disability and Society* 24 (3): 289–301.

Soreff, Stephen M., and Patricia H. Bazemore. 2006. "Confronting Chaos: Today We View Early Psychiatric Treatments as Inhumane, but During Their Time They Were State-of-the-art." *Behavioral Healthcare* 26 (6): 16–20.

Spade, Dean. 2011. *Normal Life: Administrative Violence, Critical Trans Politics and the Limits of Law*. Brooklyn, OH: South End Press.

Spivak, Gayatri Chakravorty. 1988. "Can the Subaltern Speak?" In *Marxism and the Interpretation of Culture*, edited by Cary Nelson and Lawrence Grossberg, 271–313. Basingstoke: Macmillan Education.

Steele, Linda. 2014. "Disability, Abnormality and Criminal Law: Sterilisation as Lawful and 'Good' Violence." *Griffith Law Review* 23 (3): 467–497.

Sullivan, Martin. 2008. "Subjected Bodies: Paraplegia, Rehabilitation, and the Politics of Movement." In *Foucault and the Government of Disability*, edited by Shelley Tremain, 27–44. Cambridge, MA: University of Michigan Press.

Tobis, David. 2000. *Moving from Residential Institutions to Community-based Social Services in Central and Eastern Europe and the Former Soviet Union*. Washington, DC: The World Bank.

United Nations. 1984. *Convention against Torture and Other Cruel, Inhuman or Degrading Treatment or Punishment*. New York: United Nations. December 10. A/RES/39/46.

Wadiwel, Dinesh Joseph. 2002. "Cows and Sovereignty: Biopolitics and Bare Life." *Borderlands e-Journal* 1 (2). http://www.borderlandsejournal.adelaide.edu.au/vol1no2-2002/wadiwel.html.

Walmsley, Roy. 2016. *World Prison Population List*. 11th ed. London: Institute for Criminal Policy Research, University of London. http://www.prisonstudies.org/sites/default/files/resources/downloads/world_prison_population_list_11th_edition.pdf.

Weheliye, Alexander G. 2014. *Habeas Viscus: Racializing Assemblages, Biopolitics, and Black Feminist Theories of the Human*. London: Duke University Press.

Wilderson, Frank B. 2010. *Red, White & Black: Cinema and the Structure of U.S. Antagonisms*. Durham: Duke University Press.

Wolfe, Cary. 2012. *Before the Law: Human and Other Animals in a Biopolitical Frame*. Chicago, IL: Chicago University Press.

Yoo, John C. 2005. "Letter Regarding 'The Views of our Office Concerning the Legality, Under International Law, of Interrogation Methods to be Used on Captured al Qaeda Operatives.'" In *The Torture Papers: The Road to Abu Ghraib*, edited by Karen Greenberg and Joshua Dratel, 218–222. New York: Cambridge University Press.

Mental capacity and states of exception: revisiting disability law with Giorgio Agamben

Penelope Weller

ABSTRACT

The Convention on the Rights of Persons with Disabilities (CRPD) claims a new era of disability rights – a stance that was affirmed when CRPD General Comment 1 provided its authoritative interpretation of CRPD article 12 (Equal recognition before the law). Since the publication of General Comment 1, disagreement about the meaning and significance of article 12 has heightened, particularly in response to its claim for universal legal capacity. The notion of universal legal capacity challenges a fundamental division in the law of modern liberal states – the different treatment of individuals who are unable to participate in the law as rational independent actors. This article draws on the work of Giorgio Agamben to argue that people with disabilities are placed in a 'state of exception' where they are subject to exceptional legal regimes. In modern law entry into the state of exception, where people with mental disabilities are exposed to violence and abuse, is triggered by the determination that a person lacks 'mental capacity.' This paper argues that the CRPD offers a new approach predicated on equality and inclusion.

Introduction

In 2006, the Convention on the Rights of Persons with Disabilities (CRPD) proclaimed a new era of disability rights, promising a world where people with disabilities are welcomed 'out of the shadows' to take their rightful place in the mainstream of society (Lawson 2007; Kayess and French 2008).[1] Almost 10 years on, commentators continue to grapple with the implications of the CRPD, especially the interpretation of article 12 (Equal recognition before the law). According to the Committee of the Rights of Persons with Disabilities (the Committee) article 12 affirms the principle of universal legal capacity (Dhanda 2012).[2] The principle of universal legal capacity requires all people with disabilities, including those with cognitive impairment, intellectual disabilities or psycho-social disabilities to be recognized as subjects of law entitled to the full benefits and protection of the law (CRPD 2014; Arstein-Kerslake and Flynn 2015). How the notion of universal legal capacity could or should be reflected in the law is a matter of continuing debate (see Bach and Kerzner 2010; Baldry 2014; Dhanda 2012; Flynn and Arstein-Kerslake 2014a, 2014b; Lord, Suozzi, and Taylor 2010; Minkowitz 2014; Peay 2015; Perlin 2011; Richardson 2013; Series 2015; Slobogin 2015; Steele and Thomas 2014; Szmukler, Daw, and Callard 2013; Weller 2016). At the centre of the debate is an unresolved tension between those who argue that the law in its current form provides important protections for people with disabilities, and those who pursue law reforms that facilitate the full and effective participation of people with disabilities in the law.[3] Experts in the various areas of disability related law offer a range of propositions that can be positioned along the law reform continuum.

The recognition of people with mental disabilities as people with legal capacity (that is, as people who enjoy legal standing and legal agency on an equal basis with others) challenges the most funda-mental division in the law of modern liberal states – the exclusion of people who lack mental capacity from full participation in the law. The different treatment of people with mental disabilities is found in the provisions of mental health law, guardianship law and other 'disability' focused laws such as special provisions in the criminal law for unfitness and insanity (Minkowitz 2014). It is also found in the differ-ent application of general law to people who lack mental capacity. In the latter case, mental capacity assessments operate as a threshold requirement for participation in or removal from a 'normal' legal framework (Weller 2015).

It is often argued that the various laws that apply to people with mental disabilities provide nec-essary protection to vulnerable people who would otherwise be exploited, abandoned or subject to abuse. In the years leading up to the draughting of the CRPD, however, the human rights movement drew attention to the high levels of violence and abuse experienced by people with disabilities who were under the protection of such laws (Daes 1986; Despouy 1991). Despite years of protection, rein-forced by anti-discrimination law in the law of modern developed nations (Kanter 2009, 548), people with disabilities continue to experience disproportionate levels of violence and abuse. In Australia it has been confirmed by several recent inquiries and reports (VEOHRC 2014; AHRC 2014; ALRC 2014; AGPC 2014). The almost universal experience of violence and abuse has lead the international human rights movement to argue that the marginalization of people with disabilities in society and in the law contributes to the occurrence and recurrence of violence (Hunt 2005). Critical disability scholars have argued further that the various laws permitting compulsory detention and/or medical treatment of people with disabilities constitutes a form of state sponsored or 'lawful violence' (Steele 2014; Minkowitz 2007). They point to the CRPD as the model for a new approach.

This article considers the question of violence in the law and the stance of the CRPD, through the lens of Giorgio Agamben's analysis of 'states of exception' in *Homo Sacer: Sovereign Power and Bare Life* (1998). Agamben's work is useful because it provides an analysis of the contradictory stance of the law in modern liberal states. *Homo Sacer: Sovereign Power and Bare Life* (*Homo Sacer*) is the first of seven volumes comprising Agamben's 'genealogy of contemporary government' (Whyte 2013, 143).[4] This paper considers *Homo Sacer* because it is directly relevant to question of permissible violence. The first part of this paper provides an account of Agamben's 'bare life' and 'states of exception' as they appear in modern liberal states, showing how Agamben's approach challenges the dominant liberal narrative of the law as protector. Part 2: *Agamben's bare life and the state of exception* discusses Agamben's contri-bution in light of Michel Foucault's approach to the government of freedom, arguing that Agamben's work is important because it articulates the limits of government through freedom by highlighting the historically embedded dynamic of the exclusion of people with disabilities. Part 3: *Disability and violence* considers the experience of violence, arguing that people with mental disabilities experience lawful violence in a way that mirrors the circumstance of the homo sacer described by Agamben (2008). Part 4: *Legal capacity and the CRPD* turns to the CRPD, especially article 12 (Equal recognition before the law) as a solution to the current impasse. The article argues that Agamben's approach reveals that despite the claim to universal benevolent inclusion, liberal law is predicated on the exclusion of those individuals whose bodies and minds challenge the reification of the self-governing liberal subject. The article concludes that an end to violence against people with disabilities will only be realized through a radical interpretation of the CRPD's principle of full inclusion in the law.

Agamben's bare life and the state of exception

Homo Sacer examines the outcast figure in Roman law of the 'homo sacer' who 'could not be sacrificed, but could be killed by anyone' (Agamben 1998, 86). Agamben uses the figure of homo sacer as a met-aphor for 'states of exception' in modern law, arguing that the bio-political purpose of modern law is achieved through the suspension of normal law in discrete legal spaces. States of exception are para-doxical legal spaces where an individual is simultaneously placed within and beyond the law, stripped of the legal relationships that give social value to normal life. The life of an individual in a state of exception is rendered 'bare life' – a kind of diminished or devalued form of life that is no longer connected or recognized in the same way as other living beings. For Agamben, homo sacer is a figure who is alive, and yet beyond law, inhabiting a place where all normal rights, expectations, connections, honour and meaning are suspended. Because homo sacer is a diminished life form – a 'bare life' – Agamben argues, it becomes 'an object of violence that exceeds the sphere both of law and of sacrifice' (1998, 86).

Agamben sees that the figure of *Homo Sacer* as emblematic of the complex relationship that exists between the citizen and the sovereign. In this relationship, the exercise of sovereign power occurs at the 'point of indistinction between violence and law: the threshold on which violence passes over into law and law passes over into violence' (Agamben 1998, 32). Agamben argues that the exercise of sovereign power over banned life, encapsulated in the figure of homo sacer, is the same form of power that was ultimately expressed in the phenomena of the Nazi concentration camps (1998, 111).[5]

In his exploration of the Nazi analogy, Agamben puts particular weight on the fact that in the camps there was a (permanent) suspension of constitutional law, followed by the imposition of a permanent state of emergency:

> In the camp, the state of exception, which was essentially a temporary suspension of the rule of law on the basis of a factual state of danger, is now given a permanent spatial arrangement, which as such nevertheless remains outside the normal order. (Agamben 1998, 170)

According to Agamben, the suspension of the law in the camp renders the people in them figures of bare life, people who were simultaneously within and beyond the law, and therefore able to be killed or be subjected to violence with impunity.

Rather than seeing the camp as an aberration of the past, Agamben argues that suspension of law (and the consequent imposition of permanent extraordinary law) is an essential feature of modern bio-politics.[6] For Agamben the camp 'decisively signals the political space of modernity itself' (1998, 174) in which the State assumes directly the care of the nation's biological life as one of its proper tasks (1998, 175). The key to bio-political power, he argues, requires the suspension of normal order. The difference in modernity is that the exercise of sovereign power is no longer confined to spatially defined camps, but shifts to the bodies of everyone. Modern bio-political power renders the 'transformation of a provisional or exceptional measure into a technique of government' (Agamben 1998, 144). The result is a constant reckoning in the bio-political order of who is 'inside or outside', or 'outside but within' the bio-political horizon of modern state (Agamben 1998, 13). To put this another way, Agamben sees that the process of identifying who will be made subject to the state of exception in bio-political order as being distributed, normalized and contested. The 'constant reckoning' of belonging is itself a technique of bio-political government which is implicated in the construction of the modern legal subject. In this dynamic, sovereign power retains its indistinction between violence and law which in its modern form is exercised by physicians and scientists who move into a new space of ambiguity – the crossover point between violence and law – that in the past the sovereign alone could penetrate (Agamben 1998, 140).

Agamben's analysis challenges the dominant liberal narrative that exceptional law for people with disabilities is essentially benevolent by highlighting the four key features of bio-political power. First, in bio-political power there is a constant reckoning of who is to be regarded as in or out, included or excluded. Second, medicine plays a central role in deciding the boundaries of exclusion. Third, that the power exercised by medicine over 'bare life' is a sovereign power characterized by an indistinction between law and violence, and fourth that states of exception are inherently violent. Agemben's analysis indicates that modern bio-political power maintains liberal order through the exclusion of bodies and minds that fail to confirm to the liberal vision. For people with disabilities, inclusion in the mainstream can only be achieved through a demonstration of the individual's ability to function as a rational self-actualizing liberal subject. In this kind of order, a benevolent response denotes exclusion from the mainstream. Moreover, as people with disabilities report, the struggle to avoid benevolence and achieve inclusion becomes the constant feature of the disability experience. Taking this observation further, Jessica Whyte observes that Agamben's analysis challenges the dominant assumptions of liberal political philosophy, suggesting that its not identity, belonging and protection and the rule of law, but exclusion and exception that founds sovereign power and constitutes a political community (2013, 61).

States of exception, rights and modern law

Agamben's observations articulate the limits of Michel Foucault's account of government through freedom, which rests on the acceptance of the generative capacity of 'power' as a diffuse phenomenon embedded in the structures of society and the processes of normalization (Foucault 1977, 157). The recasting of power as a productive force enabled Foucault to describe twentieth century liberalism as a complex of practices, methods and procedures that measured and enforced intervention through distally delegated actions. Such actions were aptly described by others as the 'conduct of conduct' (Gordon 1991, 3) or 'governing at a distance' (Burchell 1993, 267). Foucault demonstrated how medical rationalities in liberal regimes were deployed to govern 'freely' constituted individuals through the 'authority of expertise', becoming inextricably linked to the formal political apparatus of rule (cited in Rose 1993, 284). In short, the government of freedom provided a compelling account of the complex relationships between medicine and ordinary citizens in liberal regimes. The account of governing through freedom, however, could not be plausibly extended to encompass the government of people with mental disabilities who seemed to be placed literally and metaphorically beyond the reach of governmental apparatus and the practice of freedom. Agamben's analysis fills this gap in theory by identifying dispersed pockets of exclusion or exception around which the struggle to be included in the liberal regime occurs.

In other words, Agamben sees 'states of exception' as essential to the exercise of bio-power because the distributed pockets of exception in modern society are created within and around the structures that govern though freedom. In the ancient and modern context, those with 'bare life' are simultaneously within and beyond the law, marked by the suspension of rights:

> Precisely because they were lacking almost all the rights and expectations that we customarily attribute to human existence, and yet were still biologically alive, they came to be situated in a limit zone between life and death, inside and outside, in which they were no longer anything but bare life. (Agamben 1998, 159)

The observation that bare life and states of exception are marked by the suspension of rights provides a framework for the interrogation of modern law. As a growing body of literature attests, the various laws applying to people with disabilities, either in fact or in practice, give effect to a suspension or modification of (normal) rights, understood as the rights that are enjoyed by everyone (Weller 2010a).

At first glance, the observation that the suspension of normal rights is an indicator of exclusion sits uncomfortably with the inclusive promise of liberal law. The idea that ordinary law is suspended for people with disabilities is invisible because it is taken for granted. It is deeply embedded in the historical evolution of modern law, and always justified by a strong narrative of benevolence. For example, in the fifth century BC Roman law invoked different rules for those who were considered 'vulnerable' (Lush 2014, 3). The doctrine of *parens patriae* in sixteenth century England constituted special rules for all those in need of medical care, including children, the elderly, the sick, the disabled and the mentally ill (Carney and Tate 1997, 10; Wood 2012, 79; Then 2013, 136). In the 17th century the paternalistic doctrine of best interests was created (Carney and Tate 1997, 12). In the nineteenth century England the *Poor Law Act* of 1834 established work-houses for the 'criminally indigent' including beggars, vagrants, prostitutes and criminals (Watson 1969, 5), while several inquiries into the care of 'lunatics' culminated in the *Lunacy Act* of 1890. The 'great incarceration' of destitute individuals, including those with physical disabilities, cognitive impairments or mental health problems dominated the nineteenth century, variously justified by liberal narratives of freedom, poverty, discipline, and charity (Mill 1869, 144). The institutionalization of people with disabilities continued well into the twentieth century, justified by a narrative of asylum.

In the twentieth century new institutions and legal arrangements for people with disabilities coalesced around the principle of mental capacity (O'Neill and Peisah 2011). To be recognized as legal subject, modern law requires individuals to demonstrate mental capacity. Mental capacity in the law is generally defined as the ability to understand information relevant to a decision or action, retain the information, use or weigh the information as part of the process of making the decision and communicate the decision (whether by talking, using sign language or any other means) (e.g. see *Mental Capacity Act 2005*, England and Wales, s 3). Assessing mental capacity has become a routine aspect of day to day practice in many areas of law. It arises in medicine (whether or not the person has capacity to provide a valid consent to medical treatment); in aged and disability care (whether or not the person can make their own decisions) in the law of wills (whether or not the person can lawfully depose of his or her goods after death) and in general contract law (whether or not the person is able to buy goods and services) (O'Neill and Peisah 2011). Mental capacity is relevant to the question of whether a person may instruct a solicitor; appear as witness in a court of law or agree to sexual intercourse (O'Neill and Peisah 2011). In short, an individual must demonstrate mental capacity to be recognized as legal agent (Weller 2016). Once the many instances of different laws and mechanisms are listed, the idea that mental capacity laws articulate a modern form of exclusion seems more plausible. A determination that an individual lacks mental capacity serves to suspend 'normal' law, ushering in a legal framework in which normal rights are limited or diminished. Moreover, consistent with Agamben's description of the camp, a suspension of normal law is followed by the imposition of an alternative legal regimes. In modern law, mental capacity dictates the contours of 'states of exception'.

The imposition of an alternative regime is exemplified by the practice of appointing a substitute decision-maker for those who lack mental capacity. In the liberal view, substitute decision-making mechanisms facilitate a form of limited or approximate inclusion. In practice, however, they tend to generate legal confusion (White et al. 2011) fraud and abuse (Carney and Beaupert 2013; Kohn, Blumenthal, and Campbell 2013). Confusion, fraud and abuse are also reported when a 'substituted judgment' approach is used (Carter 2010, 200). Another example of the routine suspension of the law and its replacement with a different regime is found in mental health law. In Australia, 'rights based' mental health laws purport to balance the rights and freedoms with procedural mechanisms designed to protect vulnerable individuals (Weller 2010a). The rights based model positions medical professional discretion at the heart of mental health legislation. The laws limit the scope of the discretion by providing threshold criteria for the exercise of the power and provide 'safeguard' mechanisms of oversight and review (Weller 2010a). The decision to impose compulsory medical treatment, however, rests with the treating psychiatrist (Weller 2010b). Unlike all other areas of healthcare, people who are subject to compulsory mental health treatment are unable to appoint a substitute decision-maker of their own choosing.[7] As is explained more fully in the next section, Agamben's argument that the suspension of normal law permits lawful violence and invites unlawful violence seems apt.

Disability and violence

The salience of Agamben's analysis is the link he draws between the suspension of rights in states of exception with the occurrence of unlimited and unaccountable violence. Linda Steele argues that the violence experienced by people with disabilities is best understood as 'lawful violence' (Steele 2014). Lawful violence is unwanted violence that is authorized by law within an established legal framework. For example, Linda Steele argues that court authorized sterilization of disabled girls is lawful violence that is also cast as 'good violence' being constructed through legal discourse as a necessary intervention for the benefit of everyone. Tina Minkowitz similarly identifies nonconsensual psychiatric treatment as a kind of lawful violence that is stripped of its normal cultural meaning because it is expressly imposed by law (Minkowitz 2007). In this volume, Dinesh Wadiwel argues that in such instances violence is rendered as non-violence by being naturalized as a necessary function of the institution (Wadiwel, forthcoming).

Lawful violence also occurs when instances of unwanted bodily contact, that would otherwise be unlawful, are effectively permitted because no legal action is taken to prevent or punish the actions

(Steele 2014). Minkowitz's account of 'lawful violence' in mental health institutions describes this kind of violence as violence that is not expressly authorized by legislation (as is the case with lawful violence such as compulsory medical treatment or seclusion and restraint) but is associated with institutional and social practices that assume the exercise of power and exploit vulnerability. An example of such unregulated and permissible violence is 'rough handling', seclusion as a punishment or the denial of privileges in institutions or care homes. Such actions are sometimes justified on the basis that they fall within the acceptable boundaries of professional or institutional discretion. But as Agamben makes clear, this kind of violence is only made possible by the suspension of normal law and the consequent ambiguity of the (non-legal) subject. Disability scholars also point out that the violence experienced by people in institutions that arises from the actions of other people held in the institutions is also ambiguous and typically unrecognized. In summary, disability scholars identify four different kinds of 'lawful violence': violence that is permitted by omission; violence that is ordered by the law; violence that is incidental to legally imposed violence from professional staff; and violence from other people with disabilities.

These types of unrecognized violence are consistent with Agamben's account of the homo sacer. From Agamben's perspective, people with disabilities are placed in states of exception. In the state of exception normal law is suspended and new laws are imposed. In the state of exception, sovereign power is exercised as the point of indistinction between law and violence. This is most clearly demonstrated when a person is subject to compulsory mental health treatment. Agamben's work therefore provides a compelling account of the power relationships established by a legislative context (where violence is lawful). Moreover, a person who is subject to lawful violence may also find themselves subject to additional or incidental violence. The important observation drawn out by Agamben is that while the privilege of the sovereign is to exercise lawful violence, the creation of a relationship of violence, encourages others to act violently towards figure of the homo sacer. They are emboldened because violence is made permissible. The contemporary experience of people with disabilities invokes the homo sacer figure described by Agamben – they become figures of bare life who may be subject to unlimited and unaccountable violence precisely because the protection of normal human relationships based on respect and honour is stripped away.

Legal capacity and the CRPD

The validity of the suspension of normal law for those with disability is directly challenged by the human rights approach in the CRPD. The CRPD articulates the existing human rights framework in the context of disability by recognizing and responding to the entrenched and multifaceted discrimination experienced by people with disabilities (Dhanda 2007; Kanter 2007; Quinn and Degener 2002; Bartlett 2012). Central to the CRPD approach is the social model of disability (Weller 2008). The social model of disability recognizes that discrimination on the basis of disability is the primary mode of social oppression experienced by people with disabilities (Kanter 2009; Petersen 2015). It is expressed in the definition of disability in the CRPD that distinguishes impairment from 'disability', understood as the interaction of impairment with hostile environments and attitudes (Kayess and French 2008; Shakespeare 2013).

The key idea underpinning the social model of disability in the CRPD is the rejection of the medical model of health and illness that dominated social, institutional and political responses to disability throughout the twentieth century (Quinn and Degener 2002). The medical model equates impairment with disability, sickness and dependence (Knight 1998, 13). It promotes medical intervention, correction, the suppression of difference and paternalism. In contrast, the social model of disability highlights the problem of social exclusion on the one hand, and the benefits of social inclusion on the other (Weller 2013). In this sense, social inclusion in the CRPD is both the objective of the human rights model and the mechanism that will bring about the social change.

Article 12

The CRPD's challenge to the exclusionary stance of current law takes its most explicit form in article 12 (Equal recognition before the law). Article 12(2) requires that people with disabilities are able to 'enjoy legal capacity on an equal basis with others in all aspects of life'. They are entitled to 'support for legal capacity' (article 12(3)). CRPD General Comment 1 defines legal capacity as the dual ability to hold rights and duties (legal standing) and to exercise those rights and duties (legal agency) (McSherry 2012). As a holder of rights with legal standing, a person with legal capacity is entitled to the full protection of his or her rights by the legal system. As a legal agent, he or she is entitled to create, modify or end legal relationships (Arstein-Kerslake and Flynn 2016). The assertion of legal capacity with the principle of support denotes the 'decoupling' of mental capacity and legal capacity. The CRPD rejects the notion that one's cognitive ability or mental capacity is static, fixed or can be medically pre-determined. Rather, it is precisely because mental capacity is a fluctuating contextual and relational human attribute, that legal capacity must be respected at all times.

CRPD General Comment 1 clarifies that the obligation to provide 'support for legal capacity' may encompass many different types of support (CRPD General Comment 1, para 14). People with disabilities are not obliged to accept support (CRPD General Comment 1, paras 15 and 17), and whether or not support is sought by the person, the decisions made by people with disabilities must be respected (CRPD General Comment 1, para 16). The Committee affirms that measures that support legal capacity must respect the will and preferences of the person, and be protected by safeguards (CRPD General Comment 1, para 18). In short, the General Comment seeks to place people with cognitive impairment on an equal basis with non-disabled people, by ensuring that their 'rights, wills and preferences' will be respected in all circumstances, and supported by whatever means are necessary to recognize legal capacity. The principle of inclusion in the CRPD, especially the principle of 'equality before the law' rejects the 'states of exception' that characterize modern laws. Instead the CRPD insists on substantive equality before the law expressed in the principle of universal legal capacity.

Conclusion

From the outset, the CRPD was hailed as a 'lodestar for the future' (Dhanda 2007). It was anticipated that the CRPD would challenge the contours of modern law, not least because the CRPD re-imagines the notion of 'what it means to be human' (Quinn 2010). Ten years on, there remains significant disagreement about the relationship between mental and legal capacity and their representation in law and a reluctance to abandon the assumption that the law is benevolent.

This paper challenges the assumption that the continued exclusion of people with disabilities from full legal recognition can be justified on protective or benevolent grounds. Following Agamben, the paper argues that exceptions in the law invite and permit violence towards the figure of the homo sacer (or a person with disabilities) who is defined as those who are simultaneously within and beyond the law. It is known that people with disabilities experience high levels of violence and abuse, including violence and abuse that is clearly prohibited by the law. Inquiries into such abuse have found that unlawful violence and abuse goes unchecked because it is undetected, because people with disabilities are unable to report their experience, because access to justice is poor, because the burden of reporting is onerous, because people are fearful of the police or courts, or of the response they will receive from their families or carers (AHRC 2014). Violence also goes unchecked because abusive behaviours are unnoticed or tolerated because individual suffering is not recognized or it is not seen as important (VEOHRC 2014). These explanations for the escalated violence experienced by people with disabilities are consistent with Agamben's observations.

If Agamben is correct, the incidence of violence experienced by people with disabilities is unlikely to be reduced by traditional legal response. Instead, the underlying cause – the legal exclusion of people with disabilities – must be addressed. According to Agamben exclusion from the law will always and inevitably produce and reproduce violence. For the current approach to be overturned, however, the belief that exclusion from the law equates with protection will need to erode. The analysis contained in this paper seeks to disrupt the dominant assumption that states of exception in the law can be justified on protective grounds by revealing the dynamic of lawful violence. The paper argues for the removal of all states of exception and the introduction of measures and processes that will enable the full and effective participation of people with disability in the law. Strategies of inclusion will reduce the incidence of violence for people with disability by addressing the underlying cause of such violence.

The approach offered in the CRPD recognizes that the social construction of difference through the promulgation of exceptional legal regimes for people with disabilities. The CRPD accepts that exclusion from the law prefigures and underpins legal, political and social marginalization, that legal exception is the precursor of social exclusion. More importantly, the CRPD recognizes that the remedy for exclusion is the radical inclusion of people with disabilities in all aspect of social life. The remedy is crystallized in a requirement to regard people with disabilities as legitimate subjects of the law and as legitimate actors in the law and legal processes.

Notes

1. In this article the term 'people with disabilities' refers to individuals with impairment who are recognized under article 1 of the CRPD. The term 'people with mental disabilities' refers to those with intellectual or psych-social impairment.
2. Legal capacity refers to the dual ability to hold rights and duties (legal standing) and to exercise those rights and duties (legal agency) (McSherry 2012).
3. Mental capacity in this sense refer to the common law concept of mental capacity summarised in article 2 of the Mental Capacity Act 2005 (England and Wales) as the ability of an individual to understand information relevant to a decision, weigh the information in order to arrive at a decision and communicate the decision.
4. *Remnants of Auschwitz: The Witness and the Archive* (2002); *State of Exception* (2003); *The Kingdom and the Glory: For a Theological Genealogy of Economy and Government* (2007); *The Sacrament of Language: An Archaeology of the Oath* (2008); *Opus Dei: An Archaeology Of Duty* (2013); *The Highest Poverty*, 2013).
5. Finding an explanation for the Nazi phenomenon is a key theme in Agamben's work.
6. Cf. In *History of Sexuality* Foucault argues that sovereign power, thought of as 'the ancient right to *take* life or *let* live was replaced by a power to *foster* life' and that the power of life evolved into the two forms of *anatomo-politics*, or the disciplining of the economically useful human body and the and *bio-politics* that focused on the species body as imbued with the mechanism of life (Foucault 1978, 138, 139). In his later work, Foucault describes governmentality as a complex form of modern power encompassing disciplinary and sovereign power (Foucault 2008).
7. Queensland's new mental health laws provide an exception.

Acknowledgements

The author would like to thank the reviewers of this paper for their helpful comments.

Disclosure statement

No potential conflict of interest was reported by the author.

Primary Legal Sources

CRPD (Committee on the Rights of Persons with Disabilities). 2014. General Comment No. 1 – Article 12: Equal Recognition before the Law, Paragraphs 12–15, UN Doc. No. CRPD/C/GC/1, Adopted at the 11th Session, April.

Articles and books

Agamben, Giorgio. 1998. *Homo Sacer: Sovereign Power and Bare Life*. Stanford, CA: Stanford University Press.
Agamben, Giorgio. 2008. *State of Exception*. Chicago, IL: University of Chicago Press.
AGPC (Australian Government Productivity Commission). 2014. *Access to Justice Arrangements*. Canberra: AGPC. http://www.pc.gov.au/inquiries/completed/access-justice/report.
AHRC (Australian Human Rights Commission). 2014. *Equal Before the Law: Towards Disability Justice Strategies*. Sydney: AHRC. https://www.humanrights.gov.au/our-work/disability-rights/publications/equal-law.
ALRC (Australian Law Reform Commission). 2014. *Equality, Capacity and Disability in Commonwealth Laws*. Sydney: ALRC. https://www.alrc.gov.au/publications/equality-capacity-disability-report-124.
Arstein-Kerslake, Anna, and Elionóir Flynn. 2016. "The General Comment on Article 12 of the Convention on the Rights of Persons with Disabilities: A Roadmap for Equality Before the Law." *International Journal of Human Rights* 20 (4): 471–490. doi:10.1080/13642987.2015.1107052.
Bach, Michael, and Lana Kerzner. 2010. *A New Paradigm for Protecting Autonomy and the Right to Legal Capacity*. Law Commission of Ontario. http://www.ontla.on.ca/library/repository/mon/24011/306184.pdf.
Baldry, Eileen. 2014. "Disability at the Margins: Limits of the Law." *Griffith Law Review* 23 (3): 370–388. doi:10.1080/10383441.2014.1000218.
Bartlett, Peter. 2012. "The United Nations Convention on the Rights of Persons with Disabilities and Mental Health Law." *The Modern Law Review* 75: 752–778.
Burchell, Graham. 1993. "Liberal Government and Techniques of the Self." *Economy & Society* 22 (3): 267–282.
Carney, Terry, and Fleur Beaupert. 2013. "Public and Private Bricolage – Challenges Balancing Law, Services and Civil Society in Advancing CRPD Supported Decision-making." *University of New South Wales Law Journal* 36 (1): 175–201.
Carney, Terry, and David Tate. 1997. *The Adult Guardianship Experiment: Tribunals and Popular Justice*. Sydney: Federation Press.
Carter, Barbara. 2010. "Adult Guardianship: Human Rights, Social Justice." *Journal of Law and Medicine* 18: 143–155.
Daes, Erica-Irene A. 1986. *Principles, Guidelines and Guarantees for the Protection of Persons Detained on Grounds of Mental Ill Health or Suffering from a Mental Disorder. Report Prepared by the Special Rapporteur of the Sub-commission on Prevention of Discrimination and Protection of Minorities*. New York: United Nations. UN Doc E/CN.4./Sub.2/1993/17.
Despouy, Leandro. 1991. *Human Rights and Disability. Final Report of United Nations Special Rapporteur of the Sub-commission on Prevention of Discrimination and Protection of Minorities*. New York: United Nations Economic and Social Council. UN Doc E/CN.4/Sub.2/1991/31. http://www.un.org/esa/socdev/enable/dispaperdes0.htm.
Dhanda, Amita. 2007. "Legal Capacity in the Disability Rights Convention: Stranglehold of the Past or Lodestar for the Future." *Syracuse Journal of International Law and Commerce.* 34 (2): 429–462.
Dhanda, Amita. 2012. "Universal Legal Capacity as a Universal Human Right." In *Mental Health and Human Rights: Vision, Praxis, and Courage*, edited by M. Dudley, D. Silove, and F. Gale, 177–188. Oxford: Oxford University Press.
Flynn, Elionóir, and Anna Arstein-Kerslake. 2014a. "The Support Model of Legal Capacity: Fact Fiction Or Fantasy?" *Berkeley Journal of International Law* 32 (1): 124–143. http://dx.doi.org/doi:10.15779/Z38494G.
Flynn, Elionóir, and Anna Arstein-Kerslake. 2014b. "Legislating Personhood: Realising the Right to Support in Exercising Legal Capacity." *International Journal of Law in Context* 10 (01): 81–104.
Foucault, Michel. 1977. *Discipline and Punish: The Birth of the Prison*. London: Penguin.
Foucault, Michel. 1978. *The History of Sexuality, Volume 1: An Introduction*. New York: Pantheon Books.
Foucault, Michel. 2008. *Birth of Bio-politics: Lectures at the College du France 1978–1989*. New York: Palgrave Macmillan.
Gordon, Colin. 1991. "Government Rationality: An Introduction." In *The Foucault Effect*, edited by Gary Burchell, Colin Gordon and Peter Miller, 1–52. Chicago, IL: Chicago University Press.
Hunt, Paul. 2005. *Mental Disability and the Right to Health: Report of the Special Rapporteur on the Right of Everyone to the Enjoyment of the Highest Attainable Standard of Physical and Mental Health*. Geneva: UN Commission on Human Rights. E/CN.4/2005/51.
Kanter, Arlene. 2007. "The Promise and Challenge of the United Nations Convention on the Rights of Persons with Disabilities." *Syracuse Journal of International Law and Commerce* 34: 287–321.
Kanter, Arlene. 2009. "The United Nations Convention on the Rights of Persons with Disabilities and its Implications for the Rights of Elderly People Under International Law." *Georgia State University Law Review* 25 (3): 527–573.
Kayess, Rosemary, and Phillip French. 2008. "Out of Darkness into Light? Introducing the Convention on the Rights of Persons with Disabilities." *Human Rights Law Review* 8 (1): 1–34.
Knight, James. 1998. "Models of Health." In *Second Opinion: An Introduction to Health Sociology*, edited by John Germov, 136–155. Oxford: Oxford University Press.

Kohn, Nina, Jeremy A. Blumenthal, and Amy T. Campbell. 2013. "Supported Decision-making: A Viable Alternative to Guardianship?" *Pennsylvania State Law Review* 117 (4): 1111–1157.

Lawson, Anna. 2007. "The United Nations Convention on the Rights of Persons with Disabilities: New Era or False Dawn?" *Syracuse Journal of International Law & Commerce* 34 (2): 563–619.

Lord, Janet, David Suozzi, and Allyn Taylor. 2010. "Lessons from the Experience of U.N. Convention on the Rights of Persons with Disabilities: Addressing the Democratic Deficit in Global Health Governance." *The Journal of Law, Medicine & Ethics* 38 (3): 564–579. doi:10.1111/j.1748-720X.2010.00512.x.

Lush, Denzil. 2014. "Roman Origins of Modern Guardianship Law." In *Comparative Perspectives on Adult Guardianship*, edited by Kimberly Dayton, 3–16. Durham, NC: Carolina Academic Press.

McSherry, Bernadette. 2012. "Legal Capacity Under the Convention on the Rights of Persons with Disabilities." *Journal of Law and Medicine* 20 (1): 22–27.

Mill, John Stuart. 1869. *On Liberty*. 4th ed. London: Longmans, Green, Reader and Dyer.

Minkowitz, Tina. 2007. "The United Nations Convention on the Rights of Persons with Disabilities and the Right to be Free from Nonconsensual Psychiatric Interventions." *Syracuse Journal of International Law and Commerce* 34 (2): 405–428.

Minkowitz, Tina. 2014. "Rethinking Criminal Responsibility from a Critical Disability Perspective: The Abolition of Insanity/incapacity Acquittals and Unfitness to Plead, and Beyond." *Griffith Law Review* 23 (3): 434–466. doi:10.1080/10383441.2014.1013177.

O'Neill, Nick, and Carmelle Peisah. 2011. *Capacity and the Law*. Sydney: Sydney University Press. http://www.austlii.edu.au/au/journals/SydUPLawBk/2011/1.html.

Peay, Jill. 2015. "Mental Incapacity and Criminal Liability: Redrawing the Fault Lines?" *International Journal of Law and Psychiatry* 40: 25–35. doi:10.1016/j.ijlp.2015.04.007.

Perlin, Michael. 2011. *International Human Rights and Mental Disability Law: When the Silenced are Heard*. Oxford: Oxford University Press.

Petersen, Carole. 2015. "Reproductive Justice, Public Policy, and Abortion on the Basis of Fetal Impairment: Lessons from International Human Rights Law and the Potential Impact of the Convention on the Rights of Persons with Disabilities." *Journal of Law and Health* 28 (1): 121–163. http://engagedscholarship.csuohio.edu/jlh/vol28/iss1/7.

Quinn, Gerard. 2010. "Personhood & Legal Capacity: Perspectives on the Paradigm Shift of Article 12 CRPD." Paper Presented at the HPOD Conference, Harvard Law School, Cambridge, MA, February 20. http://www.nuigalway.ie/cdlp/staff/gerard_quinn.html.

Quinn, Gerard, and Theresia Degener. 2002. *Human Rights and Disability: The Current Use and Future Potential of United Nations Human Rights Instruments in the Context of Disability*. Geneva: United Nations Publications.

Richardson, Genevra. 2013. "Mental Capacity in the Shadow of Suicide: What Can the Law Do?" *International Journal of Law in Context* 9 (01): 87–105. doi:10.1017/S174455231200050X.

Rose, Nikolas. 1993. "Government, Authority and Expertise in Advanced Liberalism." *Economy & Society* 22 (3): 283–299.

Series, Lucy. 2015. "Relationships, Autonomy and Legal Capacity: Mental Capacity and Support Paradigms." *International Journal of Law and Psychiatry* 40: 80–91. doi:10.1016/j.ijlp.2015.04.010.

Shakespeare, Tom. 2013. "Nasty, Brutish, and Short? On the Predicament of Disability and Embodiment." In *Disability and the Good Human Life*, edited by Jerome Bickenbach, Franziska Felder and Barbara Schmitz, 93–112. Cambridge: Cambridge University Press.

Slobogin, Chris. 2015. "Eliminating Mental Disability as Legal Criterion in the Deprivation of Liberty Cases: The Impact of the Convention on the Rights of Persons with Disabilities on the Insanity Defence, Civil Commitment and Competency Law." *International Journal of Law and Psychiatry* 40: 36–42.

Steele, Linda. 2014. "Disability, Abnormality and Criminal Law: Sterilisation as Lawful and 'Good' Violence." *Griffith Law Review* 23 (3): 467–497.

Steele, Linda, and Stuart Thomas. 2014. "Disability at the Periphery: Legal Theory, Disability and Criminal Law." *Griffith Law Review* 23 (3): 357–369. doi:10.1080/10383441.2014.1017916.

Szmukler, George, Rowena Daw, and Felicity Callard. 2013. "Mental Health Law and the UN Convention on the Rights of Persons with Disabilities." *International Journal of Law and Psychiatry* 17 (3): 245–252. doi:10.1016/j.ijlp.2013.11.024.

Then, Shih-Ning. 2013. "Evolution and Innovation in Guardianship Laws: Assisted Decision-making." *Sydney Law Review* 33 (1): 133–136.

VEOHRC (Victorian Equal Opportunity and Human Rights Commission). 2014. *Beyond Doubt: The Experiences of People with Disabilities Reporting Crime*. Carlton: VEOHRC. http://www.humanrightscommission.vic.gov.au/.

Wadiwel, Dinesh. Forthcoming. "Disability and Torture: Exception, Epistemology and 'Black Sites'." *Continuum* 30.

Watson, Roger. 1969. *Edwin Chadwick: Poor Law and Public Health*. London: Aylesbury.

Weller, Penelope. 2008. "Supported Decision-making and the Achievement of Non-discrimination: The Promise and Paradox of the Disabilities Convention." *Law in Context: A Socio-Legal Journal* 26 (2): 85–110.

Weller, Penelope. 2010a. "Lost in Translation: Human Rights and Mental Health Law." In *Rethinking Rights Based Mental Health Laws*, edited by Bernadette McSherry and Penelope Weller, 51–72. Portland, OR: Hart.

Weller, Penelope. 2010b. "Right to Health – The Convention on the Rights of Persons with Disabilities." *The Alternative Law Journal* 35 (2): 66–71.

Weller, Penelope. 2013. *New Law and Ethics in Mental Health Advance Directives: The Convention on the Rights of Persons With Disabilities and the Right To Choose*. London: Routledge.

Weller, Penelope. 2015. "Reconsidering Legal Capacity: Radical Critiques, Governmentality and Dividing Practice." *Griffith Law Review* 23: 498–518.

Weller, Penelope. 2016. "Legal Capacity and Access to Justice: The Right to Participation in the CRPD." *Laws* 5 (1): 1–13.

White, Benjamin, Lindy Willmott, Pip Trowse, Malcolm Parker, and Colleen Cartwright. 2011. "The Legal Role of Medical Professionals in Decisions to Withhold or Withdraw Life-sustaining Treatment: Part 1 (New South Wales)." *Journal of Law and Medicine* 18 (3): 498–522.

Whyte, Jessica. 2013. "'The King Reigns But He Doesn't Govern': Thinking about Sovereignty and Government with Agamben, Foucault and Rousseau." In *Giorgio Agamben: Legal, Political and Philosophical Perspectives*, edited by Tom Frost, 143–161. London: Routledge.

Wood, Erica. 2012. "The Paradox of Adult Guardianship: A Solution to and a Source for Elder Abuse." *Generations* 36 (3): 79–82.

Not just language: an analysis of discursive constructions of disability in sentencing remarks

Frankie Sullivan

ABSTRACT

It is well established that people with disability (PWD) experience disproportionately high rates of domestic and family violence. Inquiries into this issue have focused on tangible barriers to accessing justice, such as onerous standards of capacity and the lack of communication aids available to those wanting to report crime or give evidence. However, relatively little research has sought to examine the social and cultural factors that compromise the justice outcomes for PWD as victims of crime. By employing the methodology of discourse analysis against a framework of critical disability studies, this research highlights how disability is constructed by judges in the sentencing remarks of those convicted of domestic homicide offences against PWD. The central argument of this article is that there appears to be underlying attitudes towards disability that affect the way family members, intimate partners and carers convicted of violent crimes against PWD are sentenced. These attitudes are reflected in the language used by judges at sentencing, resulting in statements that denigrate disability and even condone such violence. Essentially, this article seeks to demonstrate how an interdisciplinary approach that simultaneously takes into account law, language and power provides a more complete picture of the way PWD who have experienced domestic and family violence are positioned within the criminal justice system.

Introduction

On 19 March 2011, 27-year-old South Australian woman Kyla Puhle died from a lung infection. In the months leading up to her death, Kyla's parents confined her to a room of their family home and withheld food, water and medical care. At the time of her death, Kyla weighed approximately 12 kilograms. Angela Puhle – Kyla's mother – pleaded guilty to manslaughter. At her sentencing, Justice Sulan of the Supreme Court of South Australia emphasized the 'tragic' circumstances of the offence, before handing down a suspended sentence of five years (*R v Puhle* 2013). He stated that 'good reasons' existed to warrant the unusually light sentence.

At this point it should be asked: What made the circumstances of this case so exceptional and tragic? That is, when is the killing of an adult woman by her mother an act involving only minimal culpability in the eyes of the state? According to disability rights advocates and scholars, the answer hinges on Kyla having a disability.[1] Publicly commenting on the Puhle case, the late Stella Young pointed out the trend of lenient sentences being handed down to parents who kill their children with disabilities

(2013). Essentially, Young argued that instances of lethal domestic and family violence against people with disability (PWD) are treated as fundamentally different to the killing of non-disabled people. As will be demonstrated in this article, Kyla's case is indeed part of a trend – a trend that has not been given adequate scholarly attention.

This research seeks to highlight some of the discursive constructions of disability that emerge during the sentencing of people convicted of homicide or homicide related offences against PWD in the context of a domestic relationship. It will be argued that these constructions undermine the justice outcomes for PWD. Further, that the sentencing process functions as a site for the exercise of power that produces and maintains oppressive responses to disability.

It is well established that PWD – particularly women and children – experience disproportionately high rates of domestic and family violence compared to non-disabled people (Salthouse and Frohmader 2004; Baldry, Bratel, and Breckenridge 2006; Frohmader, Dowse, and Didi 2015; Senate Community Affairs References Committee 2015). It is also well recognized that few instances of this violence are reported, even fewer are prosecuted and fewer still result in a conviction (Innes 2007; AHRC 2014, [2.3]). A number of reasons have been proffered to make sense of this disparity – the social isolation and segregation of PWD, barriers to reporting and testifying, not being taken seriously by the police, reliance on the perpetrator for care, and a lack of inclusive and accessible services and information (AHRC 2014, [1.1]). In recent years, numerous inquiries, reports and legislative amendments have been directed towards addressing violence against PWD by improving access to justice. These initiatives have predominantly focused on tangible barriers to participation in the legal system, such as standards of capacity and the lack of communication aids available to those wanting to report crime or give evidence (ALRC 2014, [7.6]; AHRC 2014). Comparatively, little research has examined the role sociocultural factors play in the production of unjust legal outcomes for PWD who have experienced domestic and family violence, such as the attitudes towards disability that are held by society, including those entrusted with the role of formally responding to this violence on behalf of the state.

This article seeks to demonstrate how an interdisciplinary approach – one that identifies sentencing remarks as cultural texts and analyses them through a lens of critical disability studies – could provide a more complete picture of the obstacles PWD face within the criminal justice system. Employing the methodology of discourse analysis against a framework of critical disability studies, this research attempts to deconstruct the statements made by judges in the sentencing of those convicted of the murder, manslaughter or attempted murder of PWD within a domestic relationship. Sentencing remarks are cultural texts replete with meaning. However, the meaning that is derived from them is contingent upon the position of the reader. In undertaking this research, I will decode a discrete set of judicial texts and offer up a reading that sits in opposition to the hegemonic viewpoint on disability (Hall 2007, 103). As these texts comprised transcripts of speech, my analysis will be centred on the language that constitutes them. It will be argued that there are entrenched beliefs about disability – as evidenced through discursive constructions of disability that emerge in sentencing remarks – that permeate the criminal justice system and perpetuate the disablement of PWD, with dangerous effects.

It is vitally important to examine the way language is used throughout the legal process. Law is language. That is, law, in action, consists almost entirely of linguistic events, and language is the primary way in which it is exercised, abused or challenged (Conley and O'Barr 2005, 2). As Conley and O'Barr suggest, 'if the law is failing to live up to its ideals, the failure must lie in the details of everyday legal practice – details that consist almost entirely of language' (2005, 3). Considering that the law is used to authorize legitimate violence against perpetrators in the name of justice, these failures of language take on a particular gravity. Furthermore, language is intimately connected to the way people think and act in respect to an issue. Thus, it both reflects and produces ideologies and responses; it is both the vehicle of the power of law and power itself (Conley and O'Barr 2005, 6).

The power of language is particularly evident in sentencing. Sentencing entails a unidirectional monologue directed at the convicted by a judge (Heffer 2005, 9). Its purposes are to punish the offender, deter them and others from committing similar offences, protect the community, promote rehabilitation, make the offender accountable for their actions, denounce the conduct of the offender, and recognize the harm done by the offence (*Crimes (Sentencing Procedure) Act 1999* (NSW), s 3A). Sentencing is the culmination of the criminal process, and the moment at which justice is seen to be done. Inherent in the formulation of a sentence are value judgments about what constitutes harm, what behaviours need to be deterred, how vehemently conduct should be denounced and what an appropriate punishment is in the circumstances. As judges are located within public discourses as 'powerful, central figures, sitting in judgment on people and their lives' (Schulz 2008, 223), these value-laden assessments have pervasive effects. It will be argued that the language used by judges during sentencing betrays and bolsters the oppressive ways of thinking about and responding to disability that prevail in society. Couched in the legitimacy and formality of the legal process, the constitutive effects of this language include unjust legal outcomes and the further disablement of PWD. By focusing simultaneously on law, language and power, this article demonstrates how a criminal justice system that aspires to equality can produce a pervasive sense of injustice for PWD by providing an explication of what this injustice looks like as it happens (Conley and O'Barr 2005, 130).

To be clear, this article does not advocate for harsher sentencing for offenders who kill PWD. The use of sympathetic language as a means of mitigating the criminal responsibility of the offender raises a complex problem when those relied upon for informal care – predominantly women – are often lacking adequate support. However, empathy for the offender cannot come at the cost of the agency and acknowledgement of the value of the lives of PWD. The social inequalities tied up in care work need to be acknowledged in ways that do not reproduce the discriminatory assumptions that underpin ableist discourses. Further, they need to be addressed in ways that go beyond language and move into tangible improvements in available support. Nevertheless, the language used by judges is one of many places where agency, value and quality need to be ascribed to PWD to contribute to a cultural shift where the lives and rights of PWD are treated as equal under the law.

Methodology

A qualitative research approach is adopted as a means of interrogating the processes, thoughts and behaviours of judges, and how they connect with broader social contexts (Schulz 2014, 121). Specifically, critical discourse analysis of sentencing remarks is undertaken to reveal the way judges' language creates and reflects power relations and shared knowledge about disability (Van Dijk 2003, 93; Fairclough 2013, 178). Throughout this article, the term 'discourse' will be used to connote 'systems of statements which cohere around common meanings and values (that) are a product of social factors, of powers and practices' (Stevens and Wendt 2014, 98). The mode of discourse analysis used in this research focuses on lexicon, syntax, rhetoric, discursive formations, omissions and structure within the genre of sentencing remarks.

Domestic homicide offences are taken as the subject of analysis in this study as they represent the most severe culmination of domestic and family violence against PWD. Consequently, the discourses under scrutiny are intensified and the disparities between the protection afforded to PWD and the non-disabled – as a matter of life or death – are most evident. The category of 'domestic homicide' includes offences of murder, manslaughter and attempted murder taking place within a 'personal relationship' as broadly defined by s 5 of the *Crimes (Domestic and Personal Violence) Act 2007* (NSW). This expansive definition is apt for this research as it takes into account the types of relationships that are often the source of violence for PWD, for instance, those between givers and receivers of care, and long-term occupants of residential facilities.

Purposive sampling was used to search the case law and media databases across all Australian states and territories for the sentencing remarks of those convicted of domestic homicide offences against PWD in the last 15 years. These cases were identified using searches grouped around the terms 'disab*', 'murder', 'manslaughter', 'kill' and 'neglect'. Ten sets of sentencing remarks were located as well as one appeal of sentence decision within which the sentencing remarks of the first instance judge are extracted, and one determination of mental incompetence.[2] As a matter of convenience, these judicial texts will collectively be referred to as the 'sentencing remarks' that form the object of analysis in this study.[3]

The results were grouped into three distinct but overlapping discursive constructions of disability that emerge within the sentencing remarks. Construction one was the foundational finding that disability is inherently negative. This construction was explored by dissecting the terminology used by judges to describe impairments and those who experience them, the dominance of medical discourses of disability, and the reification of the normal and desired status ascribed to non-disabled people. The second construction entailed the way judges present subjective experiences of disability as incontrovertibly signifying a low quality of life, without reference to the lived experiences of the victims[4] or PWD generally. This assumption appeared to lead to killing being positioned as an extension of care within the sentencing remarks. Construction three saw the focus shift to how domestic relationships PWD have with those around them are construed. It appeared that relationships with PWD were constructed as inciting the offenders' violence. This emerged through the way that the needs of PWD are framed as unduly burdensome, causing the offender to 'snap' and subsequently reducing their culpability. It is this third construction that this article examines in detail.

Relationships with PWD

Having a relationship with PWD is depicted throughout the sentencing remarks as being arduous and oppressive, especially if it involves the provision of assistance. This is demonstrated through the way the victims' needs and the various acts with which they required assistance are negatively emphasised and presented as burdensome. Flowing on from this, in cases where the offender was also the primary carer of the victim, a narrative emerges in which acts of lethal violence are an inevitable response to the 'burden' of care. Essentially, the needs of PWD are cast as so unreasonable and unrelenting that they cause even the most 'ordinary' offenders to 'snap' in response. The mitigating effects of the 'burden' of caring for PWD are also evident in the formulation of the sentence, where it is suggested that the offender 'suffered enough' through the life and death of the victim, and need not be punished. By constructing relationships with PWD as a burden and then invoking narratives in which this burden excuses the offender's acts, the message sent is clear – disability incites violence.

The 'burden' of care

Throughout the sentencing remarks, the needs of PWD and the requisite acts of care required to meet them are framed as burdensome. This is evident in the way that caring for a PWD is presented as a negative experience, expressed in terms of the stress and strain it put on the offender. For instance, in *R v Sutton* (2007), assisting Matthew – the victim of manslaughter – is presented as a problem for the whole family: 'the care that they gave, however, placed a great strain on the family' ([5]) who 'began to suffer the effects of the unrelenting demands placed on them' ([8]). Similarly, in *R v Dawes* (2004, [28]), the offender being sentenced for manslaughter 'carried the burden for her husband', the burden being the needs of their son, Jason, and the offender in *R v McLaren* (2011, [36]) – a paid carer being sentenced for attempted murder – is described as 'feeling trapped and wanted to get out of it'. The language used in these comments unequivocally presents caring for PWD as an oppressive task that is, at best, endured. Furthermore, these descriptions insinuate that PWD draw upon the resources of those around them in an unreasonable and unsustainable way. As Thomas explains, the belief that PWD are dependent individuals who can only 'take from' rather than 'give to' society is so entrenched in our social consciousness that it has become a naturalized fact (2007, 61).

In being framed as a dependent category that cannot contribute, PWD become social problems whose claims to full citizenship are undermined (Thomas 2007, 88). This conception of disability overlooks two, essential facts: that care is a pre-requisite for all human development, and that relationships of care have significant value in that they establish a reciprocal sense of importance and belonging (Lynch, Baker, and Lyons 2009, 1, 2). Dependency – a devalued and stigmatized state of being – is attributed to PWD despite the actuality that all humans rely on others for support and assistance in various ways (Thomas 2007, 88). While needs themselves are neutral, they are imbued with meaning in different contexts, and 'having needs' becomes a negative quality ascribed to particular groups in society (Thomas 2007, 88). Therefore, while caring for non-disabled babies is understood as being a source of pleasure, caring for PWD is viewed as a burden (Lynch and Lyons 2009, 62). This is highlighted in the way that having a baby with a disability is described in *R v Wang* (2000, [16]) – a case involving a mother's manslaughter of her infant child – as 'obviously a severe blow', in stark contrast to the assumed joy of parenting a baby without disability.

Furthermore, undue attention is drawn to the needs of PWD through comments made by judges that catalogue the various ways in which the victims required assistance. In many cases, particularly where the offender was the primary carer of the victim, these comments appear towards the beginning of the sentencing remarks. This inverts the typical structure of sentencing remarks where the opening paragraphs are primarily focused on the offender, implying that the victim's needs are of particular relevance to the formulation of the sentence. For example, in paragraph nine of *R v Dawes* (2004), Dunford J, quoting the sentencing remarks of the judge at first instance, states:

> The practical reality was that the care in terms of daily responsibility to feed, toilet, bathe, educate, entertain and love Jason fell to his mother and the learned sentencing judge found that this was an unrelenting, tiring, frustrating and never-ending task that very few people have ever experienced or are even capable of fully comprehending.

This listing technique draws attention to the minutiae of everyday responsibility, further contributing to the notion that PWD are a burden. Not only does it foster a sense of the weighty duty felt by the offender, by foregrounding the needs of the victim in this way they become central to the commission of the offence. Additionally, the above comment cannot be mentioned without drawing attention to the way in which loving a child with a disability is framed as a 'responsibility' and a 'task' rather than a given. Furthermore, it posits the sole responsibility for feeding, toileting, educating, bathing and entertaining another as something that few people have experienced or are able to comprehend, despite this being the reality of the lives of countless carers, including many single parents. The inference that is thus drawn is that PWD is essentially different to non-disabled people, and the acts required to meet their needs goes beyond the scope of what is considered the 'normal' experience of parenthood. Interestingly, one ground of the prosecution's appeal against the inadequacy of the sentence handed down by the District Court at first instance was that this list was inaccurate (*R v Dawes* 2004, [51]). Specifically, it was argued that the evidence established that Jason did not require assistance with toileting – a fact that was confirmed on appeal (*R v Dawes* 2005, [52]). This raises another noteworthy point – the fixation on toileting habits that appears throughout the sentencing remarks.

Toileting is over-represented in discussions about the assistance the victims required. For example, the comment that 'it was difficult to toilet train him' is located in the second paragraph of *R v Eitzen* (2011), a judgement concerning whether Mrs. Eitzen was fit to stand trial for the murder of her son. Similarly, in *R v Puhle* (2013), Sulan J quotes one of Kyla's respite carers: 'Kyla was incontinent and had to wear Softies, which are disposable nappies for adults.' According to Thomas, '[c]entral to the impaired person's devalued status is the perception that impairment causes "childlike" needs to be present' (2007, 88). These references to 'nappies' and 'toilet training' are undeniably infantilizing, and reflect the way in which toileting practices are central to conceptions of 'docile' and 'civilised' bodies (Sullivan 2005, 36). Essentially, '[i]ncontinence reveals one's body, in all of its excessiveness and unruliness, as anything but productive and docile' (Sullivan 2005, 37), and toileting is used to connote the extent to which one's body can or cannot be tamed in the basest of ways, where those who cannot be 'trained' are earmarked as unable to participate in society. Ultimately, the language used to describe the impacts of caring for the victims and the cataloguing of the acts require day-to-day assistance with devalue PWD by constructing their existences as unduly burdensome to those in relationships with them.

The corollary of this is that the lives of PWD appear to be more highly valued when they are perceived as being minimally obtrusive to those around them. Even where the offender did not engage in acts of paid or unpaid care, the listing of the victim's needs still takes place. For instance, in *Harding v The Queen* the following remark is made about the victim: '[s]he lived on her own in her house in Narromine, and was visited once a day by a community nurse who assisted her with showering and other personal tasks' (2013, [25]). Similarly, in *R v Soon*, Grove J comments: '[h]e was dependent upon carers who attended him on a roster. They attended first thing in the morning, then for cleaning the premises, for lunch, to cook the evening meal, to empty his catheter bag and finally to put him to bed late at night' (2008, [4]). Despite being seemingly irrelevant, these remarks serve a distinct purpose: instead of devaluing the lives of PWD, they appear to contribute to judges' assessments of the worthiness of the victims' lives, for 'good' disabled citizens are ones who minimize the assumed inter-personal burden associated with their impairment and make their needs amenable to the labour market (Kumari Campbell 2009, 36). The criminal liability of the offenders in these cases appears to be heightened and their actions – respectively, described as 'brutal' and 'monstrous' – attract significant custodial sentences (*Harding v The Queen* 2013, [61]; *R v Soon* 2008, [41].

'Snap' narratives

One consequence of framing relationships with PWD as burdensome is the emergence of narratives in which the offender 'snaps' and loses control in response to the pressures placed on them. This narrative is embedded in *R v McLaren* (2011), *R v Dawes* (2004), *R v Eitzen* (2011), *R v Wang* (2000), and to a lesser degree, *R v Sharpe* (2005). *R v Puhle* (2013) develops along a slightly different trajectory, where the offender emotionally detaches over a period of time, corresponding with the prolonged neglect of her daughter. Nevertheless, accounts of the offender succumbing to the pressures of caring for PWD appear to some extent in the majority of cases where the offender was the primary carer of the victim. For instance, in paragraph 28 of *R v Dawes* (2004), Dunford J states:

> This was not merely a case of a mother killing her severely disabled son, but of a mother suffering from major depression occasioned not only by the need to care for her son and the devotion she gave to that task, but overwhelmed by a number of other stressors … resulting in her spontaneously snapping.

Similarly, in *R v McLaren*, Berman J comments that the offender 'himself could not really explain what he did beyond saying that he felt trapped and was at the end of his tether' (2011, [49]). Further, in *R v Wang*, Adams J remarks that '[t]he reasons which led the offender to her actions on the fatal day were powerful ones' (2000, [33]). The efficacy of this narrative of the offender 'snapping' seems to rely on the extent to which judges identify its truth, or connect the various behavioural scripts it comprise with an assumed common understanding of society (Nussbaum 2004, 19). As such, representations of disability as an unreasonable and unduly onerous burden are traded off against spontaneous acts of violence (Kumari Campbell 2005, 147).

The invocation of 'snap' narratives reveals a perturbing current that runs throughout the sentencing remarks: violence is treated as an almost inevitable reaction to being in a relationship with a PWD that involves care. For instance, commenting on giving birth to a child with cerebral palsy, Adams J states that 'any parent would readily understand the enormous anguish, anxiety and emotional turmoil which the offender would have felt in this situation', and 'even a psychologically healthy person, aware of help from government and private agencies, would have found it daunting, to say the least' (*R v Wang* 2000, [17] and [33]). Furthermore, the first instance sentencing judge in *R v Dawes* is quoted by Barr J as remarking that 'it is little wonder this offender was no longer able to cope … she had had enough and could take no more' (2004, [63]). Effectively, the violent acts of these offenders are depicted as being explicable and reasonable responses to caring for PWD. However, considering that in New South Wales alone one in five people have a disability and 82% of those requiring assistance receive it from family and friends (JCNSW 2006, [5.1]), this response is neither ordinary, nor one the courts should be sympathetic to. Additionally, research has indicated that contrary to the wear-and-tear hypothesis that dominates the public imagination of what it must be like to care for PWD, parents of children with disabilities often feel increasingly competent in their parenting and become psychologically stronger as they adapt to the role (Gilmore and Cuskelly 2012, 28). Social stressors are not accepted by judges or society generally as factors that lessen the culpability of those who commit acts of domestic violence against non-disabled people, and yet, narratives of ordinary offenders pushed to breaking point by PWD persist throughout the sentencing remarks.

Suffered enough

Narratives in which the offender, suffering under the enormous pressure of caring for a PWD, kills in a moment of hopeless desperation generally culminate in lenient sentences. Essentially, these offenders are portrayed as having 'suffered enough' and therefore, as it is put by Barr J in *R v Sutton*, 'the need for further punishment is spent' (2007, [38]). The offender's history of caring for the victim, often without support or recognition, is framed as a deprivation of their liberty that pre-empted the offence. Further, an unusual reasoning emerges where living with the knowledge of having committed the offence and the subsequent loss of a loved one is treated as sufficient penance. The results are significant, with 'exceptional' circumstances being cited to warrant the handing down of suspended sentences in response to what a less ableist society might perceive to be murdered (see, e.g. *R v Sutton* 2007; *R v Dawes* 2004; *R v Puhle* 2013). This appears to demonstrate Sherry's point that:

> there is less of a rush to judgment in cases where crimes against disabled people are committed by family members who claim to have reached their breaking point … This ambivalence reflects the unique dynamics which family members of disabled people experience. They have a duty to care after their disabled family member, particularly if the person relies on others for assistance with activities of daily living, but they often feel overwhelmed and under supported (2010, 104).

This acknowledgement of the lack of support for families, friends and partners engaged in caring for PWD is implicit within the sentencing remarks. For instance, in *R v Dawes*, the offender's life as an unsupported, primary carer for her son is described by Barr J as 'almost unbelievably cruel' (2004, [71]), and in addressing the offender in *R v Puhle* (2013), Sulan J remarks: '[y]ou have suffered enormously over the years. You have confronted adversity in a way that many others could not.' Barr J's statement in *R v Sutton* is particularly telling: '[n]obody in the community suffering under the burden that weighed on the offenders is likely to give consideration to sentences imposed on others' (2007, [33]). The judges make thinly veiled criticisms of the services provided by government agencies, and demonstrate their reticence to punish offenders who were both primary carer and parent. The offender's criminal responsibility is stripped back and their culpability is minimal; there is no need for deterrence and the unlawful nature of the killing is almost completely forgotten. This could be attributed to judges taking 'responsibility for responsibility' (Loughnan 2015, 116), that is, absorbing some of the blame of the state in failing to provide adequate support and respite to PWD and those caring for them.

It is tempting to celebrate this tacit recognition of the state's failings, particularly considering the gendered dimensions of care work (Hanlon 2009, 180). It is no coincidence that the majority of the offenders engaged in unpaid care work with minimal support are women while 'dominant definitions of masculinity exclude many aspects of caregiving from men's lives' (Hanlon 2009, 198). However, the fact that the lack of services available to support PWD and their families is often felt most acutely by women should not be used to temper the culpability of those convicted of domestic homicide offences against PWD. Shifting criminal responsibility from the offender and onto the state eclipses the central issue of how the needs of PWD are perceived. Further, it does nothing to meaningfully change the negative ways in which disability is conceived of and talked about throughout the criminal legal process, and this is the change that is needed to produce a society that is inclusive of PWD.

By constructing relationships with PWD as burdensome, and in some cases, so burdensome that they result in the psychological instability and lethal outbursts of ordinary people, the sentencing remarks suggest that disability incites violence. These 'snap' narratives are widespread and toxic in their effects. Essentially, the lives of PWD who rely on their families, friends and partners for assistance fall rung-by-rung down a hierarchy of personhood, within which not only is their existence viewed as being an imposition to those around them, but acts which bring about their deaths do not warrant punishment.

Conclusion: reconceptualizing justice

Ultimately, this research calls for a (re)conceptualization of justice for PWD that goes beyond access and considers how disability itself is constructed within the criminal justice system. Even in the few instances where domestic and family violence against PWD results in a conviction, the discursive constructions of disability that emerge at sentencing present substantial obstructions to justice and equality under the law. As Young highlights, the vast and deep injustices that characterize social oppression are suffered as a result of unconscious assumptions and reactions of well-meaning people in the processes of everyday life (1990, 41). Therefore, responses to these injustices must go beyond getting rid of rulers and making new laws; they must address the way ableist norms and assumptions are reproduced in economic, political and cultural institutions: they must address discourses of disability (Young 1990, 41). Consequently, short of a cultural audit of how judges – and society at large – conceive of disability, the justice outcomes for PWD will continue to be compromised. By way of conclusion, I will briefly discuss what might be required for this positive change.

Reflecting upon Kumari Campbell's statement that the 'subtext of disability as negative ontology has remained substantially unchallenged' (2005, 108, 109), one must ask, what might it look like to resist or subvert this subtext? Crucially, the footing of the medical model of disability must be dislodged from the legal system. As Goodley highlights, the term 'disability' is a signifier, calling out for meanings to be attached (2014, xi). Although 'disability–pathology' has become the dominant association within legal discourses, 'disability–celebration', 'disability–subversion', 'disability–desire' and 'disability–politics' are other, equally viable options (Goodley 2014, xi). PWD should be afforded agency; their quality of life not assumed to be diminished and notions of vulnerability abandoned. Interestingly, in some ways, Grove J's sentencing remarks in *R v Soon* presage what the justice outcomes for PWD might look like if this discursive shift were to occur. Stephen Chin – the victim – escapes the constructions of disability that pervade the other sentencing remarks examined in this study. He is the only wheelchair user who is not 'confined' or 'bound' to his mobility aid, nor are his daily routines and level of independence unduly emphasized to foreground the offence. A quote from his ex-wife's – the offender's – police interview is included in the sentencing remarks, indicating her belief that Stephen experienced a higher quality of life than her: 'he's better off than me' (*R v Soon*, 20). Lastly, his death is framed as a monstrous act of violence, tempered only by the offender's guilty plea and defence of substantial impairment (*R v Soon*, [41] and [54]). At this point it should be asked: what made the circumstances of this case so exceptional? The answer hinges on the way Stephen disrupts the scripts of PWD as being burdensome, having a low quality of life and lacking agency. Within the opening paragraphs of the sentencing remarks it is revealed that he broke his neck while engaging in sexual acts with a sex-worker that involved 'unusual physicality' (*R v Soon*, [4]). Pity and vulnerability cannot easily be projected onto those demonstrating agency through enacting desire. Further, Stephen's active and transgressive sexuality prevents constructions of disability premised on notions of PWD being defenceless, vulnerable and passive recipients of care from settling within the sentencing remarks. While the facts are atypical of the cases studied, this case revealed the alternate ways in which disability can be constructed in the law: as human variation as something incidental to humanity – not as something that eclipses one's status as equal under the law. Ultimately, the acknowledgement of agency – something that can be achieved linguistically – can produce a significant impact on the construction and conception of PWD: hierarchies of personhood are destabilized, resistance to dominant and denigrating constructions of disability becomes possible, and the value of the lives of PWD can be recognized.

Notes

1. The terms 'disabled' and 'disability' will be used in this article to connote the socio-medical categorisation of people who are identified as having impairments.
2. The low number sentencing remarks appeared to be the result of the lack of reporting and publication of District Court proceedings and sentencing remarks generally as well as exercises of prosecutorial discretion not to pursue certain matters.

3. See Appendix 1 for complete list of judicial texts.
4. The word 'victim' is widely recognised in feminist literature as being problematic when referring to victims of crime, as it has connotations of passivity and an inability to transcend the act. However, as the preferred term, 'survivor', is inappropriate in the context of this article, where unavoidable, the term 'victim' will be used to indicate the PWD's experience of victimization.

Acknowledgements

The author thank the Associate Professor Arlie Loughnan for her support and guidance in the development of this research. In addition many thanks go to Linda Steele, Jessica Robyn Cadwallader and Gerard Goggin and the reviewers of this paper for their helpful comments.

Disclosure statement

No potential conflict of interest was reported by the author.

References

AHRC (Australian Human Rights Commission). 2014. *Equal Before the Law: Towards Disability Justice Strategies*. Sydney: AHRC.
ALRC (Australian Law Reform Commission). 2014. *Equality, Capacity and Disability in Commonwealth Laws*. Report No 124. Sydney: ALRC.
Baldry, Eileen, Joan Bratel, and Jan Breckenridge. 2006. "Domestic Violence and Children with Disabilities: Working Towards Enhancing Social Work Practice." *Australian Social Work* 59 (2): 185–197. doi:10.1080/03124070600651895.
Conley, John, and William O'Barr. 2005. *Just Words: Law, Language and Power*. 2nd ed. Chicago, IL: University of Chicago Press.
Crimes (Domestic and Personal Violence) Act 2007 (NSW).
Crimes (Sentencing Procedure) Act 1999 (NSW).
Fairclough, Norman. 2013. "Critical Discourse Analysis and Critical Policy Studies." *Critical Policy Studies* 7 (2): 177–197. doi:10.1080/19460171.2013.798239.
Frohmader, Carolyn, Leanne Dowse, and Aminath Didi. 2015. *Preventing Violence Against Women and Girls with Disabilities: Integrating a Human Rights Perspective*. Think piece document for the development of the National Framework to Prevent Violence Against Women. Sydney: Women With Disabilities Australia and University of NSW.
Gilmore, Linda, and Monica Cuskelly. 2012. "Parenting Satisfaction and Self-efficacy: A Longitudinal Study of Mothers of Children with Down Syndrome." *Journal of Family Studies* 18 (1): 28–35. doi:10.5172/jfs.2012.1996.
Goodley, Dan. 2014. *Dis/Ability Studies: Theorising Disablism and Ableism*. Abingdon: Routledge.
Hall, Stuart. 2007. "Encoding, Decoding." In *The Cultural Studies Reader*, edited by Simon During, 90–103. 3rd ed. London: Routledge.
Hanlon, Niall. 2009. "Caregiving Masculinities: An Exploratory Analysis." In *Affective Equality: Love, Care and Injustice*, edited by Kathleen Lynch, John Baker, and Maureen Lyons, 180–198. Basingstoke: Palgrave MacMillan.
Heffer, Chris. 2005. *The Language of Jury Trial: A Corpus-Aided Analysis of Legal-Lay Discourse*. Basingstoke: Routledge.
Innes, Graeme. 2007. "Diverse and Inclusive Practice: Redrawing the Boundaries." Speech delivered at the Domestic Violence, Disability and Cultural Safety National Forum, Sydney, November 8–9.
JCNSW (Judicial Commission of New South Wales). 2006. *Equality Before the Law Bench Book*. Sydney: JCNSW.
Kumari Campbell, Fiona. 2005. "Legislating Disability: Negative Ontologies and the Government of Legal Identities." In *Foucault and the Government of Disability*, edited by Shelley Tremain, 108–130. Ann Arbor: University of Michigan Press.
Kumari Campbell, Fiona. 2009. *Contours of Ableism*. Basingstoke: Palgrave Macmillan.
Loughnan, Arlie. 2015. "'Society Owes Them Much': 'Veteran Defendants' and Criminal Responsibility in Australia in the Twentieth Century." *Critical Analysis of Law* 2 (1): 106–134. http://cal.library.utoronto.ca/index.php/cal/article/view/22517.
Lynch, Kathleen, John Baker, and Maureen Lyons. 2009. "Introduction." In *Affective Equality: Love, Care and Injustice*, edited by Kathleen Lynch, John Baker and Maureen Lyons, 1–11. Basingstoke: Palgrave MacMillan.

Lynch, Kathleen, and Maureen Lyons. 2009. "Love Labouring: Nurturing Rationalities and Relational Identities." In *Affective Equality: Love, Care and Injustice*, edited by Kathleen Lynch, John Baker and Maureen Lyons, 54–77. Basingstoke: Palgrave MacMillan.

Nussbaum, Martha. 2004. *Hiding From Humanity: Disgust, Shame, and the Law*. Princeton: Princeton University Press.

Salthouse, Sue, and Carolyn Frohmader. 2004. "Double The Odds: Domestic Violence and Women with Disabilities." Paper presented at the Home Truths Conference, Melbourne, September 15–17.

Schulz, Pamela. 2008. "Rougher Than Usual Media Treatment: A Discourse Analysis of Media Reporting and Justice on Trial." *Journal of Judicial Administration* 17: 223–236. http://www.pria.com.au/documents/item/1400.

Schulz, Pamela. 2014. "Who is the Judge? A Critical Analysis of the Discourse of Disbelief." *Journal of Judicial Administration* 24: 118–128.

Senate Community Affairs References Committee. 2015. *Violence, Abuse and Neglect Against People With Disability in Institutional and Residential Settings, Including the Gender and Age Related Dimensions, and the Particular Situation of Aboriginal and Torres Strait Islander People with Disability, and Culturally and Linguistically Diverse People With Disability*. Canberra: Senate Printing Unit, Parliament House.

Sherry, Mark. 2010. *Disability Hate Crimes: Does Anyone Really Hate Disabled People?*. Burlington, VT: Ashgate.

Stevens, Nicole, and Sarah Wendt. 2014. "The 'Good' Child Sex Offender: Constructions of Defendants in Child Sexual Abuse Sentencing." *Journal of Judicial Administration* 24 (2): 95–107.

Sullivan, Martin. 2005. "Subjected Bodies: Paraplegia, Rehabilitation, and the Politics of Movement." In *Foucault and the Government of Disability*, edited by Shelley Tremain, 27–44. Ann Arbor: University of Michigan Press.

Thomas, Carol. 2007. *Sociologies of Disability and Illness: Contested Ideas in Disability Studies and Medical Sociology*. Basingstoke: Palgrave Macmillan.

Van Dijk, Teun. 2003. "The Discourse-Knowledge Interface." In *Critical Discourse Analysis: Theory and Interdisciplinarity*, edited by Gilbert Weiss and Ruth Wodak, 85–109. Basingstoke: Palgrave Macmillan.

Young, Iris Marion. 1990. *Justice and the Politics of Difference*. Princeton: Princeton University Press.

Young, Stella. 2013. "Disability Is No Justification For Murder." *The Drum* September 3. http://www.abc.net.au/news/2013-09-03/young-kyla-puhle-death/4930742.

Appendix 1. Index of Judicial Texts

Case name	Relationship to victim	Offence	Outcome (with reference to victim's disability)
R v Wang [2000] NSWSC 447 (Unreported, Adams J, 23 May 2000)	Mother	Manslaughter	Sentence imposed of 6 years imprisonment. Partial defence of substantial impairment established. Victim's disability linked to the deterioration of the offender's mental health
R v Daniella Dawes [2004] NSWCCA 363 (Unreported, Dunford, Barr and Hoeben JJ, 5 November 2004)	Mother	Manslaughter	Defence of substantial impairment established. Appeal against non-custodial sentence dismissed. Victim's disability a mitigating factor and linked to the deterioration of the offender's mental health
R v Sharpe [2005] VSC 276 (Unreported, Bongiorno J, 5 August 2005)	Father	Murder	Sentence imposed of imprisonment for life. Victim's disability linked to the offender's motive
R v Raymond Douglas Sutton; R v Margaret Ellen Sutton [2007] NSWSC 295 (Unreported, Barr J, 4 April 2007)	Parents	Manslaughter	Non-custodial sentence imposed. Victim's disability linked to the deterioration of the offenders' mental health. Partial defence of substantial impairment established
R v Andrew [2008] VSC 138 (Unreported, Forrest J, 1 May 2008)	Intimate partner	Manslaughter	Sentence imposed of 10 years imprisonment. Victim's disability was an aggravating factor
R v Soon [2008] NSWSC 622 (Unreported, Grove J, 20 June 2008)	Ex-wife	Manslaughter	Sentence imposed of 9 years imprisonment. Partial defence of substantial impairment established. Victim's disability an aggravating factor
R v HA [2008] NSWSC 1368 (Unreported, Rothman J, 18 December 2008)	Mother	Manslaughter	Suspended sentence imposed of 2 years imprisonment. Victim's disability both an aggravating and mitigating factor
R v BW & SW (No 3) [2009] NSWSC 1043 (Unreported, Hulme J, 2 October 2009)	Parents	Manslaughter (BW); Murder (SW)	Sentence imposed of 16 years imprisonment (BW) and imprisonment for life (SW). Victim's disability was an aggravating factor
R v McLaren [2011] NSWDC 115 (Unreported, Berman J, 15 June 2011)	Paid carer	Attempted murder	Sentence imposed of 8 years imprisonment. Victim's disability was an aggravating factor, but also linked to the deterioration of the offender's mental health
R v Eitzen [2011] SASC 98 (Unreported, Sulan J, 16 June 2011)	Mother	Murder	Deemed mentally incompetent for trial. Victim's disability linked to the deterioration of the offender's mental health
Harding v The Queen [2013] NSWSC 513 (Unreported, Garling J, 16 May 2013)	Intimate partner	Murder	Sentence imposed of 27 years imprisonment. Victim's disability was an aggravating factor
R v Puhle (Transcript of Proceedings, Supreme Court of South Australia, Sulan J, 22 August 2013)	Mother	Manslaughter	Suspended sentence imposed of 5 years imprisonment. Victim's disability linked to the deterioration of the offenders' mental health. Partial defence of substantial impairment established

Policing normalcy: sexual violence against women offenders with disability

Linda Steele

ABSTRACT

This article explores police responses to sexual violence reported by women offenders designated as having cognitive and psychosocial disabilities. The article does so by reference to the critical disability studies analytical approach to disability as socially constructed 'abnormality'. This article utilizes this approach in analysing the recorded police contacts of one woman offender designated as disabled, 'Jane'. Jane has had multiple contacts with police over a period of 15 years as a victim of sexual violence, alleged offender and 'mentally ill' person. The article finds that through multiple contacts with police as victim, alleged offender and 'mentally ill' person, the police events records build a narrative of Jane as an 'abnormal' body who is reduced to a drain on police and public health resources, a dishonest and nuisance offender and an attention seeker. The article argues that it is the interlocking discourses of gender, disability *and* criminality that produce Jane as unworthy of victim status and, perversely, in need of punishment by the criminal justice system for her public displays of trauma, mental distress and requests for police assistance. Ultimately, the article concludes that we need to give greater attention to the relationship between disability and affect, and to the broader cultural, institutional, legal and economic discourses that shape individuals' affective responses, in understanding police responses to violence against women offenders designated as disabled and in contesting these women's status as 'ungrievable' victims of violence.

Women designated as having cognitive and psychosocial disabilities ('women designated as disabled') experience disproportionate rates of violence (particularly sexual violence) when compared to women and men not designated as disabled, and women and men designated with other disabilities (Frohmader and Sands 2015, 38; see also Dowse et al. 2016) Women designated as disabled also have poor justice outcomes when seeking legal redress in relation to their experiences of violence, with high attrition of complaints at various points throughout the criminal justice process. The failure of police to exercise their discretion to investigate complaints and press charges is a particularly significant issue, with stereotypes about gender and disability being commonly identified as key causes (Frohmader and Sands 2015, 19, 55–57). Thus, women designated as disabled experience significant difficulties in relation to acts of violence themselves *and* the affective and legal responses to these acts of violence.

In her groundbreaking scholarship on intersectionality, Kimberle Crenshaw emphasized that violence against women is not only shaped by gender but other dimensions of identity (Crenshaw 1991, 1242, see further 1269–1271; for a recent discussion of intersectionality which explicitly includes ability see Collins and Bilge 2016). Building on this, scholars and advocates argue that the incidence of violence and the justice outcomes for women designated as disabled must be understood at the intersection of gender and disability. For example, Stephanie Ortoleva and Hope Lewis state 'when gender and disability intersect, violence takes on unique forms, has unique causes, and results in unique consequences' (2012, 14; see also Frohmader and Sands 2015, 17, 18). Scholars and advocates argue that the complaints of women with cognitive and psychosocial disabilities about sexual violence are routinely dismissed by police by reason of their perceptions of the women at the intersection of gender and disability. Such perceptions relate to these women being oversexualized (invite sexual violence) or undersexed (incapable of engaging in sexual activity), irrational (cannot be trusted or believed) and incapable (cannot comprehend sex or violence) (for scholarly work see, e.g. Dowse, Frohmader, and Meekosha 2010, 249, 265, 266; Ellison 2015; Ellison et al. 2015a, 2015b; Keilty and Connelly 2001; Murray and Heenan 2012; Murray and Powell 2008; Razack 1995; for advocacy work see, e.g. Dowse et al. 2013; Frohmader and Sands 2015; Ortoleva and Lewis 2012; Pettitt et al. 2013).

Scholars and advocates have paid less attention to differentials *between* groups of women designated as disabled along other axes of marginalization (see, however, Baldry, Dowse, and Clarence 2012; Baldry et al. 2015, 39, 130–135; Frohmader and Sands 2015; Ortoleva and Lewis 2012). Attention to these differentials is important because, as Sherene Razack argues in the context of analysing cases of sexual assault of women with developmental disabilities, there needs to be 'a clear articulation of how power relations produce the responses of nondisabled individuals to persons with disabilities and how the subtexts of race, gender, disability, sexuality and class interlock' (Razack 1995, 919; see also Baldry and Cunneen 2014). Also, as per Razack, it is important to consider how these subtexts play out, not only in the acts of violence themselves but also in the affective and legal responses to these acts of violence, particularly by police who have a central role in the criminal justice process and the ultimate recognition of violence as unlawful and impermissible.

This paper considers the criminal justice outcomes for one group of women designated as disabled who are considerably marginalized in society and in the criminal justice system (Baldry, Dowse, and Clarence 2012; Dowse et al. 2015): those *who have had contact with the criminal justice system as offenders* ('women offenders designated as disabled'). Paying close attention to the dynamics that shape justice outcomes for these women is important because women in this group are often victims of sexual violence. Carolyn Frohmader and Therese Sands have noted that '[m]ore than half of all women incarcerated in Australian prisons have a diagnosed psychosocial disability and a history of sexual victimisation' (2015, 38). Furthermore, research suggests that there is a higher incidence of violence perpetrated against women offenders designated as disabled as compared to male offenders with disability (Baldry, Dowse, and Clarence 2012; Dowse et al. 2015; Lindsay et al. 2004, 581, 585, 586, 587). Rates of violence are particularly significant for *Aboriginal* women offenders designated as disabled (Baldry, Dowse, and Clarence 2012). It is likely that the criminal justice outcomes of women offenders designated as disabled as *victims* of sexual violence will be affected by their contact with the criminal justice system as *offenders*. This is because the criminal justice system, the space through which individuals are criminalized, is also the space that women offenders designated as disabled must be recognized as victims in order to have their complaints of sexual violence processed and ultimately recognized as unlawful and impermissible acts of violence – possibly involving the very police stations, police officers, courts and judges who have been involved with them in their capacity as offenders (see similar issue in relation to women offenders generally in Hannah-Moffat 2004, 372–376; Segrave and Carlton 2010, 292).

Mindful of Razack's point of considering how different 'subtexts' interlock, this article examines the significance of women offenders designated disabled's past contact with the criminal justice system as offenders (what I term the 'subtext' of criminality) and how this interlocks with disability and gender. To do so, I utilize the critical disability studies analytical approach to disability as 'abnormality'. This approach directs attention to the cultural relationships between disability, gender, criminality and violence and the material and legal impacts of these cultural relationships on the bodies of women with disability, including their impact on the enactment of violence on bodies of women offenders designated as disabled *and* the affective response by others to this violence which renders these acts of violence permissible and lawful.

This analytical approach is applied to an examination of the initial police contact of women offenders designated as disabled have when reporting sexual violence. For any victim this initial point of contact is significant because police determine whether a complaint will be investigated. Police also have a key role in initiating the legal process towards the state condoning (or not) this violence. For women offenders designated as disabled, the initial point of police contact is of *additional* significance for two interrelated reasons. One is that the police force (and possibly specific individual police) may also have contact with these women as offenders, as mentioned earlier. The second is that there is a state-based centralized recording system of police contacts across offending and victim contacts (as compared to the more siloed and dispersed nature of court records) and police have the capacity to check and make reference to a woman's record of past contacts with law enforcement, when having contact with her as a victim (as compared to court where there are strict rules of evidence and rules against judicial bias which restrict judges from explicitly drawing on a woman's past court files in making a judicial decision). Suellen Murray and Melanie Heenan's empirical study of police reports of rape by victims with psychiatric disability in Victoria identified past contact with police as a relevant factor in police response to complaints. However, this study did not engage in an in-depth analysis of the significance of past contact with police as an offender, nor did the authors consider women offenders with disability as a specific cohort (Murray and Heenan 2012, 357, 361, 362; see similarly Ellison et al. 2015b, 238). In examining the point of initial police contact for women offenders designated as disabled when reporting sexual violence, my focus is less on quantifying different police outcomes. Rather my analysis illuminates *how* discourses of disability, gender and criminality circulate in the ways police represent the women and their complaints of violence – both through words used and associated affect – and the material impacts of these representations on how these women's complaints of violence are responded to by police.

Methodological approach

I approach this examination methodologically by reference to the recorded police contacts of one woman offender designated as disabled by criminal justice and public health agencies: 'Jane'. Jane has multiple contacts with police over a period of 15 years as a victim of sexual violence, alleged offender and 'mentally ill' person. Jane's case study is drawn from a project consisting of ten case studies of women offenders with disability.[1] These ten case studies were derived from the 'People with Mental Health Disorders and Cognitive Disabilities (MHDCD) in the Criminal Justice System (CJS) in NSW' data-set ('MHDCD dataset') which is a cohort of 2731 men and women who have been in prison in New South Wales, Australia, most of whom have been designated by criminal justice and public health agencies as having a cognitive impairment and/or mental illness diagnosis.[2] The MHDCD data-set contains linked data on the life-long human services and criminal justice involvement of each individual,[3] and was constructed by merging extant administrative records from criminal justice and human service agencies. All ten individuals were allocated pseudonyms. De-identified data was obtained on each individual's demographics, criminal justice contacts, social and health factors, and disability service usage.

Two kinds of data are of primary importance here: what are referred to as 'events narrative', and 'incident data' respectively. The events narrative is the running written record of specific instances of contact an individual has had with police over their life – as an alleged offender ('person of interest' or 'POI'), victim and as a 'mentally ill person' under civil mental health legislation. Supplementing the events narrative is the incident data which lists in tabulated form basic information on the date, reason and associated factors of each contact. Importantly, not all contacts listed in the incident data are detailed in the events narrative. Together, these two forms of data were used to quantify and construct a chronology of each individual's police contacts. The events narrative for each individual were analysed: identifying initial reason for contact (POI, victim, mental health), police perception of each individual by end of contact (POI, victim, mental health), location upon departure of police (e.g. custody, hospital, house) and references to and relationships between disability, gender, and criminality in how police described each contact with the individual (the 'facts' of the incident, the 'facts' of their interaction with the individual and their affective response to all of these facts).

This methodological approach differs from existing empirical studies on women with disability reporting violence to police, which have focused on sampling individual instances of victim contacts with police in a specific time period, rather than building pathways of specific women across time and all of their police contacts. For example, Murray and Heenan's study referred to above drew on a random sample of 850 records of rape offences reported in a 3 year time period. While points did emerge about references by police to past contact as an offender or past 'vexatious' complaints, the authors did not examine the relationships between specific contacts which might make further sense of these references (Murray and Heenan 2012, 358, 359; see similarly Ellison et al. 2015a, 2015b, 234–236). While the methodological approach utilized in existing empirical studies usefully identifies the breadth of police victim contacts and emerging trends, it disembodies and de-temporalises the contacts and limits the significance of the findings in relation to what is happening to specific, material bodies.

Jane's case study has been selected as the focus of discussion in this article because the high number of contacts that Jane has with police enables a particularly powerful and nuanced illumination of the relationships between contact with police as a POI, victim and 'mentally ill person'. Through analysis of Jane's police contacts I argue that both within specific instances of police contact as a victim of sexual violence, and across her police contacts as victim, alleged offender and 'mentally ill' person, Jane is constructed by police as an 'abnormal' body who is a drain on resources, a dishonest and nuisance offender and an attention seeker. Ultimately, it is the interlocking of discourses of gender, disability *and* criminality that produce Jane as unworthy of victim status and, perversely, in need of punishment by the criminal justice system.

Analysing violence across discourses of disability, gender and criminality: abnormality

Analysing the significance of women offenders designated as disabled's past contact with police as offenders ('criminality') to the criminal justice outcomes of these women as victims of sexual violence is not merely an exercise in searching out references by police to past criminal acts or to the women as offenders, that is, as an identity or phenomenon, *separate* to their disability. Rather, analytically, it requires an appreciation of the complex place of criminality in the cultural representation of disability *and* the material enacting of and affective responses to violence on women designated as disabled: the 'interlocking' nature of these discourses. This is provided by the critical disability studies approach to disability as 'abnormality'.

Critical disability studies scholars have contested the concept of disability as a biomedical condition that resides within an individual. They argue that it is against social *ideals*, rather than biological *norms*, of human functioning and ability that disability becomes a socially constructed 'abnormality' (see, e.g. Davis 1995; Shildrick 2009; Tremain 2002). Feminist disability scholarship has built upon this in highlighting how disabled women are constructed as abnormal at the intersections of norms of gender, ability and sexuality (Garland-Thomson 2011; Hall 2011; Shildrick 2009). Interrogation of representations of disability as abnormality involves making apparent the contingency of these representations to broader historical and geopolitical dimensions of power and inequality related to such dynamics as colonialism, neoliberalism and globalization. Disability is not analytically approached as a discrete, additional category of difference but instead is always coming into existence co-relationally with other dimensions of difference such as gender, race and sexuality in ways that reproduce the 'normate' subject (and in turn the nation) as white and male (Connell 2011; Erevelles 2011a; Hollinsworth 2013; Razack 2002; Soldatic 2015).

Critical disability studies scholars have explored on an *abstract, discursive* level the relationship between disability and criminality as *deviancy* in the cultural representation of disability. This is on the basis that disability as abnormality is a deviancy in constituting a failure to meet social norms (see also the critical disability-critical criminology theoretical development by Baldry and Dowse 2013; Dowse, Baldry, and Snoyman 2009). Critical disability studies scholars, notably Sharon Snyder and David Mitchell, have argued that the cultural representation of disability as abnormality impacts on the social (and legal) status of people with disability (2006). Nirmala Erevelles argues that analysis of disability must consider how representations of disability as abnormality results in material violence on the actual bodies of individuals designated as disabled and how individuals marginalized on other bases such as race, gender or class disproportionately become subjected to disablement through acts of violence (Erevelles 2011a, 104–120, 142, 143; Erevelles 2011b, 119, 129–132; Erevelles 2014, 96).

Critical disability studies scholars have explored how the representation of disability as abnormality impacts on how the *bodies* of disabled individuals are viewed and acted upon. Critical disability studies scholars have typically focused on how disability is a biopolitical category that enlivens possibilities for regulation and violence on bodies designated as disabled. While such critique has typically focused on biopolitical possibilities for normalization to purportedly enhance life and bodily capacities (albeit directed towards predetermined ends) (Tremain 2005), recent scholarship is beginning to engage more directly with the violence of biopolitics (Mbembe 2003, 27), including the colonial and racial dimensions of confinement of and other non-consensual interventions in bodies designated as disabled which position individuals for greater calculated exposure to violence and death (see, e.g., Berghs 2015; Razack 2015; Wadiwel, forthcoming). Analysis also extends to considering the carnal dimensions of law's and other institutions' representational and material approaches to disability including how lawful techniques for regulating disability work *through* the body (notably through 'therapeutic' interventions such as sterilization, detention, non-consensual mental health treatment) and how discourses of care, humanitarianism and benevolence which mobilize certain affective responses to the disabled body (Sullivan, forthcoming) mask the regulative, punitive, violent, indeed even lethal, effects of these interventions on disabled bodies. Moreover, these bodies are viewed as defective, dangerous, wasteful and a parasitical drain on public resources and a threat to the health and economic prosperity of the population as a whole. Where the sexuality and reproductive capacities of women designated as disabled present a threat of *future* abnormality, violence done to the bodies of women designated as disabled to curb their sexuality is a particular focus of anxiety and intervention (Titchkosky 2007, 108, 123; see also Chapman 2014, 35, 36, 39, 40; Garland-Thomson 2011, 21, 26; Hall 2011, 6). Circulating in all of this is an important *affective* dimension to violence against people designated as disabled: how society *responds* to acts of violence. Shaista Patel (drawing on Judith Butler's discussion of grievable lives) argues, in the context of her analysis of the figure of the 'mad Muslim terrorist', that people designated as disabled are viewed as 'the excess of society, those nonhuman subjects whose lives are not worth grieving over in their pain and even in their deaths' (Patel 2014, 207).

Analysing disability as abnormality provides an opportunity to explore (to borrow from Razack) the complex ways in which discourses of disability 'interlock' with criminality in relation to police responses to women offenders designated as disabled who report sexual violence. This can go beyond a superficial analysis of criminality as equated with past instances of criminal acts, to criminality as at the core of the ontology and epistemology of disability itself, as well as central to the enactment and *affective responses to* violence against people designated as disabled. This analytical approach foregrounds examination of the relationships between cultural representations of disability in general *and* police's emotional or affective response to being confronted with the victim reports of made by specific women designated as disabled.

Jane

Jane is a non-Indigenous woman born in the 1980s who has been labelled by criminal justice and public health agencies with diagnoses including intellectual disability and a range of psychosocial disorders including depression, conduct disorder, schizophrenia and bipolar affective disorder. She experienced multiple episodes of out of home care from the age of 4. Jane has had contact with the criminal justice system since she was a child, having around 280 recorded police contact events (as POI, victim and 'mentally ill person') over a 15 year period.

Jane has a considerable level of contact with police as a victim. She has around 110 police contact events with police as a victim listed in the incident data, commencing at the age of 13 years old. The overwhelming majority of these contacts are not elaborated upon in the events narrative. There are 20 sexual violence-related victim contacts detailed in the events narrative, all for non-consensual sexual intercourse. These sexual violence victim contacts receive a variety of responses. At times police investigate (e.g. seek CCTV footage, request Jane undertake the sexual assault kit); at other times Jane chooses not to proceed with the matter beyond an initial report; at other times the police explicitly decide not to proceed. Significantly, there is no indication from the events narrative that any of Jane's reports of sexual violence ever result in a person being charged or indeed any investigations that even come close to that point, including the identification of a perpetrator. Many entries in the incident data are not discussed in the events narrative, suggesting that those *not* included were not pursued any further than the initial contact with police.

Regardless, as will emerge from the discussion below in turn of the three types of contact that Jane has with police (victim, mental health and POI), it is not merely what outcome is achieved in relation to the report of sexual violence, but that Jane's contact with police as a victim develop as a basis for her further criminalization and as such the way in which police represent Jane is significant.

'No injuries, no witnesses ...'

Throughout the events narrative of Jane's victim contacts, there are references to the ways in which Jane fails to meet many of the stock characteristics of what feminist scholars describe as the gendered 'ideal victim' of 'real rape' (see discussion and references in Brown et al. 2015, 658–666, 677–680, 693–706). For example, there are no signs of struggle or injury, she does not appear emotionally affected, there are inconsistencies in her versions of event and her reports are uncorroborated. This is demonstrated by the following comments by police:

No injuries, no witnesses …

Jane's version of events changed a number of times and was very vague. She did not appear to be visibly shaken or particularly upset either.

The Sexual Assault Protocol was collected. The protocol shows the victim has no visible injuries or bruising to the affected groin and leg areas. The lack of injuries supports the doubtfulness of this report. Further to this, the time it took, 2 days, for the victim to report this matter to anyone, supports that this report is doubtful. The victim's inconsistencies in her version make it difficult to understand what really happened. Due to the victim making so many unsubstantiated reports in the past it is difficult to give any credibility to her claims.

The events narrative also reflect the ways in which disability intersects with gender to render Jane outside the 'ideal victim of real rape', reflecting the scholarship on sexual violence against women with disability that emphasizes the significance of the intersection between gender and disability. At times, Jane's mental health is mentioned without further elaboration, as though this *per se* has certain consequences for her reports, as demonstrated by the following quote: 'report is considered doubtful due to the severe mental problems of the victim.'

At other times, police make a link between pathologized behaviour related to her disability and Jane's reports of sexual violence:

self harm attempts and other attention seeking matters including sexual assault complaints.

… the victims [*sic*] history of making false allegations over a lengthy period of time. The victim also has a history of being treated for mental health problems.

The victim has an extensive history of mental illness issues, attempted suicides and has made in excess of 10 allegations of sexual assault since [7 years ago].

These references to Jane in terms of her gender and at intersections of her gender and disability construct Jane as unbelievable and irrational, in turn invalidating her reports of sexual violence and delegitimizing her as a victim. Yet, there is a need for more careful, nuanced consideration of how these ideas of irrationality and unreliability come about in the specific, material context of Jane's contact with police. This involves turning to Jane's criminality.

'Numerous [police record] entries'

As well as being known to police as a victim, according to the incident data Jane also has 75 contacts with police as a person of interest. Jane is charged with 37 offences (generally related to public nuisance, drug possession, property theft or damage) but only ultimately convicted of 9 of these (drug possession, non-aggravated assault, two instances of offensive behaviour, theft, trespass, false representation resulting in police investigation and 2 instances of aggravated robbery). The charged property offences relate to minor theft such as taking a packet of cigarettes from a store and taking needles from a hospital. The aggravated robbery charges relate to threatening with a knife on demand of money a convenience store worker near the hospital where she had just been discharged after being held overnight for observation after having a drug overdose. The facts of the 37 charged offences relate predominantly to incidents of mental distress. One offence of making false representations resulting in police investigation related to Jane allegedly phoning 000 from a phone box at a railway station threatening self harm only to tell the ambulance officer upon arrival that she phoned 000 for a lift home. Police deal with Jane's POI contacts primarily through the mental health system (e.g. use of civil mental health powers to transport Jane to a local hospital for assessment and possible treatment), although Jane is not always admitted by the hospital and is then frequently taken home by police.

At times police refer in their narratives of victim contacts to Jane's previous contacts with police as an offender or her current offending behaviour:

> Jane has numerous [police record] entries.

> Once at the hospital the victim was given a more thorough search which located numerous items of hospital items … . She admitted stealing the property when in hospital earlier.

> Jane when conveying [report] to police appeared well effected [*sic*] by valium and details of the alleged assault were sketchy.

The particular nature of Jane's offending as relating to morally wrong acts of drug use and stealing further constructs her as an unbelievable (and unworthy) victim. Yet, as discussed earlier, the analytical significance of criminality to disability is not restricted to the superficial level of past acts of offending, it is also how criminality informs representations of disability in ways that both render permissible the violence against individuals with disability and delegitimize their status as 'grievable' victims. In order to consider these dynamics, it is important to briefly turn to the third type of contact Jane has with police: as a 'mentally ill' person.

'A history of staging such antics'

Jane has a high degree of contact with police under civil mental health legislation. Police have powers under civil mental health legislation to deal coercively with individuals if they appear to have a mental illness. In particular, under this legislation, police can take an individual to a hospital for assessment by a medical practitioner with the view to possibly 'scheduling' (that is, obtaining legal authority to coercively admit and detain) the individual to a mental health facility for involuntary containment and treatment. Criminology and legal scholars have identified the problems associated with police having these 'public health' powers insofar as they can result in criminalization of incidents of mental health distress and result in long term cycling of individuals in and out of the criminal justice system (Baldry and Dowse 2013). This is apparent in Jane's case yet with an additional, compounding effect not fully explored in the existing scholarship: the impact on her contact with police as a victim, as will now be discussed.

Jane has around 65 recorded contacts with police since the age of 19 years old which police categorize as being on the basis of mental health. Jane's contact with police in this respect generally involves Jane phoning emergency services from her house (that is, with a general threat to kill herself, reporting overdose, threatening to jump from the roof or cut herself, or alternatively some kind of hoax such as a bomb scare) or threats made at train stations (generally to throw herself in front of a train). Police explain the 'facts' both of these incidents and their related contact with Jane in ways that are far removed from anything resembling empathy or concern and instead reflect a deep scepticism and trivialization of her mental distress. In entries tinged with frustration and contempt, police refer to Jane as being motivated by attention seeking, the need for free transport and loneliness, and as generally providing false and misleading information, as demonstrated by the following quotes:

> The POI has a history of *staging such antics* [self-harm] and seems to *thrive* on the attention given to her by the emergency services. (emphasis added)

> Jane is continually tying up Emergency Services within the [area]. Jane has requested police assistance over 23 times in the past three months, mainly *claiming* she was about to commit suicide. (emphasis added)

Police categorize forty of Jane's victim incidents as 'trauma' (just over one third). It is uncertain on what basis they identify trauma and what meaning this holds for police. Yet it is apparent that they do not view them as genuine and therefore as not requiring support and a compassionate response. Their recurring nature – an attribute of trauma – ironically becomes one of the very reasons for criminalization of her distress as attention seeking, staged performance. Repeated contact in 'trauma' becomes a problem to be managed (and punished) rather than questioning *why* someone would constantly contact police. The affective response of frustration and suspicion – which at its worst results in arrest or simply indifference and inaction – raises questions about how police and how society at large can respond to trauma and to historical injustice in ways that are both supportive to the individual and address the structured framework within which that trauma and its causes are located. This is particularly necessary in relation to Indigenous women offenders with disability (Baldry et al. 2015, 130–135).

The affective response that police have towards Jane's mental distress and 'trauma' indicates that Jane simply is not worthy of being recognized as the subject of legitimate 'suffering' (Cadwallader 2012). The police's affective response also tracks onto a broader societal suspicion about people faking disability, linked to the idea of the undeserving person with disability as an intentional drain on public resources which has contemporary manifestation in scepticism about compensation sought for psychological harm (see, e.g. Campbell 2006) arguably exacerbated here by reason of her dishonesty offences. Through her public expressions of distress Jane is not only *not* a victim in need of empathy and concern, but is obversely a deviant to be criminalized.

The majority of Jane's contact with police is not initially nor directly related to alleged offending, but rather relates to mental health incidents, self-harm and attempted suicide, which at times escalates into or is read by police as a public nuisance and specifically as offences of property damage, assault and false calls to emergency services. On four occasions, Jane is charged with making false representations resulting in police investigation. Jane is referred to by police in the events narrative as a 'frequent attention seeker', a 'habitual hoax caller', a 'recidivist complainer to police threatening self harm'. This criminalization of her distress as a public nuisance constructs Jane as a parasitical drain on public resources. On one occasion when police are called to Jane's house following a call to emergency services threatening self-harm that turned out to be a 'hoax', police state that:

> She was told that she is to cease ringing Police with false claims. She was told that every time she rings and makes these false claims, she is taking Police away from people who really need our help and that one day she could be the cause of someone being seriously injured or killed.

Here the risk to her *own* life in suicide is subverted to make Jane a parasite threatening others' lives: drawing on Patel, an 'ungrievable' life threatening 'grievable' lives. While it is acknowledged that there are different levels of seriousness of emergencies and emergency services have limited resources and that there is a lack of capability of police to handle these situations, what is of concern is that there is no recognition of Jane's mental distress, to the point that she is criminalized.

'Police explained to Jane the consequences of lying to police'

The interplay of mental distress and criminalization impacts on police perception of Jane's reports of sexual violence. The manifestation of distress when Jane reports sexual violence is not considered genuine and is inserted into a narrative of Jane's attention seeking and wasting police resources and time, and places Jane at risk of being criminalized. For example, on one ocassion police state: 'due to the mental capacity of Jane and the fact that she had made so many other doubtful similar reports, Police explained to Jane the consequences of *lying* to Police.' (emphasis added)

What becomes apparent from an analysis of Jane's police contacts as a whole is that the overarching theme running through the police response to contact with Jane is dishonesty, and while this dishonesty manifests in both criminal conduct and mental distress, it is attributed to Jane as a pathological dimension of her disability and in turn her articulations of victimization. This is exemplified in a report by Jane of sexual assault in a public space while on day leave from a mental health facility. The police provide an unusually detailed list of reasons as to why they were not pursuing the report:

Police are treating the report of this incident as dubious for a number of reasons and they are as follows:

(1)   On each of the occasions where the victim spoke to a person in authority (hospital staff/ police) she made varying alterations to her story regarding the circumstances of the assault. …

(2)   … It would be difficult to believe how police would not have been notified of this incident from an independent source let alone the fact that the victim did not receive any assistance from persons in that area, taking into account the manner in which the victim alleges the incident occurred.

(3)   [In a period of 8.5 months] the victim is recorded on COPS ['computerized operational policing system'] for seven separate incidents of sexual assault where the narrative relates that the report of sexual assault is 'dubious'. The victim is also listed on [police system] for making other false reports and attention seeking activities. [11 months earlier] the victim was charged with public mischief regarding her constant threats of self harm.

(4)   [Registered nurse] stated that the victim is told that whilst out on day leave she is not to consume alcohol. [RN] stated that when the victim returned to the [mental health facility] she was moderately intoxicated. [RN] also believed that the victim had concocted this story in an effort to justify her consumption of alcohol after the incident.

Points 1 and 2 reference gendered expectations about the 'ideal victim' related to corroboration and visible injuries. Point 3 then makes a link between her report of sexual assault and her history of false reports, her attention seeking related to mental health and her criminal charges of public mischief. Point 4 illustrates the link between disability and institutional authority because Jane has broken the mental health facility's rules by engaging in the deviant activity of alcohol consumption *and then* lying to conceal it. Her challenging of the norms of power relations in mental health facilities seems to put her complaints in doubt or make her deserving of the violence (see similarly discussion of relationship between challenging behaviour, institutional authority and legitimacy of restricted practices in Dowse, forthcoming).

Disability as 'organising principle'

In their essay on the police murder shooting of 'Elanor Bumpus', an elderly, obese, black woman with mental illness, Nirmala Erevelles and Andrea Minear argue that disability was not merely a context or magnifier to the role in the incident of Ms. Bumpus's gender, race and class. They suggest it was the organizing principle that shaped the meaning attributed to these other dynamics and through which her murder by police was permissible (Erevelles and Minear 2011, 117). Likewise, my analysis of Jane's contact with police demonstrates how criminality circulates in multiple ways but it is disability (and its associations with dishonesty and waste) which is the 'organising principle' across Jane's contact with police. It is the interlocking (or, as Baldry and Dowse (2013) suggest, the 'compounding') nature of discourses of criminality, gender and disability in the production of disability as abnormality which ultimately magnifies the dishonesty of her complaints and secures her status as an un-'ideal' disabled, gendered victim *and additionally* encourages *criminalisation* of her by reason of these complaints. The way in which police represent Jane's reports of sexual violence and her mental distress as a 'nuisance' and a drain on resources reduce and dehumanize her to a problem to be managed, at times punitively. Over time, reports of sexual violence and Jane's mental distress become represented as a mundane, routine ritual to be criminalized and what is to be expected as normal for this 'abnormal' woman (see similarly Morin et al. 2005, 133, 134), rather than viewing the reports as signalling injustices or violations to be condemned and remedied.

Looking beyond Jane's case study, these discursive entanglements of criminality, disability and gender pervade the police events narratives of the nine other women in the sample – yet with slightly different formations (e.g. child familial sexual abuse, domestic violence, assault by disability service workers, violence in the context of prostitution, harassment, physical assaults) or contexts (out of home care, homelessness, drug use). The perceptions of police of their contact with these women, as recorded in the events narratives, illuminate a complex and at times contradictory interplay of dynamics: trivializing of suicide attempts and public expressions of trauma and distress, concerns for the welfare and vulnerability of these women, concerns around wastage of police and public health resources, and role of police in navigating the frequent rejection from and movement of women between various institutions (police, public health, disability services). Yet, in tracking through this project each of these women's contact with police over time, it is not only highly concerning that a common story emerges of these women as dishonest and nuisances but that the police events narrative provides the institutional possibility for the development of and reliance on this narrative. Building on these findings, further research is required, such as through interviews or focus groups with women offenders designated as disabled and with police, to examine their perceptions of these points of contact. Further research could also delve into police organizational guidelines and training material to gain greater understanding of institutional approaches to the policing of this specific group of women, including the prioritization of police resources, the operational relationships between police and public health *and* the interpretation of and reliance on the archive contained in the police events narratives.

While my analysis focused on a non-Indigenous Australian woman and on the discourses of gender, disability and criminality, further research is necessary in order to situate and further develop these findings in settler-colonial violence and its contemporary rationalizations that are increasingly relying upon scientifically 'objective' discourses of health, disability and medicine to render interventions in Indigenous bodies and communities 'noncolonial' (Chapman 2014; see also Razack 2015). It is vital to interrogate how the designation as disabled consolidates and extends the necropolitical management of Indigenous Australian women offenders and the extreme (at times lethal) violence to their bodies (Razack 2002). Where Indigeneity is itself 'lethal', and the sexualized and racialized body of the Indigenous woman is a key site for such violence (Razack 2002), future analysis should question how the deviancy of disability heightens the exposure of Indigenous Australian women to violence and death at the same time that the inherent racism and colonialism of this violence and death is negated under the guise of individual health issues which render these circumstances inevitable (Razack 2015; see, e.g. Steele 2016).

These findings have implications for current trends in criminal justice and public health to problematize individuals (particularly women) who have multiple contacts with police in relation to mental health as 'frequent presenters' (see, e.g. Baldry, Dowse, and Clarence 2012). There is a need to explore the relationship of the category of frequent presenter as a quantifier of service *overuse* to the material, economic dimensions of disability as abnormality and its association with waste (Erevelles 2011a, 143) and possible links to neoliberalism in reduction of state and public care and support (Kendall 2004, 280; Soldatic and Meekosha 2012). This exploration could draw on critical disability scholarship on disability and temporality (see, e.g. Kafer 2013). Critical interrogation of the category of 'frequent presenter' and of criminalisation of trauma more broadly is particularly pertinent in light of the current Australian Royal Commission into Institutional Responses to Child Sexual Abuse. The Commission recently released a consultation paper on criminal justice issues which focuses on criminal justice responses to the acts of child sexual abuse (Royal Commission into Institutional Responses to Child Sexual Abuse 2016). While these are essential criminal justice matters to consider, my article gestures towards the criminal justice issues related to the subsequent criminalization of the public displays of trauma and distress by those *victims* of institutional sexual abuse who (possibly by very reason of their abuse in which the state was complicit) are disabled and have ongoing contact with the criminal justice system as offenders and under civil mental health legislation. Approaching police responses to this group in the broader context of the past violence and injustices in which the state might be complicit raises further complexities about the (in)justice inherent in contemporary punitive responses to these women by the state (via the police): suggesting here the criminalization of survival and a *violent* and *punitive* disavowal of state responsibility.

Ultimately, there is a need to challenge the complex relations of disability, criminality, gender and sexuality that leave bodies subject to lawful violence and punished for their attempts to seek assistance from police. Building on the feminist scholarship and activism that has illuminated the significance of norms of gender and sexuality to the justice outcomes for women victims of sexual violence, there is a need to interrogate the significance of cultural constructions of ability *and* criminality to justice outcomes of women offenders designated as disabled and to interrogate the broader cultural, institutional, legal and economic discourses that guide the affective responses of police who inhabit a central position in the justice pathways of these women (noting that only examining disability alone and not also its intersections with criminality could legitimize violence against 'deviant' women with disability (Bromwich 2015, 204–209)). Yet beyond the specific issue of the appropriate police response to women like Jane, there is a much larger issue in need of urgent consideration: the ethical and affective response of abled members of society to individual encounters with criminalized and disabled lives already deemed ungrievable. Following from Erevelles' question, drawing on Judith Butler; 'what bodies matter and which are yet to matter' (Erevelles 2011a, 6, 7) – we need to ask why the violence to women offenders with disability does not matter and demand that it does.

Notes

1. Ethics approval was granted by the University of Wollongong Human Research Ethics Committee (HE14/168), and ratified by the University of New South Wales Human Research Ethics Committee.
2. This study is a nested study within the Australian Research Council (ARC) Linkage project, 'People with Mental Health Disorders and Cognitive Disabilities (MHDCD) in the Criminal Justice System (CJS) in NSW', University of NSW – Chief Investigators Baldry, Dowse and Webster. Ethics approval was obtained from all of the relevant ethics bodies, including from the University of New South Wales Human Research Ethics Committee. See generally *Australians with MHDCD in the CJS Project* (2015) (29 June 2012) Mental Health Disorders and Cognitive Disabilities in the Criminal Justice System http://www.mhdcd.unsw.edu.au/australians-mhdcd-cjs-project.html. See also (Baldry, Dowse, and Clarence 2012).
3. The cohort was drawn from the 2001 NSW Inmate Health Survey (IHS) and from the NSW Department of Corrective Services State-wide Disability Service Database (SDD).

Acknowledgements

Thank you to Olivia Todhunter and Julian Trofimovs for their research assistance. Thank you to the feedback received on earlier drafts from Eileen Baldry, Felicity Bell and Leanne Dowse. Thank you to feedback on related papers received at the University of Wollongong Feminist Research Network Works in Progress event and at 'Complicities' Law, Literature and the Humanities Association of Australasia Conference.

Disclosure statement

No potential conflict of interest was reported by the author.

Funding

This work was supported by the University of Wollongong Legal Intersections Research Centre under a Small Research Grant; and an Endeavour Foundation Endowment Challenge Fund Student Grant.

References

Australians with MHDCD in the CJS Project. 2015. *Mental Health Disorders and Cognitive Disabilities in the Criminal Justice System*. November 1. Accessed November 10. http://www.mhdcd.unsw.edu.au/australians-mhdcd-cjs-project.html

Baldry, Eileen, and Chris Cunneen. 2014. "Imprisoned Indigenous Women and the Shadow of Colonial Patriarchy." *Australian & New Zealand Journal of Criminology* 47 (2): 1–23.

Baldry, Eileen, and Leanne Dowse. 2013. "Compounding Mental and Cognitive Disability and Disadvantage: Police as Care Managers." In *Policing and the Mentally Ill: International Perspectives*, edited by Duncan Chappell, 219–234. Boca Raton, FL: CRC Press.

Baldry, Eileen, Leanne Dowse, and Melissa Clarence. 2012. *People with Intellectual and Other Cognitive Disability in the Criminal Justice System*. Sydney: Family & Community Services: Ageing, Disability & Home Care.

Baldry, Eileen, Ruth McCausland, Leanne Dowse, and Elizabeth McEntyre. 2015. *A Predictable and Preventable Path: Aboriginal People with Mental and Cognitive Disabilities in the Criminal Justice System*. Kensington: University of New South Wales.

Berghs, Maria. 2015. "Disability and Displacement in times of Conflict: Rethinking Migration, Flows and Boundaries." *Disability and the Global South* 2 (1): 442–459.

Bromwich, Rebecca Jaremko. 2015. *Looking for Ashley: Re-reading What the Smith Case Reveals about the Governance of Girls, Mothers and Families in Canada*. Bradford: Demeter Press.

Brown, David, David Farrier, Luke McNamara, Alex Steel, Michael Grewcock, Julia Quilter, and Melanie Schwartz. 2015. *Criminal Laws: Material and Commentary on Criminal Law and Process of New South Wales*. 6th ed. Leichhardt: The Federation Press.

Cadwallader, Jessica. 2012. "(Un)Expected Suffering: The Corporeal Specificity of Vulnerability." *The International Journal of Feminist Approaches to Bioethics* 5 (2): 105–125.

Campbell, Fiona Kumari. 2006. "Litigation Neurosis: Pathological Responses or Rational Subversion?" *Disability Studies Quarterly* 26 (1). http://dsq-sds.org/article/view/655/832.

Chapman, Chris. 2014. "Five Centuries' Material Reforms and Ethical Reformulations of Social Elimination." In *Disability Incarcerated: Imprisonment and Disability in the United States and Canada*, edited by Liat Ben-Moshe, Chris Chapman, and Allison C. Carey, 25–44. New York: Palgrave Macmillan.

Collins, Patricia Hill, and Sirma Bilge. 2016. *Intersectionality*. Cambridge: Polity Press.

Connell, R. 2011. "Southern Bodies and Disability: Re-thinking Concepts." *Third World Quarterly* 32 (8): 1369–1381.

Crenshaw, Kimberle. 1991. "Mapping the Margins: Intersectionality, Identity Politics, and Violence against Women of Color." *Stanford Law Review* 43 (6): 1241–1299.

Davis, Lenard. 1995. *Enforcing Normalcy: Disability, Deafness, and the Body*. New York: Verso.

Dowse, Leanne. Forthcoming. "Disruptive, Dangerous and Disturbing: The 'Challenge' of Behaviour in the Construction of Normalcy and Vulnerability." *Continuum*.

Dowse, Leanne, Eileen Baldry, and Phillip Snoyman. 2009. "Disabling Criminology: Conceptualising the Intersections of Critical Disability Studies and Critical Criminology for People with Mental Health and Cognitive Disabilities in the Criminal Justice System." *Australian Journal of Human Rights* 15 (1): 29–46.

Dowse, Leanne, Kimberlee Dean, Julian Trofimovs, and Stacy Tzoumakis. 2015. *People with Complex Needs Who Are the Victims of Crime: Building Evidence for Responsive Support*. Report prepared for Victims Services, NSW Department of Justice. Kensington: University of NSW.

Dowse, Leanne, Carolyn Frohmader, and Helen Meekosha. 2010. "Intersectionality: Disabled Women." In *Women and the Law in Australia*, edited by Patricia Easteal, 249–268. Chatswood: LexisNexis Butterworths.

Dowse, Leanne, Karen Soldatic, Aminath Didi, and Georgia van Toom. 2013. *Stop the Violence: Discussion Paper*. Rosny Park: Women with Disabilities Australia.

Dowse, Leanne, Karen Soldatic, Jo Spangaro, and Georgia van Toom. 2016. "Mind the Gap: The Extent of Violence against Women with Disabilities in Australia." *The Australian Journal of Social Issues* 51 (3): 341–359.

Ellison, Louise. 2015. "Responding to the Needs of Victims with Psychosocial Disabilities: Challenges to Equality of Access to Justice." *Criminal Law Review* 1: 28–47.

Ellison, Louise, Vanessa Munro, Katrin Hohl, and Paul Wallang. 2015a. "Accessible Justice? Rape Victimisation and Psychosocial Disability." *Feminists at Law* 5 (1). Online publication. http://journals.kent.ac.uk/kent/index.php/feministsatlaw/article/view/171.

Ellison, Louise, Vanessa Munro, Katrin Hohl, and Paul Wallang. 2015b. "Challenging Criminal Justice? Psychosocial Disability and Rape Victimization." *Criminology & Criminal Justice* 15 (2): 225–244.

Erevelles, Nirmala. 2011a. *Disability and Difference in Global Contexts: Enabling a Transformative Body Politic.* New York: Palgrave Macmillan.

Erevelles, Nirmala. 2011b. "The Color of Violence: Reflecting on Gender, Race, and Disability in Wartime." In *Feminist Disability Studies*, edited by Kim Hall, 117–135. Bloomington: Indiana University Press.

Erevelles, Nirmala. 2014. "'Becoming Disabled': Towards the Political Anatomy of the Body." In *Disability, Human Rights and the Limits of Humanitarianism*, edited by Michael Gill and Cathy J. Schlund-Vials, 219–233. Farnham: Ashgate.

Erevelles, Nirmala, and Andrea Minear. 2011. "Unspeakable" Offenses: Disability Studies at the Intersections of Multiple Differences." In *Disability and Difference in Global Contexts: Enabling a Transformative Body Politic*, edited by Nirmala Erevelles, 95–120. New York: Palgrave Macmillan.

Frohmader, Carolyn, and Therese Sands. 2015. *Australian Cross Disability Alliance (ACDA) Submission to the Senate Inquiry into Violence, Abuse and Neglect against People with Disability in Institutional and Residential Settings.* Sydney: Australian Cross Disability Alliance.

Garland-Thomson, Rosemarie. 2011. "Integrating Disability, Transforming Disability Theory." In *Feminist Disability Studies*, edited by Kim Hall, 13–47. Bloomington: Indiana University Press.

Hall, Kim, ed. 2011. *Feminist Disability Studies.* Bloomington: Indiana University Press.

Hannah-Moffat, Kelly. 2004. "Losing Ground: Gendered Knowledges, Parole Risk, and Responsibility." *Social Politics* 11 (3): 363–385.

Hollinsworth, D. 2013. "Decolonizing Indigenous Disability in Australia." *Disability & Society* 28 (5): 601–615.

Kafer, Alison. 2013. *Feminist Queer Crip.* Bloomington: Indiana University Press.

Keilty, Jennifer, and Georgina Connelly. 2001. "Making a Statement: An Exploratory Study of Barriers Facing Women with an Intellectual Disability When Making a Statement about Sexual Assault to Police." *Disability & Society* 16 (2): 273–291.

Kendall, Kathleen. 2004. "Female Offenders or Alleged Offenders with Developmental Disabilities: A Critical Overview." In *Offenders with Developmental Disabilities*, edited by William R. Lindsay, John L. Taylor, and Peter Sturmey, 265–288. New York: Wiley.

Lindsay, W. R., A. H. W. Smith, K. Quinn, A. Anderson, A. Smith, R. Allan, and J. Law. 2004. "Women with Intellectual Disability Who Have Offended: Characteristics and Outcomes." *Journal of Intellectual Disability Research* 48 (6): 580–590.

Mbembe, Achilles. 2003. "Necropolitics." Translated by Libby Meintjes. *Public Culture* 15 (1): 11–40.

Morin, Daphné, Shirley Roy, Marielle Rozier, and Pierre Landreville. 2005. "Homelessness, Mental Disorder, and Penal Intervention: Women Referred to a Mobile Crisis Intervention Team." In *Women, Madness and the Law: A Feminist Reader*, edited by Wendy Chan, Dorothy E. Chunn, and Robert Menzies, 127–139. London: Glasshouse Press.

Murray, Suellen, and Anastasia Powell. 2008. *Sexual Assault and Adults with a Disability: Enabling Recognition, Disclose and a Just Response.* (ACSSA Issues No. 9). Melbourne: Australian Centre for the Study of Sexual Assault, Australian Institute of Family Studies.

Murray, Suellen, and Melanie Heenan. 2012. "Reported Rapes in Victoria: Police Responses to Victims with a Psychiatric Disability or Mental Health Issue." *Current Issues in Criminal Justice* 23 (3): 353–368.

Ortoleva, Stephanie, and Hope Lewis. 2012. *Forgotten Sisters – A Report on Violence against Women with Disabilities: An Overview of Its Nature, Scope, Causes and Consequences.* Northeastern Public Law and Theory Faculty Research Paper Series No. 104-2012. Washington, DC: Women Enabled International.

Patel, Shaista. 2014. "Racing Madness: The Terrorizing Madness of the Post 9/11 Terrorist Body." In *Disability Incarcerated: Imprisonment and Disability in the United States and Canada*, edited by Liat Ben-Moshe, Chris Chapman, and Allison C. Carey, 201–216. New York: Palgrave Macmillan.

Pettitt, Bridget, Sian Greenhead, Hind Khalifeh, Varl Drennan, Tina Hart, Jo Hogg, Rohan Borschmann, Emma Mamo, and Paul Moran. 2013. *At Risk, Yet Dismissed: The Criminal Victimisation of People with Mental Health Problems.* London: Victim Support/Mind.

Razack, Sherene. 1995. "From Consent to Responsibility, from Pity to Respect: Subtexts in Cases of Sexual Violence Involving Girls and Women with Developmental Disabilities." *Law & Social Inquiry* 19 (4): 891–922.

Razack, Sherene H. 2002. "Gendered Racial Violence and Spatialized Justice: The Murder of Pamela George." In *Race, Space and the Law: Unmapping a White Settler Society*, edited by Sherene H. Razack, 121–156. Toronto: Between the Lines.

Razack, Sherene H. 2015. *Dying from Improvement: Inquests and Inquiries into Indigenous Deaths in Custody.* Toronto: University of Toronto Press.

Royal Commission into Institutional Responses to Child Sexual Abuse. 2016. *Consultation Paper: Criminal Justice.* September. http://www.childabuseroyalcommission.gov.au/getattachment/716949b2-0c54-4cca-933f-1ced55d00aa8/Consultation-paper.

Segrave, Marie, and Bree Carlton. 2010. "Women, Trauma, Criminalisation and Imprisonment …." *Current Issues in Criminal Justice* 22 (2): 287–305.

Shildrick, Margrit. 2009. *Dangerous Discourses of Disability, Subjectivity and Sexuality.* Basingstoke: Palgrave Macmillan.

Snyder, Sharon L., and David T. Mitchell. 2006. *Cultural Locations of Disability*. Chicago, IL: University of Chicago Press.

Soldatic, Karen. 2015. "Post Colonial Reproductions: Disability, Indigeneity and the Formation of the White Masculine Settler State of Australia." *Social Identities* 21 (1): 53–68.

Soldatic, Karen, and Helen Meekosha. 2012. "Disability and Neoliberal State Formations." In *Routledge Handbook of Disability Studies*, edited by Nick Watson, Alan Roulstone, and Carol Thomas, 195–210. Abingdon: Routledge.

Steele, L. 2016. "Disabling Forensic Mental Health Detention: The Carcerality of the Disabled Body." *Punishment and Society: The International Journal of Penology* 1–21. [Online First]. doi:10.1177/1462474516680204.

Sullivan, F. Forthcoming. "Not Just Language: An Analysis of Discursive Constructions of Disability in Sentencing Remarks." *Continuum*.

Titchkosky, Tanya. 2007. *Reading and Writing Disability Differently: The Textured Life of Embodiment*. Toronto: University of Toronto Press.

Tremain, Shelley. 2002. "On the Subject of Impairment." In *Disability/Postmodernity: Embodying Disability Theory*, edited by Mairian Corker and Tom Shakespeare, 32–47. London: Continuum.

Tremain, Shelley, ed. 2005. *Foucault and the Government of Disability*. Ann Arbor: University of Michigan Press.

Wadiwel, Dinesh. Forthcoming. "Disability and Torture: Exception, Epistemology and 'Black Sites.'" *Continuum*.

'The government is the cause of the disease and we are stuck with the symptoms': deinstitutionalisation, mental health advocacy and police shootings in 1990s Victoria

Piers Gooding ⓘ

ABSTRACT

The deinstitutionalization of mental health services in Australia happened first and most rapidly in the state of Victoria. In the final decades of the 20th Century, a period of immense economic and social policy reform accelerated this shift. Policy change appeared to be guided, at least in part, by ideals of human rights and citizenship. However, these same principles could be undermined in the vacuum of services created by deinstitutionalization and the broader restructuring of the welfare state. One expression of this paradox was a reported increase in violent encounters between police and those in states of distress and mental crises. Another example of paradox was rights-based mental health law, which both increased procedural safeguards for involuntary psychiatric intervention but also perpetuated differential treatment of persons with psychosocial disability on the basis of unfounded beliefs. This article will examine the intersections of policing and mental health policy in order to examine how boundaries of normality and disablement were contested during a transitional period of mental health law and policy.

Introduction

People who experience psychosocial disability[1] – whether through imputed mental disorder or the experience of profound distress, extreme mental states, and so on – have been long cast as 'abnormal' legal actors. Civil commitment laws, for example, form an entrenched anomaly in a legal system that traditionally privileges and protects individual autonomy and routinely upholds the right to refuse treatment in healthcare (Campbell 1994). Civil commitment laws indicate that rights to liberty and consent in healthcare for people with mental health diagnoses are held to a different standard compared to other citizens. It is also generally agreed that policing practices can criminalize mental distress, particularly when health and welfare service provision is flagging (Green 1997).

The closure of large-scale, standalone institutions and the introduction of 'rights-based' mental health law and policy (McSherry and Weller 2010) has disrupted – but not ended – this longstanding 'state of exception' (Agamben 2005; Spandler and Calton 2009). The policy of deinstitutionalization was accompanied by new citizenship rights, including increased procedural safeguards for involuntary psychiatric interventions (McSherry and Weller 2010) and increased community-based support services. 'Psychiatric patients' were recast in legal and policy discourse as mental health 'service users', and in Australia, as 'consumers', who experienced new forms of inclusion, even as many forms of exclusion remained.

In Australia in the 1980s and 90s, the transition from large-scale, standalone psychiatric institutions to so-called 'community-based' services happened first and most rapidly in Victoria (Gerrand 2005). Much can be gleaned from this transitional period to illuminate ongoing concerns about juridical exclusion based on psychosocial disability. During this time, the policy discourse of rights and entitlements, consumer choice and empowerment, at times stood in tension with the service void created by the dismantling of large, standalone psychiatric institutions. Critical incidents highlighted these tensions, including violent encounters between police and citizens. In 1994, for example, more people were fatally shot by police in Victoria than in all other states and territories combined (Dalton 1998, 3). Of those who died, two thirds were reported to have 'a history of emotional or mental illness' (Dalton 1998, 3). This point was seized upon by some police officials to criticise mental health policy and attribute responsibility for the shootings away from police. However, it should be stated clearly at the outset that there is no evidence of causation between deinstitutionalization and police shootings. After all, a similar spike in shootings was not seen in other deinstitutionalizing jurisdictions (Project Beacon 1995, 2) and the subsequent re-training of the Victorian Police Force led to a dramatic reduction in shootings (Kesic, Thomas, and Ogloff 2010). Yet the publicity that followed the shootings revealed a complex public exploration of the changes brought by deinstitutionalization. Importantly, this public discourse revealed how mental health service users and others with disabilities were influencing law enforcement and mental health policy and practice at the time.

This article will examine the intersections of policing and mental health policy to look at ways that boundaries of normality and disablement were contested during an important transitional period in Australian social policy. I should stress that it will not provide an empirical account of policing practices at this time, which have detailed elsewhere (see Dalton 1998; McCulloch 2000). Instead, the key issue is to consider the emerging social movement of 'former mental patients' redefined as 'consumers', and in some cases as self-identified 'psychiatric survivors' (Wadsworth 1997), who became increasingly involved in public debate related to mental health, including becoming active in training and informing police protocol (Office of Police Integrity, Victoria 2012). This engagement highlights how those most affected could resist and negotiate powerful structural changes, even as other processes continued to exclude them.

Background

Although the policy of deinstitutionalization can be seen to have begun in Australia from the 1950s onward (Gooding 2016), the final decade of the 20th century proved a crucial tipping point in the closure of large-scale standalone psychiatric hospitals in Victoria. Between 1994 and 2000, all 14 of Victoria's standalone psychiatric hospitals were closed (Gerrand 2005). In terms of the *Mental Health Act 1986* (Vic), the closures reflected policy aimed at 'treating mental illness … in the least restrictive environment possible' (MHA 1986 (Vic)). The re-configuration of services was widely applauded for its pace and magnitude (see Gerrand 2005; Lammers 2002; Meadows and Singh 2003). In 2000, for example, the Australian Governments National Mental Health Report stated that 'the degree of structural change achieved by Victoria was greater than the efforts of all other jurisdictions combined' (Commonwealth Department of Health and Aged Care 2000, 36).

Patterns of service-use were affected by changes to public administration made by the State Liberal Party Government, who were in office from 1992–1999. Costar and Economou (1999, 2) describe Jeff Kennett, the Liberal Party leader during this time, as 'the most robust example of the way the Liberal Party of Australia's approach to government and politics altered under the influence of neo-classical liberalism'. The shift to neoliberal governance – which can be broadly defined by privatization, deregulation, and the shrinking of the public sector – is evident on a number of fronts. According to Mendes, $240 million was cut from health, community services and education in the government's first mini-budget (Mendes 2001, 5). 'Client empowerment' was used as a guiding principle for transforming the government's role from one of a direct provider of services to that of a purchaser of services (Carney

2008). Hence, the term 'consumer' began to appear in official discourse to describe citizens who used mental health services.

An example of the shift brought by the new, 'mixed economy' of mental health services can be seen in the path of the most visible gatekeeper to in-patient facilities at this time – the Crisis Assessment and Treatment (CAT) services. CAT services provided mobile support to mediate between community and hospital and offered admission to acute treatment wards in mainstream hospitals. The operations of CAT teams were greatly expanded in 1994 under the new 'Framework for Service Delivery' (Department of Health and Community Services 1994). On any given day the mobile unit might visit twenty-four hour supervised residential cluster houses, a range of low-supervision suburban households, privately-run rooming houses, community support centres, drug and alcohol rehabilitation centres, homeless shelters, police cells, and family homes (Department of Health and Community Services 1994).

Within this emerging constellation of services a range of official practices could increase the likelihood of people in mental health crises interacting with police. On entering a crisis situation, an investigative journalist wrote in late 1994, the CAT might 'employ police officers using batons, and revolvers, or they might apply medication' ("Working at the brink of sanity." *The Age*, October 10, 1994). In a notable publication by the 'Melbourne Consumer Group' (Wadsworth 1997, 95), which was among the first of a number of consumer-led or co-produced publications to appear during this time (see also Cook, Jonikas, and Razzano 1995; Rosen 1994), a sense of collective concern was raised about police violence. A group discussion was captured in which one self-described 'survivor of psychiatric services', associated the twofold problems of police treatment and inaccessibility of services, when he observed:

> The way it works … is that you have to be in a crisis but you have to not be violent. And if you're in a crisis, all the CAT will do is say 'calm down, take two pills, goodbye'. And if you are violent or even just resisting the pills, then they call the police … (Wadsworth 1997, 102)

While this reflection belongs to a single person, it may suggest a broader unease, which is expressed elsewhere throughout the publication.

Mental health legislation introduced in 1986, which authorized coercive treatment in certain circumstances, may also have led to increasing encounters with police. Under the legislation, a 'person [who] appear[ed] to be mentally ill' could be detained and treated involuntarily, where 'the person [could not] receive adequate treatment for the mental illness in a manner less restrictive of his or her freedom of decision and action' (MHA 1986; s8(1)). Treatment, in the terms of the Act, had to be 'necessary for [a person's] health or safety (whether to prevent a deterioration in the person's physical or mental condition or otherwise) or for the protection of members of the public' (MHA 1986; s8(1)). According to the Human Rights and Equal Opportunity Commission, a breach of conditions could result in police entering 'premises and us[ing] reasonable force to apprehend the person subject to the order without a warrant' and the person could be then taken 'to the appropriate health care agency' (HREOC 1993, 67–68).

'Community Treatment Orders' (or 'CTOs' as they are often referred to) provided for new forms of coercive intervention *outside* the hospital (MHA 1986; s14(2)), which extended the spaces of treatment, control and regulation to homes and residences (Gooding 2016). Conditions could be imposed on former inpatients discharged from hospital and typically entailed medication compliance. Community-counselling could also be imposed. In the nearly three decades since CTOs were introduced in Victoria, three large-scale, randomized control trials and their meta-analyses have indicated that CTOs are ineffective in achieving their two principal aims: (1) lowering hospitalization rates or (2) protecting individuals subject to them (Heun, Dave, and Rowlands 2016), though no such studies have examined CTO-use in Australia. However, there is some evidence that CTOs were associated with reduced mortality rates, even when taking into consideration the use of community services, age, gender, inpatient experience, and diagnosis (Segal and Burgess, 2006). Setting aside the (limited) evidence for the utility of CTOs, questions can be raised as to why these anomalous coercive measures are applied unequally to persons with an apparent or diagnosed mental health issue. It is also noteworthy that Victoria continues to have the highest rate of people under CTOs per capita, not just within Australia but internationally (Light et al. 2012).

Disability, mental health and policing

In 1994, the first year of the new government's five-year mental health plan, there was a peak in the number of people shot and killed by Victorian police, a figure greater than all other States and Territories combined (McCulloch 2000). According to McCulloch (2000, 242), '(p)ublic controversy over public shootings of the mentally ill, peaked in September 1994 with the fatal shooting of Colleen Richman'. Richman was an Indigenous woman who was shot by police in Victoria's capital, Melbourne, after reportedly threatening police with a hatchet (Halloran 1995, 368). Ensuing controversy centred on the question of why police could not subdue a person who, in the words of one of the officers, was 'of small build and short in height' (Halloran 1995, 368). According to the coronial reports, Richman was five feet and one-inch tall (Halloran 1995, 368).

The funeral for Richman was held on 30 September 1994 at the Sacred Heart Catholic Church in St Kilda, and it was reported that over two hundred people gathered in mourning and protest (*The Age*, October 1, 1994). Father Phillip Norden, a prominent Victorian community-development worker, was reported later as saying: 'I remember the Deputy Premier ringing me on my mobile phone as I was walking down Fitzroy Street, at the funeral, to tell me he was announcing moves to retrain the whole police force' (*Sunday Age,* March 12, 1995).

It should be noted that Richman may not have identified as a person with disability or as a mental health service user. However, in the considerable media attention that followed, her death sparked a complex public exploration of Victoria's new mental health policy. For example, three days after the shooting, one charity spokesperson argued that there was not enough 'resourcing for community groups expected to take the burden of care from the closed institutions' (*The Age,* September 26, 1994). A welfare operations manager from the Smith Family reportedly stated that there was an 'increase in the number of mentally ill seeking assistance in the last two years' (*The Age,* September 26, 1994). Three months later, the Chair of the Catholic Social Services, Ben Bodna, reportedly stated that '[w]e are overwhelmed by mentally ill people looking for food and shelter' (*The Age,* December 11, 1994). Concerned with the rising number of fatal police shootings after Colleen Richman's death, Bodna initiated a reconvening of the Human Rights and Equal Opportunity Commission, *Human Rights Inquiry into the Lives of People with Mental Illness* (*The Age,* December 11, 1994).

In contrast to expressions of concern for people in mental health crises, the Victorian Police Association called for a return to asylum-style incarceration practices, reportedly arguing that the government was 'releasing dangerously mentally ill' into the community ("Police threat of action on mentally ill", *The Age,* October 28, 1994). This position was heavily criticised in public letters, editorials and in a public remonstration by the State Health Minister (see e.g. "Lawrence Slams Police", *The Age,* October 1, 1994; "Cease FIRE!" *The Age*, September 27, 1994).

It is generally agreed among commentators on this period of policing in Victoria, that the increase of shootings in 1993–94 should be seen in the context of a long history of paramilitary-style policing and the short-term effects of a violent law and order campaign in the late 1980s (see Connellan 1994; McCulloch 1998). During the campaign, twenty-one people had been shot, including police and citizens. In addition, there had been an execution-style killing of two patrol officers, dubbed the 'Walsh Street killings', and a car-bombing of a central Melbourne police station (Palmer 1995). According to, Task Force Victor, the Victorian Police Force committee in charge of 1994 police re-training titled Project Beacon (1995), this historical background contributed to a culture and training protocol that was highly adversarial, making the Force ill-prepared to respond to people in mental health crises. The 1993–94 shootings should also be seen in the context of changes to police powers by the Kennett government. For example, the *Public Sector Management Act 1992* gave increased powers to the Firearms and Operational Services Training Unit division (FOSTU), which was made up of former counter-terrorist and paramilitary officers of the Special Operations Unit (McCulloch 1998). McCulloch argues that these divisions were generally seen to be violent and confrontational (McCulloch 1998). The executive instruction accompanying the *Public Sector Management Act 1992* was 'to expand the functions and responsibilities of the FOSTU in response to Force restructuring' (Executive Instruction No. 287).

Official reports identified that police protocol was based on the idea of offenders as rational and calculated individuals. This view resonates with the policy formulation of the empowered consumer as self-interested, rationalising individuals. The Project Beacon report describes the nature of FOSTU training, in which:

> [e]mphasis was placed *inter alia* on justification of the use of deadly force by members. As understood by this Task Force, justification was taught with criminals in mind, people who were rational, and who tried to avoid being shot by police. (Project Beacon 1995, 193–194)

A member of the previously mentioned consumer interview group described how this emphasis on bringing order to a situation held 'the potential for disaster':

> The key thing is about them moving in and imposing their force, their will on the situation. They want to control it immediately through the threat of force or through the command of their voice or something. And so when that doesn't work – and why would it work with someone who is distressed, terrified or angry? (Wadsworth 1997, 100)

According to Project Beacon (1995, 55) reports, 'attitudes [were] extremely important to behaviour of police' and 'most police officers … considered mentally disturbed persons as "quite" or "very dangerous" and there was little distinction between types of illness or disability'.

Despite the argument made by the Police Association that the policy of deinstitutionalization was the *cause* for the increase in police shootings, Project Beacon identified no increase in fatal police shootings where deinstitutionalization was underway elsewhere (Project Beacon 1995, 2). Further, a longitudinal study by Kesic, Thomas, and Ogloff (2010) found that the number of fatal police shootings in the 12 years following Project Beacon was reduced by 50 per cent, despite significant increases to the Victorian population.

As with typical police forces, the Victorian Police Force had always come into regular contact with people in mental distress. The HREOC (1993, 758) raised concerns about the over-representation of people in crises being policed for 'offences such as drunkenness, offensive behaviour, disorderly conduct, loitering or vagrancy'. For police, the new mental health service framework potentially meant taking a greater workload in negotiating, detaining and transporting this more visible population.

However, it is noteworthy that police interactions with distressed people, or those imputed to be so, was not a new phenomenon. For example, it is generally agreed that police in 19th Century colonies in Australia had a central role in the passage to 'lunatic' asylums (Coleburne 2003; Finnane 2003; Garton 1994), which gives pause to consider any claim that deinstitutionalization led to a radically new role for police in responding to mental health crises. It should also be noted that Project Beacon recognized, at least in principle, the importance and need for improved mental health training of frontline officers, which served as a precursor to more recent developments in police training in which mental health consumers, carers and advocates have played an active role (Office of Police Integrity, Victoria 2012).

Responses to the shootings: deinstitutionalization 'coming apart at the seams'?

The 1993–94 shootings drew considerable criticism against police in the public sphere (see "8 in a Year", *Herald Sun*, September 24, 1994; "Mean Streets of Mentally Ill", *The Australian*, September 26, 1994; "Coming Apart at the Seams", "Lawrence Slams Police", *The Age*, October 1, 1994; "Our society on trial", *The Age,* September 29, 1994). An editorial in the State's major broadsheet newspaper summarized the criticism:

> For too long, most Victorians have given the police the benefit of the doubt about the mounting toll. But enough is enough. The problem clearly lies with the police, with their training (or lack of it), and with what the [then] coroner, Mr. Hallenstein, has identified in various reports as the police culture of the gun. (*The Age,* September 27, 1994)

Carmen Lawrence, then Federal Health Minister, called for charges to be laid on the basis of Victorian Police's 'appalling reputation' ("Open Wound" *The Age*, September 13, 1997). In response, Chief Commissioner Comrie and the Minister for Police took the unusual step of publishing an open letter to the public, stating that '[f]or the Victoria Police the issue of police shootings has led to a massive rethink on the handling of operations … The concerns of the Victorian community about police shootings have been heard by Victorian Police' ("Open Letter to All Victorians" *The Age,* October 6, 1994).

Despite the Chief Commissioner's open letter, the Police Association continued to publicly criticise the Health Department and its mental health policy, accusing the government of 'releasing dangerous mentally ill people in the community', and threatening industrial action if the policy of deinstitutional-ization was not 'reviewed' (*The Age*, October 28, 1994). In a front-page article on October 2, 1994 in *The Age*, the Police Association Secretary, Senior Sergeant Danny Walsh, reportedly stated that 'the govern-ment is the cause of the disease and we are stuck with the symptoms'. Four days after Richman's death, Walsh reportedly described police as train drivers and 'the mentally ill' as those who throw themselves in front ("Tehan raps police over fatal shooting", *The Age*, September 27, 1994). Similar sentiments were expressed by some frontline police officers in interviews undertaken as part of Project Beacon. For example, one patrol officer stated that:

> [i]n a lot of instances the decision is really not the decision of the police member. He is purely reacting to a situa-tion he has been placed in by somebody else and if the offender drops the weapon there's no need for it.' (Project Beacon 1995, 56)

The Commissioner of the Human Rights and Equal Opportunity Commission at the time, Brian Burdekin, openly criticized police actions yet also turned his attention to the Minister for Health, Marie Tehan (*The Age*, September 27, 1994). Tehan, interestingly, was reported to have replied in a letter to Burdekin, that 'private hotels were not her department's responsibility' (*The Age*, September 27, 1994), implying that those in crises beyond the bounds of hospitals and mental health facilities fell outside the remit of her department. This suggests there were some ambiguities about the governance of the 'mixed economy' of mental health services, which were comprised of public, private and quasi-private services subcontracted by government (see Gooding 2016). In the face of criticism from service users, families, professionals, and concerned public, the head of the psychiatric services division, Jennifer Williams, emphasized the slow process of systemic change: '[m]ental health reform is not going to be achieved in one year. We're in year one of a five-year reform plan' (*The Age,* November 4, 1994).

Consumer activism, 'experts by experience' and the peer workforce

Increasing attention was given to those on the receiving end of services during this time. One news report following the shootings quoted Belinda Thurlough, a representative of Victorian Mental Illness Awareness Council (VMIAC), the peak consumer organization in Victoria: 'The best time to be mentally ill in Victoria', she reportedly commented, 'is between 9 and 5, Monday to Friday, and, God, don't be ill on holidays or public holidays' (*The Age,* November 4, 1994). VMIAC was the first service-user-led organization in Victoria to receive state funding, and was founded in 1981 during the United Nations International Year of Disabled Persons in a small residence in inner-city Melbourne (VMIAC 2016). VMIAC, today remains prominent in consumer-led advocacy. Such advocacy was made increasingly prominent following the 1992 National Mental Health Service Program, which ordered the training and inclusion of paid consumer and family/carer consultants to assess services (AHMC 1992, 35–38).

By 1994 people with lived experience of mental health crises were increasingly mobilizing to contrib-ute to various levels of the service system. According to Alan Pinches, a prominent consumer advocate, 'Consumer Consultants' were employed state-wide for the first time in 1994 within Area Mental Health Services (Pinches 2014). In September 1994, the same month Richman died, Melbourne hosted the Australian and New Zealand Mental Health Services Conference, which held an inaugural conference day that was solely meant for consumers and family members (Victorian Department of Health 1994, i). The following year in Auckland, the Conference held the first Indigenous People's forum, with over 200 Indigenous service users and others in attendance. The forum was a response to the increasing need, as perceived by one group of consumers, 'to pass on consumer information to all who contribute to, impinge upon, and shape the experience of consumers, realizing that there is a widespread need for the consumer voice and a consumer perspective to be heard' (Wadsworth 1997, 3). Service users were mobilizing to influence the dimensions of deinstitutionalization at the national, state and local levels. This included contributing to committees, forums, seminars and research initiatives, and in consultant roles in community and hospital services (Pinches 2014). In this context, traditionally determined relationships between 'experts' and 'patients' were broadly contested.

In part, this negotiation was partly aided – perhaps paradoxically – by the monetarist welfare incentive to make providers accountable to 'client outcomes' through 'individual service agreements' (Department of Health and Community Services 1993; 2). However, the privatization of services and shrinking of the public sector also brought significant pitfalls. One reporter wrote after Richman's death, 'the State Government wants the community welfare sector to take on more responsibility, more clients, [even though] agencies point out they are being given less money, not more, to take on the extra load' (The Age, October 1, 1994). Mladenov (2016) has articulated how such a tension might result from marketizing public services: 'on the one hand, marketization has facilitated welfare state retrenchment, thus enhancing inequalities through maldistribution [even as] marketization has helped to bring about emancipation from top-down expertise and the paternalism of welfarist service provision'. This characterization captures some of the contradictory features of deinstitutionalization (and neoliberal governance) in Victoria and elsewhere. The complex role of people with disabilities as agents as well as potential victims of change was a strong feature of this new era of service delivery.

Richman herself was an activist for Indigenous land rights at a time when Aboriginal and Torres Strait Islander people faced systemic marginalization (The Age, October 2, 1994). Clearly, deinstitutionalization in Victoria, and its intersection with policing could be viewed from multiple axes of violence against marginalized populations, and could be considered with reference to the large literature on Aboriginal and Torres Strait Islander deaths in custody (see Australia 1988, 1998; Razack 2015). Today, the United States-based social movement, 'Black Lives Matter', could be viewed as a recent iteration of longstanding reactions to structural, race-based violence in settler democracies. For example, one major demand of the diverse group, which appears to be increasingly international in scope, are:

> […] swift and transparent legal investigation of all police shootings of black people; official governmental tracking of the number of citizens killed by police, disaggregated by race; the demilitarization of local police forces; and community accountability mechanisms for rogue police officers. (Black Lives Matter Website, 2016)

Throughout the period of deinstitutionalization across Australia, Aboriginal and Torres Strait Islander people more generally, could be seen to be engaging, resisting and negotiating the political institutions of the settler state. This is evident in the Indigenous advocacy at the Australian and New Zealand Mental Health Services Conference noted previously, as well as the advocacy of Aboriginal community-controlled health services (see Hemingway 2012).

From a theoretical perspective, the increasing involvement of 'outsider voices' may be viewed, in Michel Foucault's (1980, 9) terms, as an 'insurrection of subjugated knowledge', which is defined as knowledge that is left out, opposed or ignored by mainstreams of the dominant culture. In the specific context of disability, Steele, Dowse, and Trofimovs (2016, 181) argue that the field of critical disability studies – which positions the voices of lived experience at the centre – offers a conceptual framework that makes apparent:

> […] the social and political contingency of disability, including the intersection of disability with other dimensions of politicised identity (such as gender and Indigeneity) and the role of law and institutions (including the criminal justice system) in the disablement, marginalisation and criminalisation of people with disability.

The use of critical disability studies and other forms of contemporary theory can be seen to have informed advocacy that has boosted the participation of persons with disabilities in law, policy and practice. This is evident, for example, in the UNCRPD, which was signed and ratified by Australia in 2007, and was significantly influenced by critical disability studies and the broad, global disability movement. The UNCRPD requires participation of persons with disabilities in the laws, policies and practices that affect them as: a general principle (article 3); a general obligation for UNCRPD implementation (article 4), including in monitoring (article 33); as a specific right (articles 29 and 30); and via the inclusion of experts with disabilities on the relevant UN Committee on the Rights of Persons with Disabilities (article 34).

The UNCRPD is also noteworthy for bringing mental health issues more forcefully than ever before into the fold of international human rights law, and into the frame of disability, which may be more commonly associated in with physical disabilities. Importantly, the model of disability underpinning the UNCRPD shifts the focus to external factors, which, in interaction with impairment, create disablement. This view of disability turns the focus to societal barriers to full and effective participation in society, including strong provision for anti-discrimination and a positive obligation to provide 'reasonable accommodation' to ensure equal participation. In the mental health context, this directive is increasingly being interpreted to invite reconsideration of policy and practice which hold persons with psychosocial disability to a different standard to others (McSherry and Freckelton 2014), including ensuring sufficient resources in relevant policy areas such as health, employment, and – logically – policing.

In 1990s Victoria, the advocacy of mental health consumers, 'psychiatric survivors', and others, demonstrates the persistent forms compromise and resistance that took place at the individual and collective level. Even Richman's own family launched legal proceedings against police, including to contest the original coronial finding into her death. The original coronial findings placed sole responsibility for Richman's death and found that 'neither [of the police officers, who confronted and ultimately shot Richman] contributed to the cause of death' (West 1996, 3). While police were cleared of any wrongdoing in the final coronial finding (see "Seven-year legal wrangle," AAP, June 15, 2002), the protracted legal proceedings helped establish in common law that it was not the role of the coroner to apportion blame or connote legal conclusion (see "Keown v Kahn." Supreme Court of Victoria: Court of Appeal: No.7038 of 1996. "Keown vs. Kahn." High Court of Victoria: Court of Appeal, 1VR69, 1999).

These instances of advocacy suggest that persons with psychosocial disability, families and other supporters, despite facing considerable structural disadvantage, should not be seen as passive victims of an imposed order. Today, these groups are involved in the development of law, policy and practice at the national and international level, and in Victoria, includes the training of police (Office of Police Integrity, Victoria 2012), contribution to research agendas, and the development of the 'peer'-workforce (Lammers 2002; Lammers and Happell 2003). This participatory feature of policy in the era of deinstitutionalization is perhaps the most striking break of all from past policy and practice.

Conclusion

During deinstitutionalization in Victoria, people in mental distress appeared increasingly likely to come into contact with police, who, for reasons specific to the State at that time, tended towards adversarial confrontation and firearm use. The publicity that followed the 1994 spike in police shootings revealed broader issues to do with disability and mental health law, policy and practice.

On the one hand, persons with psychosocial disability could be cast in ideological models as the 'rational actor', presented as consumers, choosing from a range of services purchased by the state. On the other hand, they may have faced unmet need in an under-resourced community service-sector. Further, they may have faced public discourse portraying people in mental health crises as inherently risky to themselves and others, unpredictable and in need of social and legal regulation. This portrayal was seized upon by the Victorian Police Association. Although the Association's views were widely condemned in the public sphere, mental health legislation that specifically imposed differential restrictions on the rights to liberty and consent to treatment were based on similar predicates. At the time, Campbell (1994, 556) argued that such laws established 'institutional discrimination' which promoted at law 'the idea that there is something about "mental illness" itself which invites a system of control and coercion'. Similarly, Ben-Moshe, Chapman, and Carey (2014, ix) argue that deinstitutionalization left behind a landscape of authority and power in which persons with disabilities who enter services - whether voluntarily or not - are forced to negotiate 'processes of labelling, normalization, and marginalization upon which these settings rely'.

Concerns about this differential treatment continue today, and much work is needed to achieve, for example, equal recognition before the law in the mental health context (see McSherry and Freckelton 2014; McSherry and Weller 2010). Similarly, the issue of law enforcement responding to those in crises remains highly relevant. Ogloff and Thomas (2014, 1) reported that 'in 2013 alone, … [Victorian] police apprehend one person every two hours and take them to hospital for assessment'.

The snapshot of Victorian deinstitutionalization set out in this article suggests that people with psychosocial disabilities and their allies shared the experience of resisting and negotiating the changes of the era. Avenues for future research might consider a detailed history of this contribution (which is sorely missing in Australia and New Zealand), or a view of the tensions and alliances built between professionals, policymakers and consumer/survivor/disability advocates. The increasing role of those with disabilities is also likely to continue assisting law enforcement agencies, offering tools to police to engage with people in distress and their families as safely as possible, including identifying good practice in police use of force. Elevating 'subjugated voices' in this way can help achieve equality before the law for persons with disabilities and improve their access in real terms to the different systems, procedures, processes and locations involved in the administration of justice.

Note

1. The term 'psychosocial disability' is being used increasingly since the coming into force of the UN Convention on the Rights of Persons with Disabilities (UNCRPD) in 2008. This includes use of the term by the UN Human Rights Committee (2016), the WHO (2013), the UN Office of the High Commission for Human Rights (2009, para 49), various governments and a range of disabled people's organisations. This term is by no means uncontroversial, nor does it refer to a coherent and easily-defined human experience. Many people who experience mental health crises, mental illness, and so on – even the majority – may not think of their experience in terms of disability. Nor may mental health professionals be inclined to use disability to frame their practice. Nonetheless, the term is used here as a broad term that includes, in the terms of the UNCRPD (art. 1), 'those who have long-term physical, *mental*, intellectual or sensory impairments which in interaction with various barriers may hinder their full and effective participation in society on an equal basis with others'. This non-exhaustive list could include the disablement that may come from imputed disorder or from short-term crises.

Acknowledgements

I would like to thank my anonymous reviewers for their considered feedback. Moira Jenkins also provided illuminating comments on an earlier draft. Thanks also to thank Dr. Zora Simic and Associate Professor Tracey Banivanua-Mar for their support and guidance through an earlier iteration of this material.

Disclosure statement

No potential conflict of interest was reported by the author.

ORCID

Piers Gooding 🆔 http://orcid.org/0000-0001-5743-5708

References

Agamben, G. 2005. *State of Exception*. Chicago, IL: University of Chicago Press.
AHMC (Australian Health Ministers' Conference). 1992. *National Mental Health Strategy: Commonwealth of Australia*. Canberra: Australian Government Publishing Service.
Australia. 1998. Royal Commission into Aboriginal Deaths in Custody, and E Johnston. *Royal Commission into Aboriginal Deaths in Custody*. Canberra: Austlii, Council for Aboriginal Reconciliation.
Australia. 1988. Royal Commission into Aboriginal Deaths in Custody, and J. H. Muirhead. *Royal Commission into Aboriginal Deaths in Custody Interim Report*. Canberra: Australian Government Publishing Service.

Ben-Moshe, L., C. Chapman, and A. Carey, eds. 2014. *Disability Incarcerated: Imprisonment and Disability in the United States and Canada*. New York: Palgrave Macmillan.

Carney, T. 2008. "The Mental Health Service Crisis of Neoliberalism – An Antipodean Perspective." *International Journal of Law and Psychiatry* 31 (2): 101–115.

Campbell, T. 1994. "Mental Health Law: Institutionalised Discrimination." *Australian and New Zealand Journal of Psychiatry* 28: 554–559.

Coleburne, C. 2003. Passage to the Asylum: The Role of the Police in the Committals of the Insane in Victoria, Australia, 1948–1900 In *The Confinement of the Insane: International Perspectives, 1800–1965*, edited by R. Porter and D. Wright, 129–149. Cambridge: Cambridge University Press.

Commonwealth Department of Health and Aged Care. 2000. *National Mental Health Report 2000: Sixth Annual Report. Changes in Australia's Mental Health Services under the First National Mental Health Plan of the National Mental Health Strategy*. Canberra: Mental Health and Special Programs Branch, Department of Health and Ageing.

Connellan, G. 1994. "Power without Accountability." *Alternative Law Journal* 19: 203–206.

Cook, J. A., J. A. Jonikas, and L. Razzano. 1995. "A Randomized Evaluation of Consumer versus Nonconsumer Training of State Mental Health Service Providers." *Community Mental Health Journal* 31 (3): 229–238.

Costar, B., and N. Economou, eds. 1999. *The Kennett Revolution: Victorian Politics in the 1990s*. Kensington: UNSW Press.

Dalton, V. 1998. *Police Shootings 1990–97. Trends and Issues in Crime and Criminal Justice No. 89*. Canberra: Australian Institute of Criminology.

Department of Health and Community Services. 1994. *Victoria's Mental Health Service: The Framework for Service Delivery*. Melbourne: Victorian Government.

Department of Health and Community Services. 1993. *Victoria's Health Reforms: Psychiatric Services – Discussion Paper*. Melbourne: Victorian Government.

Executive Instruction No. 287, Firearms and Operational Survival Training Unit, R. Falconer, Deputy Commissioner. 10 November 1993, PROV VPRS 24/P0014/93.

Finnane, M. 2003. "From Dangerous Lunatic to Human Rights?: the Law and Mental Illness in Australian History." In *'Madness' in Australia: History, Heritage, and the Asylum*, edited by C. Coleburne and Dolly MacKinnon, 23–33. St. Lucia: University of Queensland Press.

Foucault, M. 1980. *Power/Knowledge: Selected Interviews and Other Writings*. New York: Pantheon Press.

Garton, S. 1994. "Sound Minds and Healthy Bodies: Re-Considering Eugenics in Australia, 1914–1940." *Australian Historical Studies* 26 (103): 163–181.

Gerrand, V. 2005. "Can Deinstitutionalisation Work? Mental Health Reform from 1993 to 1998 in Victoria, Australia." *Health Sociology Review: The Journal of the Health Section of the Australian Sociological Association* 14 (3): 255–271.

Gooding, P. 2016. "From Deinstitutionalisation to Consumer Empowerment: Mental Health Policy, Neoliberal Restructuring and the Closure of the 'Big Bins' in Victoria." *Health Sociology Review* 25 (1): 33–47.

Green, T. 1997. "Police as Frontline Mental Health Workers: The Decision to Arrest or Refer to Mental Health Agencies." *International Journal of Law and Psychiatry* 20: 469–486.

Halloran, P. 1995. *Homicide Squad Report, Inquest Brief Re: Death of Colleen Richman, vol 1, Coroner's Copy, Compiled, Detective Chief Inspector*. Homicide Squad, Victorian Police Force, 3 July 1995, 950311 Richman Colleen, Inquest Deposition Files, PROV VPRS 24/P0014/93

Hemingway, M. 2012. "Community Control: Aboriginal Self-Determination and Australian Settler Democracy: A History of the Victorian Aboriginal Health Service." PhD Thesis, University of Melbourne. http://hdl.handle.net/11343/37910.

Heun, R., S. Dave, and P. Rowlands. 2016. "Little Evidence for Community Treatment Orders – a Battle Fought with Heavy Weapons." *BJPsych Bulletin* 40 (3): 115–118.

HREOC (Human Rights and Equal Opportunity Commission). 1993. Human Rights and Mental Illness: Report of the National Inquiry into the Human Rights of People with Mental Illness. vol. 1 & 2. Canberra: Australian Government Publishing Service.

Kesic, D., S. Thomas, and J. Ogloff. 2010. "Mental Illness among Police Fatalities in Victoria 1982–2007: Case Linkage Study." *Australian and New Zealand Journal of Psychiatry* 44 (5): 463–468.

Lammers, A. 2002. "The Reforms to Mental Health and Their Impact on the Empowerment of Consumers and Carers." PhD Thesis, University of Melbourne.

Lammers, J., and B. Happell. 2003. "Consumer Participation in Mental Health Services: Looking from a Consumer Perspective." *Journal of Psychiatric and Mental Health Nursing* 10: 385–392.

Light, E., I. Kerridge, C. Ryan, and M. Robertson. 2012. "Out of Sight, out of Mind: Making Involuntary Community Treatment Visible in the Mental Health System." *The Medical Journal of Australia* 196 (9): 591–593.

Meadows, G., and B. Singh. 2003. "'Victoria on the Move': Mental Health Services in a Decade of Transition 1992–2002." *Australasian Psychiatry* 11 (1): 62–67.

Mendes, P. 2001. "From Minimal Intervention to Minimal Support: Child Protection Services under the Neo-Liberal Kennett Government in Victoria 1992-1999." *Children Australia* 26 (01): 4–11.

McCulloch, J. 1998. "Blue Army: Paramilitary Policing in Victoria." PhD Thesis, University of Melbourne.

McCulloch, J. 2000. "Policing the Mentally Ill." *Alternative Law Journal* 25 (5): 241–244.

McSherry, B., and I. Freckelton, eds. 2014. *Coercive Care: Rights, Law and Policy*. London: Routledge.

McSherry, B., and P. Weller, eds. 2010. *Rethinking Rights-Based Mental Health Laws*. Oxford: Hart.

Mladenov, T. 2016. "Policy Briefing: Marketisation, Direct Payments, Disability Justice and Austerity." *Discover Society*. Accessed February 2. http://discoversociety.org/2016/02/02/policy-briefing-marketisation-direct-payments-disability-justice-and-austerity/

Office of Police Integrity, Victoria. 2012. *Policing People Who Appear to Be Mentally Ill*. Melbourne: Office of Police Integrity, Victoria.

Ogloff, J., and S.Thomas. 2014. "Training Police to Better Respond to People with Mental Illness." *The Conversation* March 4: 1–3.

Palmer, D. 1995. "Excessive Force. beyond Police Shootings: Use of Force and Governing the Victorian Police Force." *Alternative Law Journal* 20 (2): 53–56.

Pinches, A. 2014. *What the Consumer Movement Says about Recovery*. Melbourne: Our Consumer Place. http://www.ourcommunity.com.au/files/OCP/PinchesRecovery.pdf.

Project Beacon. 1995. *Toward a Shooting Control Strategy*. Melbourne: Victorian Police.

Razack, S. 2015. *Dying from Improvement: Inquests and Inquiries into Indigenous Deaths in Custody*. Toronto: University of Toronto Press.

Rosen, A. 1994. "100% Mabo†: De-Colonising People with Mental Illness and Their Families." *Australian and New Zealand Journal of Family Therapy* 15 (3): 128–142.

Segal, S. P., and P. Burgess. 2006. "Effect of conditional release from hospitalization on mortality risk." *Psychiatric Services* 57 (11): 1607–1613.

Spandler, H., and T. Calton. 2009. "Psychosis and Human Rights: Conflicts in Mental Health Policy and Practice." *Social Policy and Society* 8 (2): 245–256.

Steele, L., L. Dowse, and J. Trofimovs. 2016. "Who is Diverted? Moving beyond Diagnosed Impairment towards a Social and Political Analysis of Diversion." *Sydney Law Review* 38 (2): 179–276.

UN Human Rights Committee. 2016. *Promotion and Protection of All Human Rights, Civil, Political, Economic, Social and Cultural Rights, including the Right to Development*, adopted 29 June 2016, A/HRC/32/L.26, 2 [2]. United Nations General Assembly.

UN Office of the High Commission for Human Rights. 2009. *Annual Report of the United Nations High Commissioner for Human Rights and Reports of the Office of the High Commissioner and the Secretary-General: Thematic Study by the Office of the United Nations High Commissioner for Human Rights on Enhancing Awareness and Understanding of the Convention on the Rights of Persons with Disabilities*. A/HRC/10/48. Tenth session Agenda item 2. January 26. United Nations General Assembly.

Victorian Department of Health. 1994. *Victoria's Mental Health Services: Improved Access through Coordinated Client Care*. Melbourne: Department of Health and Community Services.

VMIAC (Victorian Mental Illness Awareness Council) website. 2016. http://www.vmiac.org.au/.

Wadsworth, Y. 1997. *Do You Mind? The Ultimate Exit Survey: Survivors of Psychiatric Services Speak out*. Melbourne: Melbourne Consumer Consultant Group.

West, I. 1996. Investigation into the Death of Colleen Richman: Inquest Findings and Order Case No. 2644/94, Melbourne: Coroner's Court.

WHO (World Health Organisation). 2013. *Comprehensive Mental Health Action Plan 2013–2020*. Geneva: WHO.

Legislation and United Nations instruments

UNCRPD – Convention on the Rights of Persons with Disabilities, opened for signature 30 March 2007, Doc.A/61/611 (entered into force 3 May 2008) ('CRPD').

MHA 1959 – Mental Health Act 1959 (Vic) No. 6605.

MHA 1986 – Mental Health Act 1986 (Vic)

Public Sector Management Act 1992 (Vic)

Case law

"Keown v Kahn." Supreme Court of Victoria: Court of Appeal: No.7038 of 1996.

"Keown vs. Kahn." High Court of Victoria: Court of Appeal, 1VR69, 1999.

Disruptive, dangerous and disturbing: the 'challenge' of behaviour in the construction of normalcy and vulnerability

Leanne Dowse

ABSTRACT

Considerations of 'challenging behaviour' by people with disability have been largely associated with naturalized impairment and confined to the realms of clinical intervention and governance. This paper explores the bio-medical association between challenging behaviour and categories of diagnosed impairment and establishes its function as central to the construction of normalcy/abnormalcy for people who are deemed to show behaviours that challenge. The paper offers an alternate reading of challenging behaviour as embodied, emergent, relational and historically contingent. Through the analysis of case studies, the significance of legal, social and clinical responses is examined. It is demonstrated that people who exhibit challenging behaviour are marked as vulnerable to abnormality and on this basis are drawn into relations of intervention which ostensibly work to authorize targeted interventions aimed to restore or assist them to approach ideals of normalcy. In this context, theoretical conceptions of vulnerability are used to disentangle the ambivalent legal and social responsibilities and interventions for people constructed as having challenging behaviour. It is argued that failure to problematize the complex relationships between dependency and vulnerability can result in exacerbation of the 'challenge' of behaviour.

Introduction

While notions of normalcy have been viewed as a key counterpoint in the construction and disruption of disability and disability identities, people with disability who exhibit what is commonly referred to as 'challenging behaviour' or 'behaviours of concern' remain largely outside this analysis. Instead, their management and its oversight have been consigned to the spaces of clinical intervention and governance. This paper explores constructions of 'challenging behaviour' as tied to notions of naturalized impairment associated with intellectual disability and neurological difference and makes the argument, through the use of case studies, that these remain largely a-historical and a-political. In this context, responses to behaviours that challenge create dependencies that systemically suppress consideration of the multiple and compounding systemic factors and legitimate relations of intervention which themselves construct and reproduce vulnerability and abnormalcy.

In search of a definition

People who are identified as having 'challenging behaviour' or exhibiting 'behaviours of concern' are so categorized because the 'observable facts' of their human interaction are essentially divergent from 'normal' human behaviour. Attempts at definition typically identify abnormalities in either inwardly or outwardly directed actions which are seen to have negative physical and social consequences for the individuals and those around them. These elements are seen in the following commonly utilized definition of challenging behaviour:

> Behaviour … of such an intensity, frequency or duration as to threaten the quality of life and/or physical safety of the individual or others and is likely to lead to responses that are restrictive, averse or result in exclusion. (Royal College of Psychiatrists British Psychological Society and Royal College of Speech and Language Therapists 2007, 10)

Within a bio-medical framework, the presence of challenging behaviour is commonly associated with particular diagnostic labels including intellectual disability, autism, attention deficit hyperactivity disorder and certain genetic and/or organic disorders and syndromes (Hastings et al. 2004). For instance, it is generally accepted that challenging behaviour affects between 10 and 17% of population of people with intellectual disability (Bouras and Holt 2010) and that it occurs more commonly in men than women (Emerson et al. 2001). Evidence also suggests that for people with the label of intellectual disability, traumatic life events are associated with increased mental health symptomotology and challenging behaviour (Biswas and Furniss 2009) and such behaviours can be a major factor in relation to people with mild and moderate disabilities and their families (Tilley, Ledger, and Bardsley 2015).

Command of these diagnostic frameworks of impairment has been invested in the 'psy' disciplines (psychology and psychiatry) (Rose 1985) and grounded in professional and institutional codings and classifications of disorders associated with IQ measurement, assessment of adaptive functioning, participation and context. These are elucidated for example in internationally influential texts which guide clinicians such as the International Classification of Functioning, Disability and Health (WHO 2001) and the American Association of Intellectual and Developmental Disabilities, whose most recent Intellectual Disability: Definition, Classification, and Systems of Supports (Schalock et al. 2010) purports to 'contain the most current and authoritative information and knowledge on intellectual disability, including best practice guidelines on diagnosing and classifying intellectual disability and developing a system of supports for people living with an intellectual disability' (AAIDD 2010). While these classificatory typologies have, since the late 1990s, been revised to encompass the more complex interplay of the bio-medical, functional, social and environmental contexts of individuals so labelled, at the same time, critical and social constructionist critique has highlighted problems with the assumptions at the foundation of these identification and classificatory systems (Rapley 2004). These approaches, for example, explore life history (Goodley 1996), subjectivity (Yates, Dyson, and Hiles 2008), examine power/knowledge relations (Roets 2009) and the processes of social control of defective identities (Peter 2000) to disrupt historically accepted orthodoxy on the nature and experience of intellectual disability.

The operation of diagnosis and classification mechanisms in framing judgements about intellectual disability and eligibility for social services has been fundamentally called into question by Whitaker (2013), who provides a powerful critique from within the psy-complex itself. In examining whether the construct of intellectual disability remains 'fit for purpose' (2), Whitaker demonstrates statistically and socially that IQ and adaptive behaviour cannot be measured with any reliable accuracy, arguing that a range of such factors make diagnosis of intellectual disability 'a lottery' (134). This lottery it is argued has to do with patterns of assessment across the life course – that those who acquire a diagnosis as children may not necessarily acquire the same diagnosis if assessed as adults and vice versa; with geo-political positioning where the intellectual demands of the environment may vary across global Northern and Southern contexts; and are shaped by other dimensions of social stratification and identity including gender and social disadvantage as well as contact with social and justice services.

The significance of diagnosis and classification to conceptualization, identification and intervention in challenging behaviour goes beyond their self-evident function as categories for sorting and accessing social services. Rather, they enable the generation of an ideological conception of the abnormal mind/body (Michalko 2009) which Nunkoosing and Haydon-Laurelut (2012) argue 'enables challenging behaviour to be made to appear as part of intellectual disability itself' (198). This assignment of and association between diagnoses of impairment and challenging behaviour has the effect of linking individual biological difference with abnormal human interaction in the form of behaviours that are disruptive, dangerous or disturbing. Linking biology and behaviour makes abnormality appear as an inevitable or naturalized outcome of the presence of a diagnosed impairment which in turn legitimates existing social and care structures (Nunkoosing 2000) whose function is to identify and manage this abnormalcy.

Wilcox, Finlay, and Edmonds (2006), utilizing interviews with care staff of men and women with challenging behaviour, deepen this understanding by suggesting two key intersecting discourses at work in the construction of challenging behaviour in such service contexts: firstly, that of 'individual pathology' (202) whereby abnormal behaviours emanate from already present disordered biology, often referred to in psy-medico discourse as 'comorbidity', or acquired due to deficits of learning and socialization that accrue to impairment and as such are both stable and internal. Importantly, Wilocx et al.'s social constructionist analysis further highlights two individual pathology discourses used solely in the construction of women's challenging behaviour, associating 'the menstrual cycle with intensified "irrationality"' (209) and 'the character flaws of being "manipulative or attention-seeking"' (209) as central to the gendered construction of challenging behaviour in women. These gendered discourses they argue are necessary because 'while dominant ideologies easily associate inherent violent tendencies with maleness, this "extra work" is required to claim that women's violence is caused by internal factors' (213). Wilcox et al. (2006) also identify a 'contextual discourse' (204), where challenging behaviour might be seen as an understandable reaction to the circumstances and environments in which such people are located, a key foundation underpinning behaviourist paradigms which emphasize situational antecedents and consequences as giving rise to and sustaining challenging behaviour.

Nunkoosing and Haydon-Laurelut (2012) utilize Goffman's ([1963] 1968) concept of stigma and Foucault's ideas of disciplinary power (1977) and the power–knowledge axis (1988) to argue that responses to challenging behaviour may be read as

> the exercise of bio-power over the non-docile body, and that through the application of the pathological gaze people with challenging behaviour are constructed as in need of surveillance as a result of their defective biology or/and mind rather than the disabling social arrangements' (Nunkoosing and Haydon-Laurelut 2012, 204)

in which they are positioned. This suggests a reading of challenging behaviour that moves beyond essentialist notions of impairment and abnormality to the intersection of personal, social, cultural and regulatory practices. This opens up interrogation of the discourse of challenging behaviours and its location within spaces, places and scales of surveillance, when 'they are products of relationships and of people who do not want to subject themselves, their identities, their bodies to the disciplinary regimes of care' (Nunkoosing and Haydon-Laurelut 2012, 203). Here, historicity, politics, relationality and resistance emerge as alternate readings of challenging behaviour.

Nunkoosing and Haydon-Laurelut (2012) conceive of challenging behaviour as both excess and absence:

> too much anxiety, too much agitation, too much answering back, too much noise, too much aggression, too much seeking isolation, too much unwanted emotion, too much anger, too much love. Not enough obedience, not enough talk, not enough sociability. (198)

These excesses and absences can be observed as 'abnormal' behaviour which is both inwardly and outwardly directed and produced at an individual and a societal scale. Evidence suggests that outer directed behaviours are more likely to result in referral for specialist intervention (Lowe, Felce, and Blackman 1995) but that, despite having an equally significant negative impact, inner directed behaviours are less likely to result in referral and specialist support (Allen et al. 2006). Nonetheless, inwardly directed actions such as withdrawal and self-harm and outward aggression and outburst might both be understood as embodied reactions to psychical distress (Marks 1999). It has been recognized in the application of psychotherapeutic approaches to people with intellectual disability that 'the majority have deeply troubled lives and come with very painful histories' (Cottis 2009, 4). Histories of trauma and physical and sexual abuse cannot therefore be bracketed from presenting challenging behaviour.

At a broader scale, Clegg (2006) posits that 'promoting empowerment and autonomy pressurizes people with intellectual disability to perform at peak capacity too much of the time and loses sight of the way intellectual disability affects their lives' (132). This pressure to normalize through empowerment imposes the liberal values of autonomy and self-determination onto many for whom this is unattainable (Dowse 2009; Reinders 2000) and 'runs the risk of erasing mutuality and relationships from their lives' (Clegg 2006, 131). Together, these conditions speak to the need for a 'challenging epistemology' (Goodley 2001), not only for intellectual disability but for the challenging behaviour which is marked and labelled in the lives of many. Yates, Dyson, and Hiles (2008), invoking a Foucaldian analysis of subjectivity in intellectual disability, suggest that:

> at the heart of everything, there is a subject both constituted as an object of thought within systems of knowledge (power) and at the same time actively engaged in their own projects of selfhood and struggling with the ways that their subjectivities are constituted and power takes hold of them (256).

Moreover, as Nunkoosing and Haydon-Laurelut (2012) observe, 'the person with challenging behaviour does not just have troubles, he or she is seen as trouble' (198). This marks out challenging behaviour as inherently relational – whether as acts of resistance, as responses to existential trauma or as manifestations of unknowable pathologies of the mind, people with challenging behaviour do something to themselves selves or others which mark them as vulnerable to abnormality and social exclusion (Emerson 1995) and on the basis of which they are drawn into relations of dependency and intervention.

Responding to challenging behaviour

Responses to challenging behaviour are broadly premised on directing an individual away from abnormality and towards normalcy. It has been argued here that challenging behaviour can be understood as an embodied response that is multi-causal, multi-factorial, historically contingent and emergent which positions the individual as at risk or vulnerable to a range of negative outcomes as a result of their behaviour, primary among these being insufficient or ineffective support from services. However, responses and the interventions they necessitate are themselves determined by and deterministic of pervasive and cumulative cycles of individual, social and criminal/legal intervention. Consider the following two examples[1]:

Casey

A young Aboriginal Australian woman, Casey, has various labels including intellectual disability, Attention Deficit Hyperactivity Disorder and a range of behavioural, emotional and mental health diagnoses. She has a long history of self-harm, physical abuse and trauma as a young person, with problematic alcohol and drug use from childhood and very poor school attendance ceasing any attendance at 13. At this age, Casey begins frequent calls to the Police emergency number when 'no service is required'[2] and is on multiple occasions found walking the streets at night, 'highly agitated' and threatening suicide. Police are also called to attend incidents where Casey is found damaging property and climbing on the roof of various buildings including the School, the Hospital and the offices of the Child Protection Agency, refusing to come down. This continues for some months and as a result on the eighth occasion, she is picked up by Police, and after her mother informs Police that she is 'unable to have the child at home' she is taken to the local hospital and admitted under the Mental Health Act, where she is restrained, sedated and released the following morning. On the ninth occasion, a Doctor from the hospital informs the Police that 'it was his professional opinion that the young person was not in need of medical or mental intervention' and Casey is refused admission to the hospital. The Police and Doctor concur that 'the young person just enjoyed the attention her behaviour generated' and Casey is taken into Police custody, charged and given bail. The next day Police are again called, Casey is arrested, bail refused and charged by Police. She subsequently moves in to youth justice custody.

Curtis

A young man labelled with moderate intellectual disability, Curtis, resides in a group home to which he has recently moved from the family home after his parents indicated they could no longer manage his violent outbursts, particularly against his younger brother. Curtis is identified by staff to be 'unpredictable' and develops a dislike of a young male co-resident whom he begins to physically target. The manager of the residence calls on specialist clinical support staff to assess Curtis and a behaviour support plan is developed for his management which includes 'physically redirecting Curtis away from the co-resident and verbally reminding him that everyone has the right to be safe in the group home'. After two months, Curtis commits a 'serious physical assault' on his co-resident, resulting in injury. As an immediate result, Curtis is prescribed psychotropic medication to 'calm him down', and in the following weeks, a review of the behaviour support plan is instigated and lockable doors are installed in the premises to keep the two young men physically separated, which staff need to remember to keep locked when both residents are at home.

The challenge of behaviour in these two examples is situated not simply within the person with disability, not embodied by their gender, race or socio-economic status (Wilcox et al. 2006), nor within the relationship between the person and their intervention agents nor within the environment in which all are located. Instead, the problems are *emergent*, that is they are the outcomes of these three dynamically combined across a lifetime context of vulnerability and dependency. This approach sees the challenging behaviour as embodied and as relationally produced and constructed – that is – as residing not solely in the individual and not solely in the environment and those others within it – but emerges and is responded to and sustained or otherwise in the *interrelationship* between person, responder and environment in the context of histories of vulnerability and dependency. This reading signals a departure from approaches which premise the person and their environment and which omit scrutiny of the relational experience of vulnerability, dependence and care (an issue taken up in the following section) and the possibility of challenging behaviour as acts of resistance to these.

Taking this more emergent and relational view opens up to scrutiny the nexus of contexts of vulnerability, dependence and care in the production of and responses to challenging behaviour. As can be observed in the above examples, who, how, where and what is legitimized as the object and processes of intervention vary and are framed by what can be focused on, reported and referred to as challenging behaviour. For those predominantly outside the gaze of the disability system and who have histories of disadvantage and trauma such as Casey, their 'bio-medical abnormality' is overshadowed by other identities such as offender and victim. The ongoing complexity of trauma, marginalization and disadvantage experienced by Indigenous people as a result of colonization (Baldry and Cunneen 2014) is seldom recognized or invoked as explanatory or extenuating factors in the construction of Casey's 'abnormality' (Baldry et al. 2015). Despite the widely acknowledged and disproportionately high levels of violence experienced by Indigenous women and children (Davis and McGlade 2006) and recognition that the therapeutic needs of Indigenous persons are significantly different from non-Indigenous persons as the trauma resulting from ongoing colonization must be understood and addressed (Sherwood 2009; Westerman 2002), responses to Casey fall to Police as front-line 'care' managers (Baldry and Dowse 2013), with spatial seclusion in the hospital and eventually the prison, and where physical and chemical restraint are the key immediate responses. These forms of response to young Aboriginal Australians have also been highlighted as systemic and patterned in the recent outing in the Australian media of the use of 'spithoods', restraint chairs and tear gas on juvenile detainees in the 'Behavioural Management Unit' of the Northern Territory's Don Dale Youth Detention Centre (Meldrum-Hanna and Worthington 2016). Taken together, the treatment of Casey and the inmates of Don Dale show a unique and pervasive 'pattern of abuse, deprivation and punishment' (Meldrum-Hanna and Worthington 2016) applied to Aboriginal young people whose behaviours challenge. That this is occurring both in the community and in the spaces of juvenile incarceration demonstrates an urgent need to address the particularly pernicious and malignant approach to managing the challenge of so-called 'abnormal' behaviour in Australia's First Peoples.

For those within the disability social care system such as Curtis, where their bio-medical diagnoses precede them into social space and therefore staff are tasked more directly with responsibility for managing the person and their challenging behaviour, responses may appear more humane, as in positive behaviour support. In the reality of Curtis's life, the label of intellectual disability permits the service to intervene in his life in ways that would be intolerable elsewhere. In both cases, the intervention repertoire differs only marginally and by degree. Responses including mundane acts of physical handling through to seclusion and physical and chemical restraint occur at different scales for Casey and Curtis; however, all are invoked based on criteria associated with clinical, medico-legal and community-sanctioned modes of intervention which require various agencies to take responsibility for control of the behaviourally 'troubled'. The question remains as to whether such responses ameliorate these 'troubles' or add to them.

In the examples of Casey and Curtis, the problems of time and scale in the relations of intervention are writ large. In these examples, the modes of intervention applied to abnormal or challenging behaviours are premised on reducing ambiguity (Sewell 2016). Responses are applied clinically and operationally to particular presentations such as climbing on the roof of support and care agencies and lashing out at a co-resident as abnormal 'acts in the moment' that are open to interpretation by those tasked with intervening. The problem here is not solely the remedy that is applied to the presentation of particular instances of challenging behaviour but that the emergence of the problem is left to inference. Police, medical personnel and disability support staff responding to people who exhibit behaviours that challenge, who are often unfamiliar with individual histories, are placed in a position of having to utilize an 'inferred story' (Lipsky 2010, 83) of the actual presentation to inform their response. Here, the power to make inferences sits with those in the immediate environment or context while the presenting 'problem behaviour' is likely to have been a lifetime in the making.

In this broader context, it is only certain aspects of an inferred story that are either knowable or permissible. What is permissible is often confined to individualized instances of trauma, abuse or violence, largely dissociated from recognition of systemic or cultural violence or abuse or existential or psycho-emotional pain and suffering. The recognition emerging in Australia (Senate Community Affairs References Committee 2015) and internationally (Department of Health 2012) of endemic violence and abuse in institutional and care settings is one such example of emerging change in what can be recognized. For Casey, the failure of agencies of support to protect her from neglect and abuse is construed as 'attention seeking' and for Curtis, his perhaps existential crisis in processing his difference from his brother or his housemate is reduced to 'unpredictability'. This tendency to reductionism and the search for temporal specificity and certainty in the causation of challenging behaviour (Sewell 2016) tacitly authorize targeted interventions aimed to restore or assist the individual to approach privileged ideals of normalcy but which assume unproblematized histories and relations of vulnerability and dependence.

Whether legitimated through legal or sub-legal mechanisms such as those associated with the application of restrictive practices in disability care settings, operationalized systemically through clinical or medical practice or policing and criminal legal processes, responses to challenging behaviour are predominantly applied to the material body. These are variously premised on punishment and control of the individual (in the case of Casey) or the safeguarding of individuals and the protection of others such as staff, families and co-residents (in the case of Curtis). However, individuals experience these responses both singly and cumulatively in spaces and across time.

Hodge (2015), in examining everyday practices of seemingly innocuous and mundane physical handling, invites consideration of the ways that individuals experience such contact as non-consensual and questions what frequent low-level physical control by others might mean to individuals themselves. Codifying permissible and appropriate physical interventions in residential, clinical or policing settings – as seen for example in the UK approach to 'positive handling' – runs the risk that those doing the handling become more confident in intervening physically, perversely leading to increased physical interventions rather than reduction (Baker and Shephard 2005; Deveau and McDonnell 2009). In relation to the more serious and substantial practices of physical restraint, a recent systematic review focusing on the experiences of restraint among people with intellectual disabilities (Heyvaert et al. 2015) noted a discrepancy between those using restraint and those receiving it, where the former generally reported it was used as a last resort while the later often reported that the use of restraint had not been justified (74). Those who were the objects of restraint reported a range of negative feelings including 'general dislike, sadness, distress, desperation, anger, confusion, fear, anxiety, feeling stressed, feeling upset and feeling helpless against the degree of force used when held in restraint; physical experiences during the restraint were pain, harm, discomfort, but sometimes also comfort'. (64). Further, the review noted that 'sometimes anger and frustration experienced during the restraint resulted in more aggressive behaviour' (66). This is in line with the findings of Cambridge (1999) whose research suggests that the presence of challenging behaviour in turn makes individuals more vulnerable to abuse and attest to the challenging practices that challenging behaviour evokes.

Insights into the experiences and impacts of chemical constraint via the use of psychotropic medications as responses to behaviours that challenge (as seen for both Casey and Curtis) have been explored in the context of Mad studies. Fabris and Aubrecht (2014) provide a powerful analysis of chemical constraint based on their experiences as psychiatric survivors and, while diagnostically distinct, these reflections are similarly premised on the assumption that 'bodily experiences are organized and ordered through diagnosis' (187). Psychotropic medications, even though they are a standard treatment response for distress or social conflict, may not be safe or effective, and can have significant negative side effects which themselves change the brain's chemical processes and structures which may then require additional intervention (Whitaker 2010). In reflecting on their experiences of chemical constraint, Fabris and Aubrecht suggest that 'psychiatric prescriptions make it possible to define social suffering and dissent as signs or symptoms of the existence of personal disorder and moral weakness, rather than embodied responses to inequitable social systems' (187). Importantly, their work shows the centrality of chemical constraint to practices of normalcy in that 'psychiatric medication offers an initiation into normalcy – a rite of passage that is represented as an essential to survival within institutional settings' (186).

Notwithstanding the immediate negative consequences of both physical and chemical responses to challenging behaviour, such responses can be seen as marking out those who are vulnerable and become predictive of future consequences and responses. While responses are often directed towards the immediate cessation of harm to self or others and to modify the person's environment or circumstances so as to avoid recurrence of behaviour that challenges, for individuals in both disability and in criminal justice contexts, systemic markers of their vulnerability accrue from multiple preceding and often mundane interventions. Those who are diagnosed and serviced by the disability system have their abnormality clinically and procedurally recognized resulting in their vulnerability sanctioned as deserving of intervention since it is the mandate of systems of social care to do this very thing. Their disorder and the disruption it entails are then seen to be the legitimate object of legally and socially sanctioned interventions in their behaviour. For those with challenging behaviour who are largely outside systems of social care, their vulnerability is constructed as 'attention seeking' or as criminal offending and is dealt with via similarly sanctioned processes of medicalization and criminalization. In both contexts, the presence of vulnerability is tied to dependency and in particular, dependency on interventions applied via behavioural management or sanction to move the individual towards normalcy. This ascription of individual vulnerability is itself a relational intervention invested in systems to diagnose and of individuals to submit to the label. This designation and the dependencies it creates suppress consideration of the multiple and compounding systemic factors at play, which are beyond the individuals themselves.

Normalcy and vulnerability

Theoretical conceptions of vulnerability provide a useful framework for disentangling the ambivalent legal and social responsibilities and interventions for people whose behaviour is identified as challenging. The notion of vulnerability however has long had a problematic relationship to disability. Leach Scully (2014) identifies this unease as associated with the pernicious application of 'ascribed global vulnerability to all people with disabilities, identifying it with the tendency on the part of nondisabled people to extrapolate particular vulnerabilities to a blanket assumption across the whole of a person's life' (209), resulting in 'exclusion from full social and political citizenship' (210). While recognizing this uneasy positioning of vulnerability, the utility of the concept in examining the challenge of behaviour, already deeply inured with discourses of abnormality and dependency, lies in its attention to emergent mechanisms that perversely exacerbate vulnerability through particular relations of intervention.

At its broadest level, theorizing of vulnerability applied to disability highlights processes whereby 'those whose bodies or behaviours diverge from the norm are singled out as dependent and in need of extraordinary treatment, either to restore them to normal or to offer them ongoing protections that normal people do not need' (Leach Scully 2014, 206). The presence of abnormality is therefore inherently implicated in the ascription of vulnerability. For people whose behaviours challenge, their abnormality and vulnerability are seen to be embodied in the performance of behaviours that are socially disruptive, individually dangerous or culturally or morally disturbing. These in turn become connected in time and space with certain forms of dependency, most particularly dependency on others to intervene to direct behaviour towards normative ideals of functioning for the purpose of safeguarding, well-being and inclusion. The responsibility for this identification and amelioration falls to agencies of social care and control and their practices of intervention and management. However, as we have seen in the experiences of Casey and Curtis, these interventions are not simply benevolent and restorative, but rather may be generative of further vulnerability. Being conferred the status 'vulnerable' has the potential to be a new stigma, an invisible administrative status that legitimizes 'interventions' and special procedures. Vulnerability is created as a power–knowledge relation of the psy-professional (Ecclestone and Goodley 2014) and being seen as vulnerable serves to justify treatments that would not be conscionable in almost any other context.

Dodds (2014) provides a useful perspective on vulnerability as embodied and relational, forging particular links between vulnerability and dependency, which help to explain the potentially perverse and damaging impacts of responses to people with challenging behaviour such as Casey and Curtis. In arguing that

> a more extensive account of the relationships among dependency, vulnerability and responsibility for care is needed to understand fully the way in which attributions of responsibility arising from vulnerability generate further vulnerabilities for the person taken to be responsible as well as for the vulnerable person (189)

Dodds posits the concept of 'pathogenic vulnerability' (197). This calls attention to the ways that socio-institutional structures generate dependency which may exacerbate vulnerability 'if institutional arrangements fail to address the complex relationships between dependency and vulnerability' (196).

Conclusion

It is not difficult to see that for Casey and Curtis, their initial vulnerability is exacerbated through the sequence of responses to their challenging behaviour. These responses importantly are generally a-historical in that they are point in time reactions to various 'behavioural' incidents and are premised on the safeguarding of those who are attributed the challenging label as well as the protection of families, co-residents, social care workers and the community at large. Responses then systemically produce and reproduce multiple relations of dependency. Enactment of these relations of intervention occur through institutional arrangements of care and control which are ultimately determined by policy settings which address vulnerability as an anomaly and those who experience it as dichotomized from 'normal' human life. While ever structural conditions and the limited interventions they permit via legal, medical and social policy mechanisms fail to take account of these complex relations of dependency and care, those whose behaviour challenges will continue to be made vulnerable.

Notes

1. Examples used in this paper are excerpts of cases studies drawn from the Mental Health and Cognitive Disability in the Criminal Justice system data-set compiled from Australian Research Council (ARC)

Linkage project, 'People With Mental Health Disorders and Cognitive Disabilities (MHDCD) in the Criminal Justice System (CJS) in NSW', University of NSW – Chief Investigators E. Baldry, L. Dowse and I Webster. www.mhdcd.unsw.edu.au. The MHDCD data-set links extant human service and criminal justice administrative data on a cohort of people whose diagnoses are known. Case study narratives are produced by extraction and compilation of all available data on an individual and then de-identified. Ethics approval for the MHDCD study was obtained from all relevant human service and criminal justice agency ethics bodies, from the Aboriginal Health and Medical Research Council Ethics Committee and from the University of New South Wales Human Research Ethics Committee.

2. Quotation marks indicate direct quotes taken from Police narratives.

Disclosure statement

No potential conflict of interest was reported by the author.

Funding

The Intellectual Disability Behaviour Support Program at UNSW Australia is supported by funds from the NSW Department of Family and Community Services, Ageing Disability and Home Care.

References

AAIDD (American Association of Intellectual and Developmental Disabilities) 2010. *User's Guide to Intellectual Disability: Definition, Classification, and Systems of Supports.* https://aaidd.org/publications/bookstore-home/product-listing/user's-guide-to-intellectual-disability-definition-classification-and-systems-of-supports#.VyWCGxp94_U.

Allen, D., K. Lowe, E. Jones, W. James, T. Doyle, J. Andrew, and S. Brophy. 2006. "Changing the Face of Challenging Behaviour Services: The Special Projects Team." *British Journal of Learning Disabilities* 34 (4): 237–242.

Baker, P., and J. Shephard. 2005. "The Rebranding of Behavioural Approaches for People with Learning Disabilities and Challenging Behaviour." *Tizard Learning Disability Review* 10: 12–15.

Baldry, E., and C. Cunneen. 2014. "Imprisoned Indigenous Women and the Shadow of Colonial Patriarchy." *ANZ Journal of Criminology* 47: 276–298.

Baldry, E., and L. Dowse. 2013. "Compounding Mental and Cognitive Disability and Disadvantage: Police as Care Managers." In *Policing and the Mentally Ill: International Perspectives*, edited by D. Chappell, 219–234. Boca Raton: CRC Press.

Baldry, E., R. McCausland, L. Dowse, and E. McEntyre. 2015. "*A Predictable and Preventable Path: Aboriginal People with Mental and Cognitive Disabilities in the Criminal Justice System.*" Sydney: UNSW. https://www.mhdcd.unsw.edu.au/.

Biswas, A. B., and F. G. Furniss. 2009. "Life Events and Mental Illness in People with Learning Disabilities." *Psychiatry* 8 (11): 445–447.

Bouras, N., and G. Holt. 2010. *Mental Health Services for Adults with Intellectual Disability.* New York: Psychology Press.

Cambridge, P. 1999. "The First Hit: A Case Study of the Physical Abuse of People with Learning Disabilities and Challenging Behaviours in a Residential Service." *Disability and Society* 14 (3): 285–308.

Clegg, J. 2006. "Understanding Intellectually Disabled Clients in Clinical Psychology." In *Disability and Psychology*, edited by D. Goodley and R. Lawthom, 123–140. Basingstoke: Palgrave Macmillan.

Cottis, T. 2009. "Introduction." In *Intellectual Disability, Trauma and Psychotherapy*, edited by T. Cottis, 1–8. Hove: Routledge.

Davis, M., and H. McGlade. 2006. "International Human Rights Law and the Recognition of Aboriginal Customary Law." Background Paper 10. In *Aboriginal Customary Laws: Background Papers*. Project No 94, 381, 415–419. Perth: Law Reform Commission WA.

Department of Health. 2012. *Transforming Care: A National Response to Winterbourne View Hospital Department of Health Review: Final Report.* London: Department of Health. https://www.gov.uk/government/uploads/system/uploads/attachment_data/file/213215/final-report.pdf.

Deveau, R., and A. McDonnell. 2009. "As the Last Resort: Reducing the Use of Restrictive Physical Interventions Using Organisational Approaches." *British Journal of Learning Disabilities* 37: 172–177.

Dodds, S. 2014. "Dependence, Care, and Vulnerability." In *Vulnerability: New essays in ethics and feminist philosophy*, edited by C. Mackenzie, W. Rogers and S. Dodds, 204–221. New York: Oxford University Press.

Dowse, L. 2009. "'Some People are Never Going to be able to do that'. Challenges for People with Intellectual Disability in the 21st Century." *Disability and Society* 24 (5): 571–584.

Ecclestone, K., and D. Goodley. 2014. "Political and Educational Springboard or Straight Jacket? Theorising Post/human Subjects in an Age of Vulnerability." *Discourse: Studies in the Cultural Politics of Education* 37 (2): 175–188. doi: 10.1080/01596306.2014.927112.

Emerson, E. 1995. *Challenging Behaviour: Analysis and Intervention in People with Intellectual Disabilities*. Cambridge: Cambridge University Press.

Emerson, E., C. Kiernan, A. Alborz, D. Reeves, H. Mason, R. Swarbrick, L. Mason, and C. Hatton. 2001. "The Prevalence of Challenging Behaviours: A Total Population Study." *Research in Developmental Disabilities* 22: 77–93.

Fabris, E., and K. Aubrecht. 2014. "Chemical Constraint: Experiences of Psychiatric Coercion, Restraint and Detention as Cerceratory Techniques." In *Disability Incarcerated: Imprisonment and disability in the United States and Canada*, edited by L. Ben-Moshe, C. Chapman and A. Carey, 185–199. New York: Palgrave Macmillan.

Foucault, M. 1977. *Discipline and Punish: The Birth of the Prison*. London: Allen Lane, Penguin.

Foucault, M. 1988. *Technologies of the Self: A Seminar with Michel Foucault*. Edited by H. Martin, H. Gutman, and P. H. Hutton. London: Tavistock Publications.

Goffman, E. [1963] 1968. *Stigma: Notes on the Management of Spoiled Identity*. Harmondsworth: Penguin.

Goodley, D. 1996. "Tales of Hidden Lives: A Critical Examination of Life History Research with People Who Have Learning Difficulties." *Disability and Society* 11 (3): 333–348.

Goodley, D. 2001. "'Learning Difficulties', the Social Model of Disability and Impairment: Challenging Epistemologies." *Disability and Society* 16 (2): 207–231.

Hastings, R. P., C. Hatton, J. L. Taylor, and C. Maddison. 2004. "Life Events and Psychiatric Symptoms in Adults with Intellectual Disabilities." *Journal of Intellectual Disability Research* 48 (1): 42–46.

Heyvaert, M., L. Saenen, B. Maes, and P. Onghena. 2015. "Systematic Review of Restraint Interventions for Challenging Behaviour Among Persons with Intellectual Disabilities: Focus on Experiences." *Journal of Applied Research in Intellectual Disabilities* 28 (2): 61–80.

Hodge, N. 2015. "Protecting the Rights of Pupils with Autism When Meeting the Challenge of Behaviour." *British Journal of Learning Disabilities* 43 (3): 194–200.

Lipsky, M. 2010. *Street-level Bureaucracy: Dilemmas of the Individual in Public Services*. New York: Russell Sage Foundation Publications.

Leach Scully, J. 2014. "Disability and Vulnerability: On Bodies, Dependence, and Power." In *Vulnerability: New Essays in Ethics and Feminist Philosophy*, edited by C. Mackenzie, W. Rogers and S. Dodds, 204–221. New York: Oxford University Press.

Lowe, K., D. Felce, and D. Blackman. 1995. "People with Learning Disabilities and Challenging Behaviour: The Characteristics of Those Referred and Not Referred to Specialist Teams." *Psychological Medicine* 25: 595–603.

Marks, D. 1999. *Disability: Controversial Debates and Psychosocial Perspectives*. London: Routledge.

Meldrum-Hanna, C., and E. Worthington. 2016. "Evidence of 'Torture' of Children Held in Don Dale Detention Centre Uncovered by Four Corners." *ABC News*. www.abc.net.au/news/2016-07-25/four-corners-evidence-of-kids-tear-gas-in-don-dale-prison/7656128.

Michalko, R. 2009. "The Excessive Appearance of Disability." *International Journal of Qualitative Studies in Education* 22 (1): 65–74.

Nunkoosing, K. 2000. "Constructing Learning Disability: Consequences for Men and Women with Learning Disabilities." *Journal of Learning Disabilities* 4 (1): 49–62.

Nunkoosing, K., and M. Haydon-Laurelut. 2012. "Intellectual Disability Trouble: Foucault and Goffman on 'Challenging Behaviour'." In *Disability and Social Theory: New Developments and Directions*, edited by D. Goodley, B. Hughes, and L. Davis, 195–211. Basingstoke: Palgrave Macmillan.

Peter, D. 2000. "Dynamics of Discourse: A Case Study Illuminating Power Relations in Mental Retardation." *Mental Retardation* 38 (4): 354–362.

Rapley, M. 2004. *The Social Construction of Intellectual Disability*. Cambridge: Cambridge University Press.

Reinders, H. S. 2000. *The Future of the Disabled in Liberal Society: An ethical analysis*. Notre Dame, IN: University of Notre Dame Press.

Roets, G. 2009. "Unravelling Mr. President's Nomad Lands: Travelling to Interdisciplinary Frontiers of Knowledge in Disability Studies." *Disability and Society* 24 (6): 689–701.

Rose, N. 1985. *The Psychological Complex: Psychology, politics and society in England, 1869–1939*. London: Routledge.

Royal College of Psychiatrists and Royal College of Speech and Language Therapists. 2007. *Clinical and Service Guidelines for Supporting People with Learning Disabilities Who are at Risk of Receiving Abusive or Restrictive Practices*. London: RCP.

Schalock, R. L., S. A. Borthwick-Duffy, V. J. Bradley, W. H. E. Buntinx, D. L. Coulter, E. M. Craig, S. C. Gomez, et al. 2010. *Intellectual Disability: Definition, Classification, and Systems of Supports*. 11th ed. Washington: American Association on Intellectual and Developmental Disabilities.

Senate Community Affairs References Committee. 2015. *Violence, Abuse and Neglect Against People with Disability in Institutional and Residential Settings, Including the Gender and Age Related Dimensions, and the Particular Situation of Aboriginal and Torres Strait Islander People with Disability, and Culturally and Linguistically Diverse People with Disability*. Canberra: Commonwealth of Australia. file:///Users/z9400323/Downloads/report%20(5).pdf.

Sewell, A. 2016. "Complex Needs: Multiple Disadvantage and Reductionism in the Enactment of Policy." PhD. thesis, University of NSW, Sydney.

Sherwood, J. 2009. "Who is Not Coping with Colonization? Laying out the Map for Decolonization." *Australasian Psychiatry* 17: s24–S27.

Tilley, E., S. Ledger, and J. Bardsley. 2015. *A Review of the Literature Concerning Learning Disability, Challenging Behaviour and Social Work*. Open University. http://cdn.basw.co.uk/upload/basw_111416-3.pdf.

Westerman, T. G. 2002. "Psychological Interventions with Aboriginal People." *Connect Magazine*, Health Department of Western Australia.

Whitaker, R. 2010. *Anatomy of an Epidemic: Magic bullets, Psychiatric Drugs, and an Astonishing Rise in Mental Illness in America*. New York: Crown.

Whitaker, S. 2013. *Intellectual Disability: An Inability to Cope with an Intellectually Demanding World*. Basingstoke: Palgrave Macmillan.

WHO (World Health Organisation) 2001. *International Classification of Functioning, Disability and Health*. http://www.who.int/classifications/icf/en/.

Wilcox, E., W. M. Finlay, and J. Edmonds. 2006. "'His Brain is Totally Different': An Analysis of Care-staff Explanations of Aggressive Challenging Behaviour and the Impact of Gendered Discourses." *British Journal of Social Psychology* 45: 197–216.

Yates, S., S. Dyson, and D. Hiles. 2008. "Beyond Normalization and Impairment: Theorising Subjectivity in Learning Difficulties – Theory and Practice." *Disability and Society* 23 (3): 247–258.

Making the abject: problem-solving courts, addiction, mental illness and impairment

Claire Spivakovsky and Kate Seear

ABSTRACT

The advent of 'problem-solving courts' (e.g. drug courts, mental health courts) is claimed by some to represent a significant shift in the administration of justice. Problem-solving courts purport to address the underlying social, medical and/or psychological issues that are often understood as driving certain populations' contact with criminal justice systems. Although there is a large body of research examining the operation and efficacy of such courts, there is minimal critical research on how these courts have been conceptualized by governments as logical, suitable 'solutions' to both particular 'problems' in society and 'problem populations', and the various implications thereof. In this paper, we examine these issues through an adaptation of Australian post-structuralist theorist, Carol Bacchi's theoretical framework. Bacchi argues that policy 'problems' do not precede policy interventions, but that 'problems' are instead constituted by and given meaning through implicit policy representations. In this paper we consider how two Australian problem-solving courts – Victoria's Drug Court and the Assessment and Referral Court List for people with cognitive impairments or mental illness – have been conceptualized by Victoria's Parliament to target their populations, the 'problems' they purport to address, and with what effects for targeted populations.

Introduction

This article is concerned with the ways that certain 'problems' and 'solutions' of normalcy and disability become associated with, constituted by, and given meaning through political, discursive representations. Specifically, we are interested in tracing how the growing number of people with cognitive impairments, mental illness and/or alcohol or other drug (AOD)[1] dependence in Australian prisons has emerged as a central 'problem' of law and justice in the past two decades, and the effects that occur when 'problem-solving' courts take shape as the logical, necessary 'solution'. To do this, we analyse the parliamentary debates surrounding the creation of two problem-solving courts in the Australian state of Victoria: the Drug Court, and the Assessment and Referral Court List (a specialist court list for people with cognitive impairments and/or mental illness). Adapting Carol Bacchi's (2009) theoretical framework for analysing policy 'problems' to the study of law, we draw out the different ways that these specialist jurisdictions have been conceptualized in political, formative debates, focusing on the 'problems' they are purportedly designed to solve, and the effects for their target populations. We reflect on the ways that these debates provide access to deep-seated presuppositions and pervasive cultural logics about agency, capacity, disability and crime, and enable certain modes of governance to take form.

The emergence of 'problem' populations and therapeutic 'solutions'

There are a growing and disproportionate number of people entering Australian prisons who experience AOD dependence, cognitive impairments and/or mental illness. While only 15 per cent of Australia's general population use illicit drugs (AIHW 2011), this number increases to 70 per cent for prison entrants, with many experiencing AOD dependence (AIHW 2013). At the same time, 31 per cent of prisoners have been treated for a mental health disorder (AIHW 2012) – a figure which is approximately 2.5 times higher than the general population (ABS 2010) – and somewhere between 25 per cent (Morrell, Merbitz, and Jain 1998) and 82 per cent (Schofield, Butler, and Hollis 2007) of prisoners are living with a traumatic brain injury. These figures have prompted important questions about the reasons why people experiencing AOD dependence, cognitive impairments and/or mental illness are over-represented in criminal justice systems, as well as queries about the appropriateness and effectiveness of criminal justice interventions (see Butler et al. 2005; Lamberti et al. 2001; Prins 2011). In response to such questions, specialist, 'problem-solving' courts have emerged.

Problem-solving courts are purposely designed, specialized jurisdictions which aim to address the underlying social, medical and/or psychological issues that are believed to underpin certain populations' contact with criminal justice systems. Derived from the therapeutic jurisprudence movement of the United States, the courts operate on the premise that law, its personnel and processes can have therapeutic effects on participants' wellbeing (Wexler and Winick 1996). The courts aim to foster the therapeutic potential of the law by taking into consideration both the treatment and justice concerns of the accused and any victims. The result of this consideration can take several forms, including diversionary processes (that is, processes which divert people from the traditional court system, offering a chance to avoid a criminal record), and providing intensive, mandatory, medical and psychological treatments in the community.

Scholars have interrogated the development of problem-solving courts from a number of fronts. Predominately, research has been evaluative in nature, measuring the courts' clinical effects (e.g. Boothroyd et al. 2005; Cosden et al. 2003), or their capacity to manage risk and reduce recidivism (e.g. Herinckz et al. 2005; McNeil and Binder 2007; Steadman et al. 2011). Some have also investigated the consequences of merging adversarial and therapeutic court approaches, raising concerns about the extended periods of time offenders spend in contact with criminal justice systems through these approaches, and the intrusive nature of the interventions imposed (e.g. Boldt 2002; Hanna-Moffat and Maurutto 2012; Moore 2007). This article seeks to engage with problem-solving courts in another way. Rather than focusing on the putative impacts of these courts – intended or otherwise – we are interested in tracing the different processes of 'problem' construction that have informed the development of Victoria's Drug Court and Assessment and Referral Court List, the pervasive cultural logics which inform this construction process, and the effects this have for targeted populations. To draw out these different facets, we turn to the analytical strategy of the highly influential Australian post-structuralist theorist, Carol Bacchi.[2]

Bacchi, policy problematization and the law

Inspired by Michel Foucault's (1977) work on 'problematisation', Bacchi is concerned with 'thinking problematically' about policy-making. For Bacchi, policy 'problems' are not fixed or stable phenomena; they 'do not exist "out there" in society, waiting to be "solved" through timely and perspicacious policy interventions' (Bacchi and Eveline 2010, 111). Rather, working with Foucault's observation that discursive and non-discursive practices produce things as 'objects for thought' (Foucault 1988, 257), Bacchi proposes that policies *give shape* to "problems"; they do not *address* them' (2009, x, emphasis original). Bacchi argues that 'problems' are constituted through and given meaning by the *representations* embedded within public policy. Bacchi thus encourages us to critically interrogate the presuppositions and conceptual logics which underpin policies and policy-making practices, unearthing the problem representations that purport to naturally 'pre-exist' the policy-making process.

Interrogating presuppositions and conceptual logics is important because, as Bacchi points out, policy representations are 'political interventions' (2009, 35) which 'imagine' problems, 'in particular ways that have real and meaningful effects' (Bacchi and Eveline 2010, 111). Bacchi identifies three main 'effects':

(1) *discursive effects* – the ways in which problem representations limit what can be thought or said;
(2) *subjectification effects* – the ways in which particular kinds of subjects and subject positions are discursively produced; and
(3) *lived effects* – the 'real' and material repercussions of these problematizations in people's lives (Bacchi 2009; Bacchi and Eveline 2010).

To draw out problem representations and their effects, Bacchi (2009) offers an analytical strategy called 'What's the Problem Represented to be?' This strategy comprises six questions, which can be undertaken together or selectively.[3] The questions are:

(1) What is the 'problem' represented to be in a specific policy or policy proposal?
(2) What presuppositions or assumptions underpin this representation of the 'problem'?
(3) How has this representation of the 'problem' come about?
(4) What is left unproblematic in this problem representation? Where are the silences? Can the 'problem' be thought about differently?
(5) What effects are produced by this representation of the 'problem'?
(6) How/where has this representation of the 'problem' been produced, disseminated and defended? How has it been (or could it be) questioned, disrupted and replaced? (adapted from Bacchi 2009, xii)

In recent years, this strategy for examining policy 'problems' has been adapted to analyses of the law (Lancaster, Seear, and Treloar 2015; Seear and Fraser 2014). Seear and Fraser (2014) argue that Bacchi's strategy is well suited to the study of law and legal processes, because – like policy – it is possible to:

> see the law as reflecting, and in turn re-enacting, the (always changing) values of a given society. If we read legal discourse as does Bacchi on policy, we can expose its role in formulating social problems rather than simply address-ing them. Doing this allows us to create space to critically assess these formulations for their assumptions and oversights, and for the ways in which they might reinforce or exacerbate social inequalities or exclusions as much as ameliorate them. (Seear and Fraser 2014, 828)

In this paper, we extend this work further, analysing the pervasive cultural logics which enable specialist court systems to emerge as logical, wholly beneficial 'solutions' to the growing number of people with AOD dependence, cognitive impairments and/or mental illness entering prisons. We further consider how this process of defining 'solutions' limits what can be said about the lives of people with AOD dependence, cognitive impairments and/or mental illness, and their criminal activity. As such, our focus is not on the everyday operations of the specialist systems themselves, but on the legislative processes through which these courts came about. We explore these processes through an analysis of parliamentary debates pertaining to the development of both the Victorian Drug Court and the Assessment and Referral Court List. Such debates (including the second reading speech) enable us to access the deep-seated presuppositions and claims (both express and implied) about the purported 'true nature' of the particular 'problem' requiring this specialist response. Focusing in particular on questions 1, 2 and 5 of Bacchi's strategy, we trace a few of the effects (discursive, subjectification and lived) on the targeted populations of the courts.

The Victorian drug court

The Victorian Drug Court was established as a division of the Magistrates' Court by the *Sentencing (Amendment) Act 2002* (Vic). Under s4B of the *Magistrates Court Act 1989* (Vic), a proceeding can be adjourned to the Drug Court if it appears that the accused:

- might be eligible for a drug treatment order (DTO),
- resides within a postcode area covered by the Drug Court, and
- consents to the adjournment.

To be eligible for a DTO, several conditions must be satisfied (s18Z *Sentencing Act 1991* (Vic)). Among other things, the accused must be willing to plead guilty and submit to a DTO; they must not be charged with a sexual or violent offence; and crucially, the court must be satisfied on the balance of probabilities that the accused is dependent on drugs or alcohol, and that such dependency contributed to the commission of the offence.

Agency, capacity and the criminogenic addict

The Bill to propose a Drug Court in Victoria was debated in November 2001 and February 2002. These debates reveal a consistent but internally contradictory conceptualization of the 'addicted' subject's agency and capacity to independently make changes in their lives. Although addicts are described as having 'complex individual needs' (Mr Hulls, Parliament of Victoria, Legislative Assembly, 29 November 2001, 2193), they are also constructed as largely predictable, with 'chaotic lifestyles' (Mr Hulls, Parliament of Victoria, Legislative Assembly, 29 November 2001, 2191) that hinder their ability to function normally. Most often, addicts are positioned as incapable of change, rational action and/or self-control, being 'desperate and usually driven by one urge, and that is to get the next hit or whatever you would call it' (Mr Savage, Parliament of Victoria, Legislative Assembly, 27 February 2002, 131). According to members of the Legislative Assembly, addicts live a life of 'despair', trapped by virtue of 'being permanently *caught in a web* of addiction' (Mr Savage, Parliament of Victoria, Legislative Assembly, 27 February 2002, 131; our emphasis). These are people 'who probably will not rehabilitate for the rest of their life' (Dr Dean, Parliament of Victoria, Legislative Assembly, 27 February 2002, 104).

Here, the presumed effects of addiction are represented as harmful, restrictive and devastating for the individuals so affected. Yet despite the apparently significant personal costs of addiction, the 'true problem' to be addressed by law and policy is that of addiction-fuelled crime. Indeed the then Attorney-General Rob Hulls lamented the traditional criminal justice system's approach towards drug use and offending, suggesting that it 'punishes their offending without addressing the *cause* of that offending: drug addiction' (Mr Hulls, Parliament of Victoria, Legislative Assembly, 29 November 2001, 2191; our emphasis).

Hulls' comments reveal an important set of assumptions about the 'problem' at play during the parliamentary debates of 2001–2002: the notion that drug addiction is *inherently criminogenic*. Indeed, 'anti-social behaviour'[4] is described as being '*a result* of their dependency on drugs' (Ms McCall, Parliament of Victoria, Legislative Assembly, 27 February 2002, 121; our emphasis); a 'reality' whereby 'this person is breaking into people's houses *because* he [sic] is a drug addict and that *will continue for so long as he* [sic] *is a drug addict*' (Dr Dean, Parliament of Victoria, Legislative Assembly, 27 February 2002, 103; our emphasis). Similarly, burglary and assault are portrayed as things often done 'to get the money to provide for their drug habit' (Mr Wells, Parliament of Victoria, Legislative Assembly, 27 February 2002, 125). In fact, not only does criminality follow drug use and/or addiction, but there appears to be a pathway of gradually increasing severity that can be identified in many instances:

> Many of those who have been associated with drug dependency have moved from actions within the family circle to petty theft and more serious crime to support their drug habits. The pattern of progression is well and truly established and can be seen in the many cases that we are all aware of. (Mr Stensholt, Parliament of Victoria, Legislative Assembly, 27 February 2002, 123)

This representation of the relationship between crime and addiction has important implications for the construction of the addict's agency. Paradoxically, addicts are largely positioned as lacking agency and the capacity for change, while being simultaneously responsible for their behaviour, and for altering it. In the following passage, for instance, offending is positioned as an 'effect' of addiction, at the same time as the addict is reprimanded for *persisting* with offending. The emphasis on *discouraging* people who use drugs from so doing, while also purportedly *deterring* addicts through the threat of future imprisonment suggests a subject who is agentive, responsive, responsible and capable of change:

> I would hope that what we are looking for in the drug courts is the opportunity to discourage those who have not reached the stage of addiction from continuing their antisocial behaviour. We should therefore view the drug courts in the light of prevention rather than cure. They should in some ways act as part of a package of deterrents that establish that people who persist in antisocial behaviour as a result of their dependency on drugs will end up in a much more severe environment and will potentially end up serving custodial sentences behind bars for an indefinite period of time. (Ms McCall, Parliament of Victoria, Legislative Assembly, 27 February 2002, 121)

In Bacchi's terms, these passages reveal how the 'problem' of addiction, drugs and drug-related crime emerged within the context of the parliamentary debates. The principal problem to be addressed is the (paradoxically, simultaneously) non-agentive/choosing subject whose poor choices have rendered them unable to bring their 'anti-social behaviour' under control.

This configuration of the addict is somewhat familiar. It is, for example, largely consistent with traditional tropes of addiction, where the subject is positioned as chaotic, false, dependent, irrational and lacking control (e.g. Fraser and Seear 2011; Keane 2002), while simultaneously being enjoined to action, and responsibilized (e.g. Fraser 2004). Yet by rehearsing this familiar narrative within the context of the Drug Court's development, certain discursive and subjectification effects take hold. Not only do drug users paradoxically become simultaneously non-agentive/choosing subject, but other ways of conceptualizing their crimes are foreclosed. It is no longer possible to imagine, for example, that some 'addicts' may not partake in criminal offending, or that where they do, the origins of such offending might be either more complex, or undertaken for reasons unrelated to drug use. Drugs and addiction, it would seem, are the sole/principal causes of crime and 'anti-social behaviour' because, once chosen by the subject, they become all-controlling. This is an important conceptual logic, and one which carries certain familiar repercussion in law and policy. It is to these repercussions we turn now.

Rehabilitating lesser citizens back to their full potential

Bacchi and Beasley (2002, 325) argue that much of Australian social policy is underpinned by 'a demarcation between full and lesser citizens which hinges precisely upon assumptions about bodies'. They propose that two kinds of political subjects are often produced through policy responses: 'those deemed to be in control of their bodies [full citizens], and those considered to be controlled by their bodies [lesser citizens]' (2002, 325). Bacchi and Beasley (2002, 338) argue that the 'control over body'/'controlled by body' dichotomy is often deployed within social policy as a means of justifying the 'illiberal treatment of some citizens'. They propose that through locating the division of citizenship within a medicalized discourse of the body, certain constraints, restrictions and intrusions upon the 'autonomy' of citizens becomes palatable (as long as they are overseen by the medical profession). This appears to be what has taken place in the context of the development of the Drug Court.

Having rendered drugs and addiction as inherently criminogenic, and the 'addict' as controlled by this criminogenic addiction (which, at the same time, they have poorly chosen), a neatly aligned yet highly intrusive 'solution' emerges. With its focus on finding ways to 'cure people's problems by freeing them from their addictions' (Mr Savage, Parliament of Victoria, Legislative Assembly, 27 February 2002, 131) – as opposed to simply imprisoning the person for their crimes – the Drug Court is purported to simultaneously 'facilitate the rehabilitation of the offender' (Mr Hulls, Parliament of Victoria, Legislative Assembly, 29 November 2001, 2192) and 'protect the community' (Mr Hulls, Parliament of Victoria,

Legislative Assembly, 29 November 2001, 2191) from the 'anti-social behaviours' associated with their poor choice. In other words, by drawing upon the conceptual logic surrounding bodies, control and citizenship, members of the Legislative Assembly both exclude the prospect that other forms of criminal justice interventions (not focussed on rehabilitation and 'cure') may be warranted or useful with such individuals (i.e. interventions that focus on addressing other factors that may in some way be associated with crime, including homelessness and poverty, past trauma and abuse, and more)[5], but at the same time, make the prospect of subjecting someone to up to two years of restricted freedoms, drug treatment and drug testing for a non-serious crime appear as an 'innovative' and 'modern' (Mr Hulls, Parliament of Victoria, Legislative Assembly, 29 November 2001, 2191) solution.

Crucially in interlocking the conceptualizations of both the 'problem' and 'solution' around bodies, control and citizenship, the addict is discursively produced as abject[6]: as *always already* criminal, and as a threat to community, public safety and more.[7] Indeed, addicts are positioned as subjects who are external to and distinct from 'the community' (and the protections typically offered to the community), precisely because their lack of control renders them a *threat* to full citizens. Such a configuration not only reinforces the dominant cultural imaginary of the addict as being a lesser citizen, but further strengthens the elevated status of the disease models of addiction (as 'disease of the will') within medicine and law, justifying an expanded role for medicine in 'curing' the addict in order to restore them to full citizenship. Thus it would seem that in the case of the Drug Court's creation, the state is willing to cede power to medicine in the pursuit of caring for the 'disordered' and 'irrational' addict – not for his or her own sake – but for the sake of others to whom they pose an unending threat.

The assessment and referral court list

The Assessment and Referral Court List ('the List') was established by the *Magistrates' Court Amendment (Assessment and Referral Court List) Act 2010* (Vic). Like the Drug Court, cases heard under the List are pre-sentence, and exclude violent or sexual offences (s4S(3) *Magistrates Court Act 1989* (Vic)). Matters eligible for handling through the List must meet the following criteria:

(1) *Diagnostic criteria* – the accused must be diagnosed as living with either a mental illness, intellectual disability, acquired brain injury, autism spectrum disorder or a neurological impairment such as dementia (s4T(2) Magistrates Court Act 1989 (Vic)).

(2) *Functional criteria* – the impairment with which the accused is diagnosed must substantially reduce their capacity to undertake self-care, self-management, social interactions or communication (s4T(3) Magistrates Court Act 1989 (Vic)).

(3) *Needs criteria* – the accused must be able to derive benefit from receiving services from an individual support plan, this includes services pertaining to disability, mental health, housing, welfare and/or health (s4T(4) Magistrates Court Act 1989 (Vic)).

Faultless individuals suffering from a criminalizing affliction

The List was debated in Victoria's Parliament in December 2009, February 2010 and March 2010. Like the Drug Court, these debates provide access to a number of deep-seated presuppositions surrounding the purported lives of people with cognitive impairments or mental illness. In particular, members of the Legislative Assembly appear to rely on a medicalized and protectionist discourse of disability and mental health. This discourse positions cognitive impairments and mental illness as inherently negative conditions which produce lives characterized by tragedy and constant struggle, and which require intervention for the sake of 'the vulnerable' (see Oliver 1990). In this vein, members of the Legislative Assembly present people with cognitive impairments or mental illness as 'some of the most vulnerable people in the state' (Mr Drum, Parliament of Victoria, Legislative Council, 25 February, 2010, 545), who are 'suffering' (Mr Donnellan, Parliament of Victoria, Legislative Assembly, 3 February, 2010, 137; Mr Wakeling, Parliament of Victoria, Legislative Assembly, 3 February 2010, 138; Mr Clark, Parliament of Victoria, Legislative Assembly, 2 February, 2010, p. 54) from a devastating 'affliction' (Mr Drum, Parliament of Victoria, Legislative Council, 25 February, 2010, p. 545) which is 'not the fault' of the person (Ms Thomson, Parliament of Victoria, Legislative Assembly, 2 February, 2010, 59), but rather a 'medical condition' (Ms Thomson, Parliament of Victoria, Legislative Assembly, 23 March, 2010, 937). Indeed we are told that 'people with mental illness are often the most unhappy, the most disturbed, the most troubled persons in our society, who have the greatest difficulty in dealing with day-to-day life' (Mr Scott, Parliament of Victoria, Legislative Assembly, 2 February, 2010, 68). What is of interest for our purposes however, is what this familiar medicalized and protectionist narrative facilitates when it appears within broader discussions of law and order; that is, it's discursive, subjectification and lived effects.

By rendering people with cognitive impairments or mental illness 'faultless' victims of a debilitating 'affliction', members of the parliamentary debates give rise to the notion that crimes committed by people with cognitive impairments or mental illness are subject to the same restrictions. Indeed, members explain that many people with cognitive impairments or mental illness find themselves before the courts 'through no fault of their own' (Mr Herbert, Parliament of Victoria, Legislative Assembly, 23 March 2010, 935), and that this occurs 'primarily as a consequence of their various afflictions' (Mr Drum, Parliament of Victoria, Legislative Council, 25 February, 2010, 545).

In Bacchi's sense, these passages provide access to some important, underpinning conceptual logics. There is a clear assumption that a person's cognitive impairment or mental illness somehow *creates*, or at the very least, *facilitates* criminality. Indeed, regardless of whether we are told that crime occurs because the person's 'affliction' causes them to act in ways 'they do not fully understand' (Mr Clark, Parliament of Victoria, Legislative Assembly, 23 March, 2010, 932), or because there are, apparently, 'parents trying to help through the system children found guilty of criminal offences when we as a community should have seen that behaviour as the workings of their medical condition' (Mr Carli, Parliament of Victoria, Legislative Assembly, 23 March, 2010, 937), it is a clear that criminality is understood as being linked to a person's cognitive impairment or mental illness; that it is derived from their 'medical condition'.

This is a familiar narrative as well. Mental illness in general, and schizophrenia in particular, often appear within our cultural imaginary as catalysts for uncontrolled violent behaviour (Glover-Thomas 2011). Similarly, it is often suggested in court hearings that people with cognitive impairments are standing before the court because their impairment is simply, 'unruly' (Spivakovsky 2014, 2015). Yet there is a slightly different representation of the 'problem' under construction here.

What is being problematized through members of the Legislative Assembly's discussion of the List, is the person's agency. That is to say, it is not simply that people with the cognitive impairments or mental illness are assumed to be more likely to commit a crime because of their 'affliction', rather, their crimes occur because their 'affliction' determines all actions they take, criminal and non-criminal. The 'problem' with people with cognitive impairments or mental illness, is that they are both inherently criminal and entirely 'faultless' for being so.

This is a different construction of the 'problem' than that which underpinned the advent of Victoria's Drug Court. Indeed, even though in both cases members of the Legislative Assembly identify the 'affliction' (i.e. AOD dependence, cognitive impairment, mental illness) as the primary cause of crime, the parliamentary debates surrounding the development of these courts bring into being two very different 'afflicted' individuals. The addict has the capacity to change, but 'persists' in making poor choices. The person with the cognitive impairment or mental illness, on the other hand, neither has a choice in how they behave nor the capacity to change; they are wholly controlled by their unrelenting medical condition, and for this reason, they become 'faultless'.

The assumed presence of this different kind of 'afflicted' individual within the parliamentary debates is significant. Having been rendered both agentless and 'faultless' by their apparent 'affliction' (as opposed to defiant or illogical, as was the 'addict'), this figure opens up the possibility that both the blame for their presence *and* the responsibility for change can be found elsewhere. Indeed we are told that:

it is the failure of the government to invest in community-based and acute mental health services and the inability of people to get access to the mental health care that they need that is leading to such people ending up in the justice system. (Ms Wooldridge, Parliament of Victoria, Legislative Assembly, 2 February, 2010, 63)

It is suggested that 'if more was being done at a government level' (Ms Duncan, Parliament of Victoria, Legislative Assembly, 3 February, 2010, 139), people wouldn't be at 'a greater risk of falling through the cracks' (Ms Mikakos, Parliament of Victoria, Legislative Council, 25 February, 2010, 537). Or that people with cognitive impairments or mental illness: 'Require ongoing intervention to prevent [themselves] from hurting themselves or others. It is not their fault that they have these illnesses. We cannot turn our backs on them once they are out of the system' (Mrs Fyffe, Parliament of Victoria, Legislative Assembly, 2 February 2010, 67).

Such statements produce a number of effects, in Bacchi's sense. Discursively, they draw a significant distinction between the *object* responsible for people with cognitive impairments or mental illness' crimes – their 'affliction' – and the *subject* responsible for their contact with the criminal justice system – the state. Subjectively, such a distinction allows for the actual person with cognitive impairments and/or mental illness – their subjecthood and agency – to be effectively removed from the problem representation itself, relocating all of their actions, behaviours, and now even, responsibilities and possibilities within and between the realms of medicine and governance. This move, in turn, sets the foundations for some new material, regulatory repercussions.

A civilized response to an ongoing problem

Because the 'problem' of people with cognitive impairments or mental illness' contact with the criminal justice system lies not with the person themselves, apparently, but instead within and between their unrelenting medical condition and their history of poor governance, it is no longer conceivable to hope for 'rehabilitation' and a 'cure', nor is it logical to pursue deterrence (as it was with the more agentive 'addict'). Rather, for this problem representation, the only suitable, necessary approach would be to first assess the exact nature of the person's medical condition – to understand its propensity to 'control the body' – and to then provide 'coordinated' and extensive health and welfare services which are consistently monitored by the magistrate (i.e. 'good' governance).[8] This, it is claimed, will finally 'stabilise' the accused (Mr Clark, Parliament of Victoria, Legislative Assembly, 2 February, 2010, 53; Mr Hulls, Parliament of Victoria, Legislative Assembly, 10 December 2009, 4604).

Conceptualizing the 'solution' in this way gives foundation to a new logic about people with cognitive impairments and mental illness. This conceptualization gives rise to the notion that people with cognitive impairments and mental illness *require ongoing government intervention* in order to live in the community, that to provide anything different than this form of intervention would 'lead to a "revolving door phenomenon" where mentally impaired defendants continue to cycle through the criminal justice system with diminishing prospects for reintegration in the community' (Mr Hulls, Parliament of Victoria, Legislative Assembly, 10 December 2009, 4602).

Yet this concerning regulatory repercussion is largely obscured from critique by the dominant, medicalized and protectionist discourse that underpins this problem representation. That is to say, we are reminded by Attorney-General Hulls that 'The fairness of our system, our institutions and our democracy is measured by the manner in which we treat the most vulnerable members of our community, including mentally impaired individuals' (Mr Hulls, Parliament of Victoria, Legislative Assembly, 10 December, 2009, 4604).

Accordingly, it is understood that it is okay to subject people with cognitive impairments and mental illness to significant intervention and surveillance because this, we are told, is 'a civilised' way of dealing with the 'problem' (Mr Donnellan, Parliament of Victoria, Legislative Assembly, 2 February, 2010, 70). It protects these 'vulnerable' populations from the harshness of prison, offering them a 'more dignifying and more humane' (Mr Hulls, Parliament of Victoria, Legislative Assembly, 10 December, 2009, 4602) way of being treated. Indeed, the List is claimed to provide people with cognitive impairments or mental illness with the 'dignity and understanding' (Mr Somyurek, Parliament of Victoria, Legislative Council, 25

February, 2010, 548) that has been absent in the past; it is both 'more humane and thoughtful' (Mr Scott, Parliament of Victoria, Legislative Assembly, 2 February, 2010, 68) than anything that has come before.

It is at this point that we can draw some final conclusions about the dominant cultural imaginary underpinning the development of the Drug Court and Assessment and Referral Court List in Victoria.

Conclusion

The advent of 'problem-solving courts' over the past 20 years is claimed by some to represent a significant shift in the administration of justice, offering a more 'holistic' and 'generous' approach to offenders. At a time when calls to expand such courts are on the rise, including, in the Victorian context, the Drug Court (Law Reform, Drugs and Crime Prevention Committee 2014), we considered it as important to examine the presuppositions and conceptual logics underpinning the creation of such courts, along with the effects for targeted populations.

We argued that politicians responsible for developing specialist 'problem-solving' courts rely upon a dominant cultural imaginary about agency, capacity, control and the body that draws upon and is bolstered by dominant medical discourses of addiction, disability and mental health. In parliamentary debates leading up to the establishment of these courts, key figures conceptualized people living with AOD addiction, mental illness and/or cognitive impairment as inherently criminal, through repeated and extensive discussions about the multiple ways that criminal activity was produced by their respective 'afflictions'. Importantly, however, we noticed two distinct narratives emerging in relation to agency in the context of criminal offending. In the case of people experiencing AOD dependence, the 'problem' of AOD-related offending was ultimately understood as a choice/self-induced. For people with cognitive impairments or mental illness, the problem was externalized (it was the 'fault' of their all-controlling medical condition and the state's neglect). Here, the 'addict' is simultaneously and paradoxically constituted as beholden to their affliction and yet responsible for it (and for making change). On the other hand, people living with mental illness or cognitive impairment are conceptualized as beholden to their affliction but not to blame for their predicament, nor for changing it: instead, the state is seen to have failed them through inadequate resourcing and supports. We suggest that the process of tracing how these respective 'problem' populations are constituted tells us much about how policy and lawmaking processes imagine particular subjects ('addicts', the 'disabled' and the 'mentally ill') as abnormal, fixing connections, in the process, between drugs, disability, mental illness, normalcy, crime and the state. We also argued that these conceptualizations have implications for the extent to which such subjects are viewed as citizens, and that such rationalities are often used (albeit in distinct ways) to justify seemingly novel mechanisms for the regulation, intervention and control of such populations. Although we draw no firm conclusions about the overall advantages and disadvantages of specialist court systems here, we find these processes of mutual co-constitution troubling, especially insofar as these logics appear to justify and enable long-term, intensive, medico-legal interventions into the lives of subjects that are often already marginalized and stigmatized.

We also consider it to be particularly problematic that sweeping generalizations are being made about large, diverse populations of subjects such as 'the mentally ill', without proper consideration of the many differences and distinctions between people who experience mental illness. Although it may seem obvious, it is worth pointing out that people understood to be addicts, experiencing mental health issues or cognitive impairment are a heterogeneous population with diverse subjectivities, histories and motivations. In the materials we analysed here, we see a tendency in spite of this for parliamentarians to discursively produce both groups as one-dimensional, inherently dangerous and otherwise predictable cohorts with a deep-rooted propensity for criminal behaviour. In Bacchi's sense, these debates reflect the limits on what can be thought or said about these subjects, producing them instead as 'abject', abnormal, risky and *always already* a threat to society. Arguably, these processes may enhance the stigmatization and marginalization experienced by these populations. At the same time, other ways of thinking about the origins and solutions to crime are foreclosed, including the possibility that multiple, compounding factors contribute to their contact with criminal justice systems. In our view, there is a need for more research into how the statements of policy-makers and legislators reflect dominant cultural imaginaries, shaping the ways by which 'problems' are constituted and foreclosing other possible problematizations. Future work may include an analysis of the presuppositions of vulnerability and risk that are often invoked to justify these alternative approaches to criminal justice, the effects that follow for targeted populations, and the possible benefits of alternative problematizations.

Notes

1. AOD is commonly used in alcohol and other drug research as a descriptor to encapsulate substances that are associated with elevated risks and harms. It is a broad and fluid category that may incorporate both licit and illicit substances.
2. We acknowledge that there are many useful frameworks for approaching this task, with post-structural theorists and interlocutors in particular offering a range of useful approaches, including Psychological Jurisprudence (PJ). We follow Bacchi's approach because unlike similar approaches such as PJ, Bacchi's work offers a way for this paper to open up a space for critical discussion of the conceptual logics underpinning the establishment of specialist courts (as well as how they overlap and diverge) without prescribing precisely how things might be otherwise.
3. According to Bacchi (2009), authors should also undertake to apply the questions to their own problem representations.
4. This is not the only reference to an (imprecise and undefined) notion of the 'anti-social'. Although it is beyond the scope of this paper to explore this issue in more depth, we note the strong normalizing tendency of this descriptor. We suggest that it is important, in examining the pervasive cultural logics in these debates, to consider who gets to judge what counts as 'anti-social' and how the anti-social is conceptualized. Conceptualizations of what is 'social' or 'anti-social' enable and sustain, among other things, particular practices of governance, with implications – material and discursive – for subjects.
5. We acknowledge that these associations are themselves contested and complex, and offer no opinion, here, on the validity of them (for more, see Seear and Fraser 2014).
6. Here, our use of the word 'abject' is informed by the work of Judith Butler: particularly, *Bodies that Matter* (1993) and *Gender Trouble* (1990). Butler defines the 'abject' as a concept that

   relates to all kinds of bodies whose lives are not considered to be "lives" and whose materiality is understood not to "matter". To give something of an indication: the U.S. press regularly figures non-Western lives in such terms. Impoverishment is another common candidate, as is the domain of those identified as psychiatric "cases". (Meijer and Prins 1998, 281)

7. See, for example, the Hansard record (Parliament of Victoria, Legislative Assembly, 27 February 2002, 118), where Mr Wynne MP claimed that: 'The government is committed to safety on our streets, in our homes and workplaces, and has tackled the problems of drug addiction in a creative way'.
8. As Thomson explains, '

   it is not about just having services there, which at the moment is the situation in most courts: an assessment of what may be needed by an individual is being made and service links are being made, but no single monitoring of the needs of that person is going on. This program will change that … (Ms Thomson, Parliament of Victoria, Legislative Assembly, 2 February, 2010, 59).

Acknowledgements

The authors are grateful for the useful suggestions offered by the anonymous reviewers.

Disclosure statement

No potential conflict of interest was reported by the authors.

Funding

This work was supported by an Australian Research Council DECRA Fellowship [grant number DE160100134].

References

ABS (Australian Bureau of Statistics) 2010. *National Health Survey: Summary of Results, 2007–2008 (Reissue)*. Canberra: ABS.

AIHW (Australian Institute of Health and Welfare) 2011. *2010 National Drug Strategy Household Survey Report*. Drug statistics series No. 25. Cat. No. PHE 145. Canberra: AIHW.

AIHW (Australian Institute of Health and Welfare) 2012. *The Mental Health of Prison Entrants in Australia 2010*. Bulletin No. 104. Cat. No. AUS 158. Canberra: AIHW.

AIHW (Australian Institute of Health and Welfare) 2013. *The Health of Australia's Prisoners 2012*. Cat. No PHE 170. Canberra: AIHW.

Bacchi, C. 2009. *Analysing Policy: What's the Problem Represented to Be?*. Sydney: Pearson Education.

Bacchi, C., and C. Beasley. 2002. "Citizen Bodies: Is Embodies Citizenship a Contradiction in Terms?" *Critical Social Policy* 22 (2): 324–352.

Bacchi, C., and J. Eveline. 2010. "Approaches to Gender Mainstreaming: What's the Problem Represented to be?" In *Mainstreaming Politics: Gendering Practices and Feminist Theory*, edited by C. Bacchi and J. Eveline, 111–138. Adelaide: University of Adelaide Press.

Boldt, R. 2002. "The Adversary System and Attorney Role in the Drug Treatment Movement." In *Drug Courts in Theory and Practice*, edited by J. Nolan, 115–144. New York: Aldine de Gruyter.

Boothroyd, R., C. Mercado, N. Poythress, A. Christy, and J. Petrilia. 2005. "Clinical Outcomes of Defendants in Mental Health Court." *Psychiatric Services* 56 (7): 829–834.

Butler, J. 1993. *Bodies that Matter: On the Discursive Limits of 'Sex'*. New York: Routledge.

Butler, J. 1990. *Gender Trouble: Feminism and the Subversion of Identity*. New York: Routledge.

Butler, T., S. Allnutt, D. Cain, D. Owens, and C. Muller. 2005. "Mental Disorder in the New South Wales Prisoner Population." *Australian and New Zealand Journal of Psychiatry* 39 (5): 407–413.

Cosden, M., J. Ellens, J. Schnell, Y. Yamini-Diouf, and M. Wolfe. 2003. "Evaluation of a Mental Health Treatment Court with Assertive Community Treatment." *Behavioral Sciences and the Law* 21: 415–427.

Foucault, M. 1977. *Language, Counter-memory, Practice: Selected Essays and Interviews*, edited and translated by D. F. Bouchard. Ithaca, New York: Cornell University Press.

Foucault, M. 1988. "The Concern for Truth." In *Michel Foucault: Politics, philosophy, culture: Interviews and other writings, 1977–1984*, edited by L. D. Kritzman, Translated by A. Sheridan, 255–267. New York, NY: Routledge.

Fraser, S. 2004. "'It's Your Life!': Injecting Drug Users, Individual Responsibility and Hepatitis C Prevention." *Health: An Interdisciplinary Journal for the Social Study of Health, Illness and Medicine* 8 (2): 199–221.

Fraser, S., and K. Seear. 2011. *Making Disease, Making Citizens: The Politics of Hepatitis C*. Aldershot: Ashgate.

Glover-Thomas, N. 2011. "The Age of Risk: Risk Perception and Determination Following the Mental Health Act 2007." *Medical Law Review* 19: 581–605.

Hanna-Moffat, K., and P. Maurutto. 2012. "Shifting and Targeted Forms of Penal Governance: Bail, Punishment and Specialized Courts." *Theoretical Criminology* 16 (2): 201–219.

Herinckz, H., S. Swart, S. Ama, C. Dolezal, and S. King. 2005. "Rearrest and Linkage to Mental Health Services Among Clients of the Clark County Mental Health Court Program." *Psychiatric Services* 56 (7): 853–857.

Keane, H. 2002. *What's Wrong with Addiction?*. Melbourne: Melbourne University Press.

Lamberti, J., R. Weisman, S. Schwarzkopf, N. Price, R. Ashton, and J. Trompeter. 2001. "The Mentally ill in Jails and Prisons: Towards an Integrated Model of Preventions." *Psychiatric Quarterly* 72 (1): 63–77.

Lancaster, K., K. Seear, and C. Treloar. 2015. "Laws Prohibiting Peer Distribution of Injecting Equipment in Australia: A Critical Analysis of Their Effects." *International Journal of Drug Policy* 26 (12): 1198–1206.

Law Reform, Drugs and Crime Prevention Committee. 2014. *Inquiry into the Supply and Use of Methamphetamine in Victoria*. Melbourne: Parliament House.

McNeil, D., and R. Binder. 2007. "Effectiveness of a Mental Health Court in Reducing Criminal Recidivism and Violence." *American Journal of Psychiatry* 164 (9): 1395–1403.

Meijer, I. C., and B. Prins. 1998. "How Bodies Come to Matter: An Interview with Judith Butler." *Signs: Journal of Women in Culture and Society* 23 (2): 275–286.

Morrell, R., C. Merbitz, and S. Jain. 1998. "Traumatic Brain Injury in Prisoners." *Journal of Offender Rehabilitation* 27: 1–8.

Moore, D. 2007. "Translating Justice and Therapy: The Drug Treatment Court networks." *British Journal of Criminology* 47 (1): 42–60.

Oliver, M. 1990. *The Politics of Disablement*. Basingstoke: Macmillian and St Martin's Press.

Prins, S. 2011. "Does Transinstitutionalisation Explain the Overrepresentation of People with Serious Mental Illness in the Criminal Justice System?" *Community Mental Health Journal* 47: 716–722.

Schofield, P., T. Butler, and S. Hollis. 2007. *October 2007 Forum – Injury Control Council of Western Australia. Hunder Forensic Head Injury Project*. Perth: National Drug Research Institute.

Seear, K., and S. Fraser. 2014. "The Addict as Victim: Producing the 'Problem' of Addiction in Australian Victims of Crime Compensation Laws." *International Journal of Drug Policy* 25 (5): 826–835.

Spivakovsky, C. 2014. "From Punishment to Protection: Containing and Controlling the Lives of People with Disabilities in Human Rights." *Punishment & Society* 16 (5): 560–577.

Spivakovsky, C. 2015. "Making Dangerousness Intelligible in Intellectual Disability." *Griffith Law Review* 23 (3): 389–404.

Steadman, H., A. Redlich, L. Callahan, P. Robbins, and R. Vesselinov. 2011. "Effect of Mental Health Courts on Arrests and Jail Days: A Multisite Study." *Archives of General Psychiatry* 68 (2): 167–172.

Wexler, D., and B. Winick, eds. 1996. *Law in a Therapeutic Key: Therapeutic Jurisprudence and the Courts*. Durham: Carolina Academic Press.

Legislation and Parliamentary Debates

Magistrates' Court Act 1989 (Victoria).

Magistrates' Court Amendment (Assessment and Referral Court List) Act 2010 (Victoria).

Parliament of Victoria, Legislative Assembly, Parliamentary Debates, Thursday 29 November 2001. http://www.parliament.vic.gov.au/hansard

Parliament of Victoria, Legislative Assembly, Parliamentary Debates, Wednesday 27 February 2002. http://www.parliament.vic.gov.au/hansard

Parliament of Victoria, Legislative Assembly, Parliamentary Debates, Thursday, 10 December 2009. http://www.parliament.vic.gov.au/hansard

Parliament of Victoria, Legislative Assembly, Parliamentary Debates, Tuesday, 2 February 2010. http://www.parliament.vic.gov.au/hansard

Parliament of Victoria, Legislative Assembly, Parliamentary Debates, Wednesday, 3 February 2010. http://www.parliament.vic.gov.au/hansard

Parliament of Victoria, Legislative Council, Parliamentary Debates, Thursday, 25 February 2010. http://www.parliament.vic.gov.au/hansard

Parliament of Victoria, Legislative Assembly, Parliamentary Debates Tuesday, 23 March 2010. http://www.parliament.vic.gov.au/hansard

Sentencing Act 1991 (Victoria).

Sentencing (Amendment) Act 2002 (Victoria).

Cripwashing: the abortion debates at the crossroads of gender and disability in the Spanish media

Melania Moscoso 🆔 and R. Lucas Platero 🆔

ABSTRACT

On 11 September 2015, the Spanish Senate passed the second reform of the Abortion Act, promoted by a Conservative Government. It was the last step in the parliamentary process of a law that bans 16- and 17-year-old girls from accessing abortion without parental consent. In this article, we explore how the debates between physicians, the Catholic Church, disability activists and pro-choice activists reached the Spanish media. We focus on the use the Conservative Government has made of disability rights movement (DRM) discourse to undermine the reproductive rights of women in force in the country since the 1986 Law on Voluntary Termination of Pregnancy. We unveil the intricacies of the voices of a minority group in justifying agendas against women's rights, stressing the challenges that dismantling the Spanish public health system poses for people with disabilities. We suggest that the Conservative Government was using the DRM to undermine women's rights, and we call this operation *cripwashing*. Similar to the term 'pinkwashing' used by the LGBT community, cripwashing refers to the practice of using the rights protections of one group to conceal abuses towards other groups. In the following three sections, we explore how the budget cuts imposed on the Spanish national healthcare system pose a greater danger to disabled people than the abortion laws that allow the termination of pregnancy on the basis of congenital malformations. We then focus on how the Conservative Party capitalized on the discourse of the DRM in order to undermine women's reproductive rights.

Introduction

Disability has been a recurrent topic in international abortion debates. Since prenatal testing practices came into use in the 1950s (Santesmases 2016), medical practitioners have often cited congenital malformations as a reason to terminate pregnancies. In the 1970s, the medical discourse that framed disability as pathology and thus justified a termination of pregnancy was contested by the very same disability activists who would later gather in the Society of Disability Studies (Saxton 2000, 150). Since then, the debate around abortion and disability has been framed as two competing positions, between those who argue that prenatal testing or extended periods to terminate pregnancies of foetuses with congenital malformations discriminate against people with disabilities, and those who privilege pregnant women's right to choose. The strength of these polarized representations has had the power to silence other and more nuanced standpoints.[1]

In spite of the remarkable theoretical development of disability studies since then, including approaches that challenge normalcy such as queer theory and, more recently, crip theory, the abortion debate seems to have incorporated little from these perspectives. Therefore, it is our aim to take on these critical approaches to explore the recent turns of the abortion debate regarding disability in the Spanish political agenda. In an interview given to the conservative newspaper *La Razón* on 22 July 2012, Spanish Minister of Justice Alberto Ruiz-Gallardón announced the upcoming reform of the Sexual and Reproductive Health and Voluntary Termination of Pregnancy Law (known as 'the 2/2010 abortion law'), in force since 2010. This law was passed by the former Social-Democratic government of José Luis Rodríguez-Zapatero and allowed the voluntary termination of pregnancy with no restrictions within the first 14 weeks of pregnancy, provided to women who had already given their written consent and had had at least three days to reflect on their decision. The National Health Service would cover the procedure for all women willing to terminate their pregnancies within 14 weeks; in the case that the unborn child had any congenital disease, this period was extended to 22 weeks. In an interview, Ruiz-Gallardón stated:

> I do not understand why the unborn children are unprotected, and abortion is allowed, because of the fact that they have some kind of handicap or deformity. It seems to me ethically inconceivable we have lived so long with this legislation and I think that the same level of protection that is given to an unborn child without any type of handicap or deformity should be given to those who are known to lack some of the abilities that other unborn children have. (Flotats 2012)

In Ruiz-Gallardón's view, allowing an abortion in the case of congenital malformations is incompatible with the rights of people with disabilities. Ruiz-Gallardón was not alone in this, however. In 2013, the European People's Party (Christian Democrats) banned a report aimed at ensuring access to safe and legal abortion for all women in the EU, and in the US, debates regarding prenatal testing have been going on for decades (Parens and Asch 2000).

This article focuses on the media debate following Ruiz-Gallardón's interview on July 22. We aim to discuss the apparent confrontation between women's sexual and reproductive rights and the disability rights movement (DRM) in the political and cultural context of Spain from 2012 to 2016. Spain was hit hard by the European debt crisis and the austerity policies that were implemented by the Conservative Government when the 15-M movement[2] broke out. According to our view, the Spanish Government of the conservative Popular Party (PP) was capitalizing on the DRM discourse in order to undermine women's sexual and reproductive rights that have been in force in Spain since 1986. We call this strategic operation *cripwashing*: the use of disability rights to undermine women's sexual and reproductive rights (Moscoso 2014). Following the lead of Puar (2011), we use the concept of cripwashing with the same meaning that the Center for LGBTQ Studies (CLAGS) website[3] gives for 'pinkwashing': 'using right protections for one group [in this case, people with disabilities] to conceal the rights of and abuses toward other people [in this case, women]'. We have coined this concept in an attempt to update the rather stagnated abortion and disability debate with the recent contributions that queer theory has made to disability studies. Among the authors whose contributions are rooted in knowledge produced by social movements, we want to cite the influential work of Jasbir Puar's. Puar's concept of homonationalism[4] has inspired conceptual tools such as whitewashing, purplewashing and greenwashing, among others. The use of terms like crip[5] (or white, purple or green) as prefixes serves to name the group of people on whose behalf the protection measures are put into action, while the verb 'wash' serves to denounce the co-opting strategies that use minority rights to maintain or enhance structural forms of discrimination, such as ableism,[6] racism, sexism and capitalism. Likewise, pinkwashing is rooted in the notion of homonationalism (Puar 2007, 2) and addresses the regulatory codes that make homosexuality a sign of exceptionalism; cripwashing is rooted in ablenationalism (Snyder and Mitchell 2010), the convergence of ableism and patriotism that privileges those who are able-bodied.

Accordingly we explore how the rights not only of women, but also, according to Mariano Rajoy's government, of people with disabilities, have become 'symbols of civilizational aptitude' (Puar 2011). To do so, we analyse media follow-up of the debate as it was presented in 19 articles in major Spanish newspapers and on social movements' websites. By privileging the media debate analysis, we emphasize the process in which the construction of social problems takes place. The abortion framing process illustrates how certain areas of reality that are forged in community interactions are imbued with certain meanings, through which they offer a particular course of action (López Rodríguez 2011, 16). We are aware that intersectionality is a salient feature of contemporary oppression, and we certainly want to foreground the historical contexts in which the categories of race (in our case, gender) and disability intersect (Erevelles and Minear 2010, 131). However, the goal of our research on cripwashing is not to make apparent how these two categories – gender and disability – come together to afflict a multi-faceted oppression on a person or group of people, but rather to show how the language of disability rights can be used to undermine the reproductive rights of women, whether they are disabled or not.

The article is divided into five sections; first, we introduce the methodology. Second, we provide a brief overview of the development of abortion rights in Spain. Third, we cover how the budget cuts imposed on the Spanish national healthcare system pose a greater danger to disabled people than the abortion laws that allow the termination of pregnancy on the basis of congenital malformations. Fourth, we analyse the different representations that emerge in the media debate, including the political actors involved, and lastly, we present our conclusions.

Methodology

We have analysed a total of 19 journal articles from the main Spanish news media, tracking the reactions to Ruiz-Gallardón's 2012 announcement of abortion law reform. These articles were published in leading national newspapers such as *El País, La Razón* and *Público*. Additionally, we have also examined the responses of Esparza (2012, 2013), a neurosurgeon; and Gloria Muñoz, the mother of a child who passed away from the complications of type I spinal atrophy (Muñoz 2012). We comment on interviews with Matía (2012), the president of the Spanish Federation of People with Down Syndrome – and the first person to voice support for the Minister of Justice's statement – in the *Nosotrasdecidimos* blog, as well as with CERMI [Spanish Committee of Representatives of Disabled Persons]) and the *Foro de Vida Independiente* [Independent Living Movement] activist Antonio Centeno, who posted a lengthy piece on the matter.

Our analysis is focused on Carol Bacchi's (2009) 'What's the problem represented to be?' (WPR), a Foucauldian approach that unveils both how social actors use discourses and how these discourses build political actors. Applied to the media debate on the abortion reform, WPR addresses both the hegemonic and the subaltern discourses in regard to how abortion and disability rights are presented in confrontation to one another, taking into account the specific context of Spain. According to WPA, certain social actors are able to articulate not only what the problem is, but also the solutions, thereby creating relevant mobilizations. This framework implies asking questions such as: What is the problem represented to be in the abortion reform led by Ruiz-Gallardón? What assumptions underlie the representations led by different political actors? How did these representations come about? What are the silences in these debates? What effects are produced by the different representations? How could they be questioned?

Therefore, the representation and framing process involves selecting 'some aspects of a perceived reality and mak[ing] them more salient in a communicating text', thereby 'promot[ing] a particular problem definition, causal interpretation, moral evaluation, and/or treatment recommendation for the item described' (Entman 1993, 52). Following Ruth Lister (2011), our analysis conceives the study of context as having a political value, in which the embodied and situated citizenship is materialized; this perspective thus avoids taking the context only as part of a global scenario that may (or may not) follow a global trend in regard to equality standards. By using both an analysis of the discourses (based in textual and contextual reflections) and an intersectional approach to abortion and disability rights, we can critically discuss the representations and framings.

Abortion rights in Spain

Spain has undergone important transformations since the democratic transition that began in 1975, experiencing changes that break the linkage among sexuality, procreation and marriage. This rupture was only possible once women had access to birth control (1974), abortion became legal (the 9/1985 act allowed three circumstances for the legal termination of pregnancy: risk for the mother, rape or fetal abnormality[7]) and divorce was made possible[8] (1981). These rights were achieved thanks to important feminist mobilizations, whose struggles introduced abortion into the mainstream agenda and created important resistances. These political debates had a smaller impact in Spain than they did in other European countries, probably due to Spain's recent democratic status as well as the configuration of Spanish feminism, political parties and social mobilizations at the time (Valiente Fernández 2001, 229–245).

Abortion was fiercely debated in the eighties, and it wasn't until 2010 that abortion returned to the Spanish political agenda. This revival took place under a Social-Democratic government that promoted a legal reform based on an important social consensus, which also caused relevant conservative mobilizations by the PP, the Catholic Church and anti-abortion groups. The legal reform of the 1985 law materialized in the passing of the 2/2010 Law[9] organized according to a stage system based on gestational age: women can undergo abortion within 14 weeks of gestation without needing to claim any particular reason (art. 14). This abortion period can be extended if a woman's life is in danger or the foetus has abnormalities that have yet to be detected. Under the 2/2010 Law, 16- and 17-year-old women could undergo abortion, even without parental consent (art.13). This act was repealed by the Conservative Party on 20 December 2013 in the Constitutional Court, which has not yet ruled on this appeal.

The impact of the economic crisis and the decline of President Rodríguez-Zapatero facilitated the victory of the conservatives, in government from 2011 to 2015, who imposed cuts in social policies that eliminated the discourse of gender equality from the agenda (López and Platero 2015). Under the government of Mariano Rajoy Brey, abortion became as relevant as it once was in 1985, since the banning of abortion rights was a relevant proposal in the conservatives' electoral programme, as was same-sex marriage. Ruiz-Gallardón led the conservative backlash against both rights, abortion and same-sex marriage, which were appealed to the Constitutional Court at that time. In 2012, the Constitutional Court ruled in favour of same-sex marriage, and Ruiz-Gallardón stated that 'he would respect their decision.' In regard to abortion rights, Ruiz-Gallardón announced the reform five times (Calvo and Agudo 2013), but the law proposal was not presented until December 2013 due to lack of consensus in the Conservative Party, and probably as a result of the calculation of electoral costs. Meanwhile, the feminist movement actively fought for abortion rights, demanding the permanence of the 2010 law.

The conservatives argued that there was no social consensus around abortion rights, presenting their reform as a *citizenry mandate*. According to Toharia (2013), data from the 1970s, 1980s and 2010s suggest that Spaniards never reached a consensus on banning abortion, especially when there were foetal abnormalities. The law amendment proposal presented by Ruiz-Gallardón created disputes, even within the Conservative Party, while promoting big mobilizations within social movements. The conservative proposal, more restrictive than the 1985 law, limited the circumstances in which the termination of pregnancy was legal. Abortion would only be allowed in cases of extreme risk to a woman's life, and required documentation from two doctors other than the one terminating the pregnancy. This controversial proposal was rooted in the argument of defending of the unborn child, excluding the possibility of terminating pregnancies with foetuses that showed 'abnormalities' and making healthcare professionals responsible if laws were broken.

This proposal was finally withdrawn in September 2014, long before the December 2015 elections. The failed reforms of abortion and same-sex marriage proved that sexual and reproductive rights are not lesser issues and prompted the resignation of Minister Ruiz-Gallardón. In a society that understands these rights as part of the 'common good', the expectation of an electoral cost had political consequences.

Measuring the scope of the austerity cuts

On 12 May 2010, the Social-Democratic Party announced a set of budget cuts in order to reduce the country's deficit, estimated at 15 billion euros. The restrictions affected the salaries of civil servants

(4000 million euros), retirement benefits (1500 million euros) and pharmaceutical spending (Garea 2010). Most importantly to those with disabilities, the Socio-Democratic Party placed restrictions not only on the funding of the 39/2006 Dependence Law, but also on services that targeted gender equality policies.

The 39/2006 Law on Personal Autonomy and Dependent Care (known as the 'Dependence Law'), passed in November 2006, was widely announced as the flagship of the Social-Democratic Party along with the same-sex marriage and gender violence laws. The 39/2006 Dependence Law started the network of independent living offices and the regional system of care for the elderly, people with disabilities and the sick. Unevenly developed throughout the country, the law depended on the budgets of the autonomous regions. Severely underfunded, this budget did not match 0.5% of Spain's GDP, even before the outbreak of the European debt crisis in 2010 (Morán 2010). Intended to relieve the burdens of caregivers, the law hardly developed beyond an experiment (Moscoso 2009; Guzmán, Moscoso, and Toboso 2010).

The situation became worse when Mariano Rajoy's *Partido Popular* won the 2011 Spanish elections with an absolute majority. Being hit hard with unemployment amidst the hardships of the European debt crisis, the new government increased the restrictions imposed by the Social-Democratic government on the national healthcare system and social services. The restrictions left the 39/2006 Dependence Law, which regulated independent living programmes by funding personal assistants for disabled people, without resources, and ignored the social security coverage of orthotics and dietary supplements. The cuts strongly affected the caretakers of people with disabilities and the elderly, mostly women who no longer had benefits from the healthcare system (Ruiz 2012). The conservative rhetoric on people in circumstances of dependence shifted in this legislature, challenging the true nature of their problems and demanding stricter standards in order to qualify for already underfunded public assistance (Del Burgo 2012).

On 27 July 2012, Luis Cayo, president of CERMI, asked the Minister of Justice to repeal Article 156 of the Penal Code of 1995, which allowed the forced sterilization of people with disabilities under the provision of their best interest (Flotats 2012). This contravenes Article 23 of the UN Convention on the Rights of Persons with Disabilities of 2003, which explicitly states: 'Persons with disabilities, including children, retain their fertility on an equal basis with others' (UN (United Nations) 2003). The government not only ignored CERMI's petition, it launched a reformation of Article 98, the aforementioned Penal Code, which limited reclusion for people with mental disorders to five years on grounds of outdated notions of 'social danger'.[10] According to associations such as the AGIFES [Federation of Families of the Mentally Ill], this reform 'stigmatizes people with mental disabilities' and 'opens up the possibility of life-long institutionalization in penitentiary psychiatric wards for people with mental illness and developmental disorders' (Aldaz 2014).

Cripwashing the right to undergo an abortion

The analysis of the debate on abortion includes different social actors, who frame abortion according to their ideologies, representing the political problem in a way that offers both the genesis of the issue as well as a course of action (for a summary of all frames and representations analyzed, see Table 1). The WPR approach shows how these actors make strategic representations built on previous ideas, present in their discourses and geared towards the achievement of a political problem.

Focusing on the conservative approach, Minister Ruiz-Gallardón framed the abortion reform as a confrontation between women's rights and rights of people with disabilities. Ruiz-Gallardón highlights a confrontation between the rights promised in Article 15 in the 2/2010 Abortion Law, and those promised in Article 10 of UN Convention on the Rights of Persons with Disabilities of 2003, which declares: 'every human being has the inherent right to life' (UN 2003).[11] The implication of this representation, which we call a 'conflicting rights frame', is that the 2/2010 abortion law would allow women to 'abuse' the law, since most claim harm to their health as cause for their termination of pregnancy. Therefore, there is a need (1) to ensure that the law is really applied (since harm 'is not sufficiently proved') and (2) to protect the unborn child.

Table 1. Summary of frames and representations analyzed.

Conflicting rights frame	Espoused by Minister of Justice Alberto Ruiz-Gallardón and Magistrate Andrés Ollero, akin to the Catholic organization *Opus Dei*. It posits a conflict between women´s reproductive rights and the rights of unborn children with disabilities. The solution is to protect the rights of unborn children. With some nuances this is also espoused by Agustín Matía and CERMI
Liberal bioethics frame (a fate worse than death) Eugenics frame	Neurosurgeon Andrés Esparza, Gloria Muñoz, Jesús Mosterín (utilitarian philosopher, close to Peter Singer's views). Favors extended periods for termination of pregnancy on the basis of the quality of life of the children to be born with a disability and their families. A proponent of a more extreme version of this frame is Arcadi Espada, who opposes the birth of children with disabilities because of the burden placed on the national healthcare system (eugenics frame)
The right to choose frame	The feminist movement, represented by the Women's Participation Board in Andalusia, Alba Dobla
Human rights frame	Activists Antonio Centeno y Javier Romañach from Foro de Vida independiente. They oppose the extended deadline for pregnancies with congenital malformations

In statements made by the magistrate of the Constitutional Court, Andrés Ollero (who wrote the appeal of the aforementioned law and is a member of the Catholic ultraconservative *Opus Dei*), there is a similar but nuanced framing. He said that when a woman has an abortion, she is committing an 'act of war against her own son or daughter' (Ollero 2012). Ruiz-Gallardón also found allies in the Down Syndrome Federation who noted in an interview given on 26 July 2012, that 'abortions based on birth defects should be banned, not being a debatable issue' (Matía 2012). Matía added:

> It is enforced by international law, not subject to opinion. It is plain common sense. Even people with Down syndrome understand it as discrimination when they become aware of the abortion issue. They know they have limitations other people do not have and are different in some way, but they do not understand discrimination or prevention of the birth of people like them.

Related to these representations, in 2013, CERMI (Lucio 2013b) also endorsed the initial declaration of Minister of Ruiz-Gallardón, asserting: 'CERMI remembers that the United Nations Committee on the Rights of Persons with Disabilities (CRPD), has pointed out to Spain its commitment to avoid any discrimination on the basis of disability in the legal regulation of abortion' (Lucio 2013b). Both CERMI and the president of the Down Syndrome Federation stressed that abortion on the grounds of birth defects is prohibited by the UN Convention on the Rights of Persons with Disabilities of 2003, which Spain signed in 2007. Since then, Spain, along with the rest of the signatory countries, has committed to fulfilling the entire text of the aforementioned convention. According to CERMI and the Down Syndrome Federation, Spain must amend Article 15 of the 2/2010 Abortion Law, which extends to gestational age limit to terminating a pregnancy to within 22 weeks in the case of congenital malformations, in order to ensure the right to life of people with disabilities on a basis equal to others. The same conflict between the rights of the unborn child and those of the woman appears as well in Sahuquillo (2012).

In an interview given to *El País* on 25 June 2012, Gloria Muñoz pointed out how the attempted amendment imposes great suffering on both the people to be and their families, a representation that we call a 'fate-worse than death' frame. According to this frame, the birth of a child with disabilities should be prevented on the basis of the future well-being of the child and her family. The liberal bioethics approach favours extended periods for termination of pregnancy when the foetus presents congenital malformations on the basis of the quality of life argument defended by liberal bioethicist Peter Singer.

> Do you even know what preventing the abortion of a fetus with severe malformations would imply? Severe malformations carry great suffering to both the child and to their parents. May I dare to ask why is it that you feel entitled to force thousands of people to live with illness and terrible suffering, or with the premature death of their children? (Singer and Kuhse 1985, 72).

Similarly, in another article published in *El País* entitled 'No one has the right to impose suffering', paediatric neurosurgeon Javier Esparza (2012) declared:

> I'll summarize the vital prognosis and the quality of life of these children: as a result of so many interventions, their stay in hospitals can be a very prolonged one, even, in some cases, reaching several years of hospitalization: proper schooling is therefore impossible. But, worst of all, the sanitary, social, and familial efforts, as well as the efforts of the child him- or herself, will end before the second decade, for most of these children will have passed away, since this malformation presents numerous late and difficult-to-solve complications.

In a continuation of the article, on 23 December 2013, Esparza also decried the 2/2010 Abortion Law amendment, and suggested instead improving the quality of life of the nearly four million people already living in Spain: 'Since the budget cuts have undermined the 39/2006 Dependence Law, has the government anticipated any provision for this upcoming population with severe disabilities?' A year later, Esparza moved from a vantage point that considers a life with a disability a 'fate worse than death' (Parens and Asch 2000) to a more progressive framework, considering the incompatibilities between using the discourse of the DRM to ban abortions on the basis of congenital malformation while defunding the 39/2006 Dependence Law.

In an article in *El País*, 12 May 2013 entitled 'A "covert" indication', María Sahuquillo pointed out that, under the new law, abortions of foetuses with congenital malformations could still be performed under the provision of the mother's well-being. Since psychological well-being would be 'an easy way in, the stage system in force since 1985 would cause legal uncertainty to both practitioners and the women themselves' (Sahuquillo 2013). Without delving into the ideological motivations, both Esparza and Sahuquillo stressed the inconsistencies of the Minister of Justice's reform. While Esparza espoused a rather tragic perception of disability, Sahuquillo focused on the strategic use of the new law in which the Minister of Justice was planning to expose women's abuse of the welfare state, since her article is directly pointing out the possibility of circumventing the law.

From a more progressive framing, utilitarian philosopher Jesús Mosterín, a well-known follower of Peter Singer's liberal bioethics, recounted the story of a young mother who had recently had an abortion of a foetus with several malformations. While insisting that prenatal testing is one of the 'greatest achievements of our civilization' (Mosterín 2013) and asserting that disability is a personal tragedy – a fate worse than death framing. In line with the liberal bioethics approach – the philosopher nonetheless pointed out that.

Both the Republican Party in the US and the PP in Spain are conglomerates that include right-wing Christian extremists, along with libertarians and conservatives. The extreme Christian right wing is obsessed with the reproductive freedom of women and celebrates foetal malformation as a divine proof; a challenge sent by God to make us suffer in this valley of tears.

The representation of disability as a personal tragedy is widespread among many political actors and can be also found in Arcadi Espada's article (2013). Rooted in a eugenic framing, Espada remarked that a more restrictive legislation is needed since 'having children with disabilities is a crime against humanity':

> We should propose the application of some sort of legislation similar to that for crimes against humanity (…). If someone allows a sick baby to be born, while being able to avoid it, that someone should be subject to the possibility of being sued for this crime by the ill person, as well as by society itself, and have to pay for the treatments costs. (…) They are trying to impose on us freely their particular eugenic design: stupid, sick and worse children. (Espada 2013)

Even though they approached the issue from different perspectives, Javier Esparza, María Sahuquillo, Gloria Muñoz and Jesús Mosterín all shared the view that women should retain the right to terminate their pregnancies within 22 weeks in the event of congenital malformations. For these actors, the problem to be solved is the disability itself; they depict disability as non-compatible with a good quality of life, and people with disabilities as a burden to their families. This is what we call a 'liberal bioethics' frame.

According to the feminist movement [The Women's Participation Board in Andalusia], reforming the law would 'take Spain back to a time of secrecy and health and legal insecurity' (Lucio 2013a). Similarly, Alba Dobla, from the United Left Party, demanded an 'increase [in the] legal rights' included in the legislation, as well as a consideration of the 'total depenalization of voluntary abortion, eliminating the criminalization in the Penal Code' (Lucio 2013b). Interestingly, the feminist movement did not engage in Ruiz-Gallardón's framing of a confrontation between women's rights and rights of people with disabilities, but rather framed their mobilization from the perspective of 'the right to choose'. In this regard, the DRM articulated its response as a denouncement of ableist representation, as well as a refusal to engage with Ruiz Gallardón's anti-feminist approach. Using a human rights frame, Antonio Centeno, a member of the DRM, remarked that:

> Some arguments presented to justify the de-penalization of abortion (or even to make it mandatory) in cases of fetal 'abnormality' are built on judgments of the lives of the people who are already alive. I am not worried about the rights of the fetus (in my opinion there is not such a thing), but I am rather concerned about the right to a legislation that includes a dignified treatment of those that are born (with or without disabilities) and to guarantee women's right to their own bodies. (Centeno 2012)

Lastly, we examined the framing of the activists of the *Foro de Vida Independiente* (FVI), for whom the stage system is a discriminatory law with eugenic undertones. In an open letter in *El mundo*, FVI activist Antonio Centeno engaged Arcadi Espada over the aforementioned article 'A crime against humanity', stating 'It is undeniable that abortion is not practiced with children who are born, but some arguments supporting the legalization of abortion do in fact imply value judgments over born people with disabilities" (Centeno 2012).

Conclusion

We have applied Bacchi's WPR analysis to map the conflicting approaches of five different actors in the debates around the attempted amendment of the 2/2010 Abortion Law. Bacchi's WPR approach allows us to explore how the problem has been represented by the main actors in these debates. Minister of Justice Ruiz-Gallardón views women's reproductive rights, and specifically the right to an abortion, as detrimental to the dignity of people with disabilities. On the other hand, the Social-Democrats tend to frame this opposition between women's rights and the rights of people with disabilities as equally incompatible; they also tend to decry disability as a fate worse than death.

In tune with most western countries, the Spanish abortion debates play a relevant role in polarizing political debates and creating differences among political actors. The Conservative Party's capitalization on DRM discourse to undermine women's reproductive rights created allies among conservative disability organizations, Catholic citizens and family organizations. On the other hand, this capitalization also caused fragmentation among the conservative MPs and provoked resistance from ultraconservatives.

The context and timing in which the conservative amendment was presented is extremely relevant. The economic crisis and the changing political scenario make it all too plausible that the Conservative Government was using the UN Convention on the Rights of Persons with Disabilities of 2003, and more specifically, Article 10, to justify dismantling the welfare system. The defunding of the 39/2006 Dependence Law makes it clear that the use of the DRM discourse is an ideological manoeuvre to disguise the limitations of reproductive rights as social responsibility on behalf of people with disabilities. This strategic use of the confrontational discourse in order to justify austerity cuts has material consequences for women and people with disabilities, who lose rights, and further excludes women with disabilities, who make up 60% of all people with disabilities in Spain (INE 2012). This single-issue approach, missing the intersectional analysis of abortion rights, contributes to make the needs of women with disabilities invisible.

The answer proposed by the DMR and the feminist movement, along with the centre-left parties, of strengthening the maintenance of the 2/2010 Law was supported by a relevant majority of Spanish society. Ultimately, the effort to reform the 2010 abortion legislation failed due to the lack of a strong and unified position among conservatives, as well as the resistance efforts and complex positions adopted by the feminist and DRMs. All these movements have refused to see their claims co-opted so that the government could save face.

In terms of the achieved impact, the Minister of Justice succeeded in polarizing the debate, creating a division between second-wave feminists and the DRM movement. The conservatives also facilitated the co-optation of voices of people with disabilities at the same time that massive cuts in public spending were put into place. Cripwashing describes this strategic use of DRM discourse to disguise the dismantlement of the Spanish social welfare system and the curtailment of women's reproductive rights, in force during the last 30 years.

The Social-Democrats have succeeded in putting in common parlance the liberal bioethics assumptions of quality of life, such as those espoused by Peter Singer and Helga Kuhse (1985). Most notable are the discourses of Gloria Muñoz, Javier Esparza and Jesús Mosterín, all of whom construct disability as something that should be prevented before birth, framing disability as a fate worse than death. Nonetheless Esparza, Mosterín and Gloria Muñoz showed little awareness as to how their representations of disability may affect people born with disabilities. Marginally, the neoliberal journalist Arcadi Espada supported eugenics and engaged FVI activist Antonio Centeno in a public exchange of letters. The DRM argument considered the stage system a discriminatory law with eugenic undertones, rapidly evolving to report the infringement of the dependent care law and the aforementioned Penal Code modifications of Articles 98 and 156.

The attempted reform served to expose the reluctance of institutionalized feminism to include the women with disabilities, as well as the subaltern situation of feminist leaders with disabilities contesting the attempted conservative reform (Arnau 2012; Moscoso 2012). Similar debates between reproductive rights' advocates and 'prolife movements' are taking place in Germany (Achtelik 2015).

Lastly, the analysis of the representations of the abortion debates has unveiled (1) the impact of the framing process in diminishing the rights of already disenfranchised social groups; (2) the political use of confronting the rights of women and people with disabilities, with relevant benefits for the conservatives; (3) the usefulness of using Bacchi's WPR framework, combined with the new term crip-washing, in understanding the Spanish debate on abortion; (4) the resistance of social movements as key factor for why the abortion reform never took place; and (5) new areas for future research, such as the creation of conflicts of interest between disadvantaged populations, which obscure conservative backlash or further polarize the positions.

Notes

1. The very same positions seem to be recurring in the recent Zika virus crisis. In an article published by *The Huffington Post* on 4 February 2016, journalist Nicole Cliffe presents a position that could be framed according to what we call a liberal bioethics position: 'It's days off work, it's out-of-pocket therapies until diagnoses kick in, it's fighting your insurance, it's becoming a full-time advocate.' On the other hand, Disability Studies scholar Rosemarie Garland-Thomson presents a social model perspective: 'Somehow, what got written into the idea of reproductive choice and freedom and self determination for women is the assumption that no woman is prepared or would want to parent a child with a disability' (see Angyal 2016).

2. The 15-M movement is a series of ongoing demonstrations that started in the city of Madrid on 15 May 2011, and quickly spread throughout the country. This grassroots movement, which demands radical changes, emerged following the Egyptian and Tunisian revolutions.

3. The CLAGS was founded in 1991 as the first university-based research centre in the USA and belongs to the graduate centre of the City University at New York dedicated to the study of the issues of concern to LGBT, and queer individuals.

4. Homonationalism is 'an assemblage of geopolitical and historical forces, neoliberal interests in capitalist accumulation both cultural and material, biopolitical state practices of population control and affective investments in discourses of freedom, liberation and rights' (Puar 2013, 336).

5. 'Crip' is derogatory term for a person with a disability, short for 'cripple', and implies a severe impairment; such a person is unable to walk or move properly due to a disability or injury to their back or legs. According to Disability Studies theorist Carrie Sandahl, 'crip' destabilizes the normative point of view of mainstream society:

   Queering describes the practices of putting a spin on mainstream representations to reveal latent queer subtexts; of appropriating a representation for one's own purposes, forcing it to signify differently; or of deconstructing a representation's heterosexism. Similarly, some disabled people practice 'cripping'. Cripping spins mainstream representations or practices to reveal able-bodied assumptions and exclusionary effects. Both queering and cripping expose the arbitrary delineation between normal and defective and the negative social ramifications of attempts to homogenize humanity, and both disarm what is painful with wicked humor, including camp. (Sandahl 2003, 37)

6. Ableism is the discrimination or prejudice against people who have disabilities.

7. 9/1985 Law reforming the 417bis article of the Penal Code. BOE 166, July 12, 1985.

8. 30/1981 Law modifying the Civil Code in regard to the regulation on marriage, void marriage, separation and divorce. BOE 172, July 20, 1981, 16457–16562.
9. 2/2010 Act on sexual and reproductive health and termination of pregnancy. BOE 55, March 4, 2010, 21001–21014.
10. During the Francoist dictatorship the notion of 'social dangerousness' was used to vilify certain behaviours and label as outlaws individuals whose life experiences defied the national-Catholic standards of decency.
11. The article 10 of the UN Convention of the Rights of people with disabilities states that: 'States Parties reaffirm that every human being has the inherent right to life and shall take all necessary measures to ensure its effective enjoyment by persons with disabilities on an equal basis with others'. Convention on the Rights of Persons with Disabilities, available at: http://www.un.org/disabilities/convention/conventionfull.shtml.

Acknowledgements

The authors want to thank Gerard Goggin, Jess Cadwallader, Linda Steele and Rosemary Curtis and two anonymous reviewers for their comments and suggestions on this manuscript. Finally, we want to thank to the vibrant feminist movement of Spain and to the Disability Rights activists of the *Foro de Vida Independiente* for their relentless fight in favour of civil rights.

Disclosure statement

No potential conflict of interest was reported by the authors.

Funding

This research was done under the funding of three projects, firstly, of the MINECO (Ministerio de Economía y Competitividad de España), *Responsabilidad causal de la comisión por omisión: Una dilucidación ético-jurídica de los problemas de la inacción indebida* [Ref. FFI2014-53926-R], [Ref. FFI2015-65947-C2-1-P]. Also, it has been funded by the VOSATEC project funded by the Spanish R&D Programme of MINECO (2016–2018). And thirdly, supported by the European Collaborative Research Project 'Cruising the 1970s-CRUSEV' (2016–19), funded by the European Science Foundation, reference CRP 5087-00242A.

ORCID

Melania Moscoso iD http://orcid.org/0000-0002-8754-8786
R. Lucas Platero iD http://orcid.org/0000-0002-7196-6983

References

Achtelik, Kirsten. 2015. "Es gibt feministische Argumente gegen Abtreibungen [A new Feminist Argument gainst Abortion]". http://www.sueddeutsche.de/leben/praenataldiagnostik-es-gibt-feministische-argumente-gegen-abtreibungen-1.2751102.
A. F. 2012. "Los discapacitados piden a gallardón que elimine la esterilización forzosa." *Diario Público*, July 27. http://www.publico.es/espana/discapacitados-piden-gallardon-elimine-esterilizacion.html.
Aldaz, Arantza. 2014. "La reforma del código penal estigmatiza la enfermedad mental [Penal Code Reform Stigmatizes Mental Health Patients]". *El Diario Vasco*, November 2. http://www.diariovasco.com/sociedad/201411/02/reforma-codigo-penal-estigmatiza-20141102010721-v.html.

Angyal, Chloe. 2016. "Zika Virus Threat Puts Abortion Rights and Disability Rights on Collision Course." *The Huffington Post*, February 5. http://www.huffingtonpost.com/entry/zika-virus-us-abortion-disability_us_56b2601be4b04f9b57d83192.

Arnau, Soledad. 2012. "El aborto eugenésico desde la mirada bioética feminista de /desde la diversidad funcional [On Disability/ Functional Diversity Eugenic Abortion from Feminist Bioethics]". *Con la A*, 17.

Bacchi, Carol. 2009. *Analysing Policy: What's the Problem Represented to Be.* Frenchs Forest: Pearson.

Calvo, Vera Gutiérrez, and Alejandra Agudo. 2013. "Gallardón pone fecha a una reforma del aborto cuatro veces aplazada [Gallardón Sets the Date for the Abortion Law Reformation]". *El País*, September 2. http://politica.elpais.com/politica/2013/09/02/actualidad/1378109123_663116.html.

Centeno, Antonio. 2012. "Aborto libre sí, aborto eugenésico no" [Yes to Free Abortion. Not to Eugenic Abortion]. In *El blog de Antonio Centeno*. http://antoniocenteno.blogspot.com.es/2012/08/sobre-el-aborto-eugenesico_3.html.

Del Burgo, Pedro. 2012. "Nos quitan los asistentes que son nuestros pies y nuestras manos [Devoid of the Personal Assistants We need So Much]". *El Mercantil Valenciano*, October 5. http://www.levante-emv.com/comunitat-valenciana/2012/10/05/quitan-asistentes-son-pies-manos/941616.html.

[Dependence Law] Ley 39/2006, de 14 de diciembre, de Promoción de la Autonomía Personal y Atención a las personas en situación de dependencia [Law 39/2006, 14 December on Personal Autonomy and Dependent Care]. *BOE* 299, January 15: 44142–44156.

Entman, Robert M. 1993. "Framing: Toward Clarification of a Fractured Paradigm." *Journal of Communication* 43 (4): 51–58.

Erevelles, Nirmala, and Andrea Minear. 2010. "Unspeakable Offenses: Untangling Race and Disability in Discourses of Intersectionality." *Journal of Literary & Cultural Disability Studies* 4 (2): 127–145.

Espada, Arcadi. 2013. "Un crimen contra la humanidad [A Crime against Humanity]". *El Mundo*, May 9. http://www.elmundo.es/blogs/elmundo/elmundopordentro/2013/05/09/un-crimen-contra-la-humanidad.html.

Esparza, Javier. 2012. "Nadie tiene derecho a obligar al sufrimiento [No One has the Right to Impose Suffering (I)]". *El País*, July 24. http://sociedad.elpais.com/sociedad/2012/07/24/actualidad/1343153808_906956.html.

Esparza, Javier. 2013. "Nadie tiene derecho a obligar al sufrimiento (II) [No One has the Right to Impose Suffering (II)]". *El País*, December 23. http://sociedad.elpais.com/sociedad/2013/12/23/actualidad/1387828772_474921.html.

Flotats, Ana. 2012. "La malformación del feto no será ya un supuesto para abortar" [Fetal Abnormality is not Longer a Allowed Circumstance for (Legal) Abortion]. *La Razón*, July 22. http://www.elperiodico.com/es/noticias/politica/malformaciondel-feto-sera-supuesto-para-abortar-segun-gallardon-2121601.

Garea, Fernando. 2010. "Las nuevas medidas con las que el gobierno quiere ahorrar 15.000 millones." *El País*, May 12. http://elpais.com/elpais/2010/05/12/actualidad/1273652221_850215.html.

Guzmán, Francisco, Melania Moscoso, and Mario Toboso. 2010. "Por qué la ley de dependencia no constituye un instrumento para la promoción de la autonomía personal." *Zerbitzuan: Gizarte Zerbitzuetarako Aldizkaria= Revista De Servicios Sociales* (48): 43–56.

INE. 2012. *Encuesta de Integración Social y Salud Año 2012*. Madrid: Instituto Nacional de Estadística.

Lister, Ruth. 2011. "From the Intimate to the Global: Reflections on Gendered Citizenship." In *The Limits of Gendered Citizenship*, edited by Elżbieta Oleksy, Jeff Hearn, and Dorota Golańska, 27–41. New York: Routledge.

López, Silvia, and R. Lucas Platero. 2015. "Diskurser som märker kroppar." *Fronesis* 50–51: 128–133.

López Rodríguez, Silvia. 2011. "¿Cuáles son los marcos interpretativos de la violencia de género en España? Un análisis constructivista." *Revista Española de Ciencia Política* 25: 11–30.

Lucio, Lourdes. 2013a. "El Pacto por la igualdad rechaza la reforma de la ley del aborto [The Pact on Gender Equality Rejects Abortion Law Reformation]". *El País*, May 17. http://ccaa.elpais.com/ccaa/2013/05/17/andalucia/1368794463_688995.html.

Lucio, Lourdes. 2013b. "IU empuja al PSOE a votar en el Parlamento a favor del aborto [The Leftist Party Pushes the Socialist Party to Vote in Favor of Abortion at the Parliament]". *El País*, May 23. http://ccaa.elpais.com/ccaa/2013/05/23/andalucia/1369326877_014290.html.

Matía, Agustín. 2012. "Tienen que suprimir el aborto por malformaciones. No es algo opinable [Abortion in Fetal Abnormality has to be Banned. It is not Subject to Opinion]". *Nosotras decidimos*, July 26. http://nosotrasdecidimos.org/down-espana-cree-que-hay-que-prohibir-aborto-por-malformaciones/.

Morán, Carmen. 2010. "No sólo falta dinero para dependencia, falta control." *El País*, May 2. http://elpais.com/diario/2010/05/02/sociedad/1272751201_850215.html.

Moscoso, Melania. 2009. "A propósito de la ley de promoción de la autonomía personal y de ayuda de la dependencia" [On Personal Autonomy and Dependent Care Law]. *Intersticios. Revista Sociológica De Pensamiento Crítico* 3 (2): 217–221.

Moscoso, Melania. 2012. "El patriarcado por otro nombre: el discurso feminista y las mujeres con discapacidad [Patriarchy by other Name: Feminism and Women with Disabilities]". *Con la A*, 17.

Moscoso, Melania. 2014. "No en mi Nombre [Not in my Name]". *Pikara Magazine*, January 15. http://www.pikaramagazine.com/2014/01/no-en-mi-nombre/.

Mosterín, Jesús. 2013. "Una cruzada contra la libertad reproductiva" [A crusade against reproductive freedom]. *El País*, May 21. http://elpais.com/elpais/2013/05/16/opinion/1368723975_483486.html.

Muñoz, Gloria. 2012. "Si me quedase embarazada de otro bebé tan enfermo iría a abortar fuera [If I Would become Pregnant again with a Very Ill Child, i Would go Abroad to get an Abortion]". *El País*, July 25. http://sociedad.elpais.com/sociedad/2012/07/25/actualidad/1343241210_620587.html.

Ollero, Andrés. 2012. "Los no nacidos no han ganado para sustos [The Unborn on Shock]". *El País*, August 13. http://politica.elpais.com/politica/2012/08/13/actualidad/1344892603_108028.html.

Parens, Erick, and Adrienne Asch. 2000. *Prenatal Testing and Disability Rights*. Washington, DC: Georgetown University Press.

Puar, Jasbir. 2007. *Terrorist Assemblages: Homonationalism in Queer Times*. Durham: Duke University Press.

Puar, Jasbir. 2011. "Citation and Censorship: The Politics of Talking About the Sexual Politics of Israel." *Feminist Legal Studies* 19 (2): 133–142. doi:10.1007/s10691-011-9176-3.

Puar, Jasbir. 2013. "Rethinking Homonationalism." *International Journal of Middle East Studies* 45 (2): 336–339.

Ruiz, Amelia. 2012. "El gobierno abandona a los dependientes a su suerte y sus cuidadoras ya no cotizan a la Seguridad Social [Government le aves d ependent people Unattended and their Caregivers Without Benefits]". *Elplural.com*, December 1. http://pre.elplural.com/2012/12/01/el-gobierno-abandona-a-los-dependientes-a-su-suerte-y-sus-cuidadoras-ya-no-cotizan-a-la-seguridad-social/.

Sahuquillo, María R. 2012. "La ley de plazos no incrementa el número de abortos [Stage System does Not Increase Abortions]". *8 de marzo*. http://sociedad.elpais.com/sociedad/2012/03/08/actualidad/1331213258_104482.html.

Sahuquillo, María R. 2013. "Una indicación encubierta [A 'Covert' Indication]". *El País*, May 12. http://sociedad.elpais.com/sociedad/2013/05/12/actualidad/1368391369_435284.html.

Sandahl, Carrie. 2003. "Queering the Crip or Cripping the Queer? Intersections of Queer and Crip Identities in Solo Autobiographical Performance." *GLQ: A Journal of Lesbian and Gay Studies* 9 (1): 25–56.

Santesmases, María Jesús. 2016. "Discriminación *in vitro*: cuerpos y cariotipos en los orígenes de la genética del síndrome de Down [*In vitro* Discrimination; Bodies and Karyotype at the Origins of Down Syndrome Research]". In *Justicia ¿Para todos?: Perspectivas filosóficas*, edited by Concha Roldán, en David Rodríguez-Arias, Jordi Maiso, and Catherine Heeney, 79–93. Madrid: Plaza y Valdés.

Saxton, Marsha. 2000. "Why Members of the Disability Community Oppose Mental Diagnosis and Selective Abortion." In *Prenatal Testing and Disability Rights*, edited by Erick Parens and Adrienne Asch, 147–163. Washington, DC: Georgetown University Press.

Singer, Peter, and Helga Kuhse. 1985. *Should the Baby Live?: The Problem of Handicapped Infants*. Oxford [Oxfordshire]: Oxford University Press.

Snyder, Sharon, and David Mitchell. 2010. "Introduction: Ablenationalism and the Geo-politics of Disability." *Journal of Literary & Cultural Disability Studies* 4 (2): 113–125.

Toharia, José Juan. 2013. "Los españoles ante el aborto (1976–2013) [Spaniards on Abortion: 1976–2013]". *El País*, May 3. http://sociedad.elpais.com/sociedad/2013/05/03/actualidad/1367598751_549991.html.

UN (United Nations). 2003. *Convention on the Rights of Persons with Disabilities*. http://www.un.org/disabilities/convention/conventionfull.shtml.

Valiente Fernández, Celia. 2001. "Gendering Abortion Debates: State Feminism in Spain." In *Abortion Politics, Women's Movements, and the Democratic State: A Comparative Study of State Feminism*, edited by Dorothy McBride Stetson, 229–244. Oxford: Oxford University Press. doi:10.1093/0199242666.003.0011.

'Figurehead' hate crime cases: developing a framework for understanding and exposing the 'problem' with 'disability'

Ryan Thorneycroft and Nicole L. Asquith

ABSTRACT

The horrific stories of James Byrd Jr., Matthew Shepard and Stephen Lawrence are forever etched in criminal law. In each of these cases, activists, family members, politicians, academics, the public and media all reacted in their unique way to bring the problem of 'hate crime' onto the agenda. There are many other cases that have activated such a public imagination, or what we call 'figurehead' cases, yet the factors pertinent to figurehead recognition remain under-explored within hate crime scholarship. Using a case study analysis, three racist and heterosexist hate crime cases are examined in order to assess the individual and collective conditions that facilitated their place on the public agenda. This analysis has important implications for the category of 'disability', and highlights several shortcomings that forestall the recognition of 'disablist hate crime' publicly, legislatively and judicially. It is argued that the positioning of disability as 'abject' has inhibited the operationalization of disablist violence within the hate crime framework, and within criminal justice systems more generally.

Introduction

The horrific stories of James Byrd Jr., Matthew Shepard and Stephen Lawrence are forever etched in criminal law. In each of these cases, activists, family members, politicians, academics, the public and media all reacted in their unique way to bring the problem of 'hate crime' onto the agenda. Cases of violent crime, other than prejudice-related violence, have activated such a public imagination, or what Asquith (2015) calls 'figurehead' cases, yet these three cases continue to shape how hate crimes are understood in the U.K., U.S. and elsewhere. While social movements have brought the issue of minority rights onto the political agenda, and brought in an array of protections such as hate crime law, figurehead cases can also initiate (or renew) public discussion about our responses to this form of violence (Jenness and Grattet 2001). Many figurehead cases have represented the precipitous tipping point at which criminal justice and broader public recognition is delivered (Jenness and Grattet 2001). These cases have become crystallized within our social memory, yet the role they play – and the factors pertinent to figurehead recognition – remain under-explored within hate crime scholarship (Asquith 2015).

Using a case study analysis, we examined three racist and heterosexist hate crime cases in order to assess the individual and collective conditions that facilitated their place on the public agenda as figurehead hate crimes. A figurehead hate crime refers to a case of prejudice-related violence that garners considerable media and public attention, consequently shaping policy and practice, and broader understanding about the nature of 'hate crime'. As hate crimes are reported almost daily within local news and current affairs in the Western world (particularly in the U.K. and U.S.), media attention alone does not lead to figurehead status. We suggest that one prerequisite for figurehead status is that it must reach beyond the jurisdiction in which the crime occurred. The cases of Shepard, Byrd Jr. and Lawrence are considered in this analysis because they have received unparalleled significance within hate crime scholarship and public imagination, and each case resulted in landmark changes to policy, practice and/or law (Cottle 2005; Holohan 2005; Petersen 2011).

In contrast to these three cases, no case of disablist hate crime has been able to capture the necessary preconditions for figurehead hate crime status. Our analysis, therefore, has important implications for the category of 'disability' and the operationalization of provisions aimed to reduce disablist violence. This article highlights how the abjectification of disabled people, and the dis/ableism that pervades society, has rendered their existence within the hate crime rubric unintelligible. According to Butler, the abject 'relates to all kinds of bodies whose lives are not considered to be "lives" and whose materiality is understood not to "matter"' (cited in Meijer and Prins 1998, 281). Linking the themes of family, shame and celebrity inherent to the Shepard, Byrd Jr. and Lawrence cases, the article highlights some of the necessary constituents for figurehead hate crime status. The objective of this analysis is to provide a framework of analysis (not a model of action), which highlights the circumstances that facilitate figurehead status.

Figurehead cases concretize what is, and can be, known about hate crime. The figurehead cases under study in this analysis are exemplars of 'stranger-danger'. They are also extreme acts of violence by men against men. Not only does this complicate how criminal justice agencies respond to reports of hate crime, it also shapes public opinion about ideal (deserving) victims. In selecting these three cases for analysis, and to counterpoise these 'ideal' victims with the experiences of disabled people, we do not seek to homogenize disability or, in fact, the experiences of hate crime. Rather, we foreground how homogenous hate crime policies and practices result in inequitable outcomes that erase disablist violence from what can be known about hate crime.

The invention of hate crime

While acts of 'hate crime' are not new, it was not until the latter half of the twentieth century the name and concept was operationalized (Jenness and Grattet 2001). What were once examples of bigotry – including the Shoah in Second World War, the lynchings by the Ku Klux Klan and everyday instances of violence against minorities – are now viewed through the conceptual lens of 'hate crimes' (Jenness and Grattet 2001). Consisting of crimes motivated by hatred or bias, the concept originated from the various rights movements of the 1950s, 1960s and 1970s (Jenness and Grattet 2001). This type of victimization has since been criminalized in over 35 jurisdictions through the enactment of laws aimed to address hate crime (or bias crime, or prejudice-related crime) by penalizing the commission of crimes motivated by the victims' perceived identity or social membership. In some jurisdictions, hate crimes have been constituted as a unique form of victimization, which is complemented by penalty enhancements (for example, the *Hate Crime Enhancement Act 1994* in the U.S.A. and the *Crime and Disorder Act 1998* in U.K.). In other jurisdictions, the motivational aspects of hate crime are considered an aggravating factor in sentencing (for example, Victorian *Sentencing Act 1991*). A largely Western concept, the historical development of these laws has often proceeded from responding to anti-semitic violence, which has been closely followed by provisions for racist, heterosexist, faith-based (including Islamophobic), cissexist and disablist violence. Some jurisdictions recognize a wider range of attributes while other jurisdictions have enacted outlier provisions. For example, in the U.K., violence against women and sub-cultures (such as Goths) have been defined as hate crimes and operationalized by some policing agencies (Garland, Chakraborti, and Hardy 2015). In contrast to these attribute-based definitions, in some U.S.A. jurisdictions, hate crime definitions have been widened to professions, such as police and emergency workers.

As 'disability' has been considered a medical problem for almost all of human history, its relatively recent emergence as an 'identity' has complicated social attitudes to disability (Siebers 2008). While racial, religious, sexuality and gender minorities are firmly ensconced in hate crime laws in line with the identity politics that brought their experiences to the attention of the criminal justice system (Siebers 2008), disabled people are essentialized, making their corporeal vulnerability difficult to translate into hate crime laws. Price and Shildrick (1998, 226) label 'disability' the rubric of 'and so on', whereby 'disability' is routinely last on the list. Siebers (2008) suggests that the ideology of ability is so powerful that disability becomes invisibilized and Swain and Cameron (1999, 68) argue that able-bodiedness is presumed 'unless otherwise stated'. Disabled people are constituted as abject within a 'domain of abjected bodies' (Butler 1993, 16). Within a hate crime context, disability again is last on the list. Disablist violence is not legislatively recognized in many jurisdictions, and even where it is, widespread non-recognition, under-policing, under-reporting and under-recording occurs (Thorneycroft and Asquith 2015). Moreover, many cases of disablist violence are reconceptualized as motivated by opportunism and vulnerability rather than prejudice (Thorneycroft forthcoming).

The analysis of three racist and heterosexist figurehead hate crime cases in this article highlights several factors that perpetuate the unintelligibility of disablist violence. While some jurisdictions have attempted to respond to disablist violence (the U.K., for example), this has not translated to a renewed definition of hate crime, altered public perceptions of hate crime or increased the recognition and reporting of disablist violence.

Contextualizing the analysis

Some victims garner greater public recognition and media attention than others, and a range of individual and collective factors help transform these singular events into (inter)national tragedies. To date, public and professional understandings of such cases interpret these victims as 'ideal victims', a term shaped by Christie (1986, 18) to denote those people 'when hit by crime – most readily are given the complete and legitimate status of being a victim'. However, it is when examples of 'ideal victims' are scrutinized it becomes apparent that Christie's conceptualization is not definitive or exhaustive. For example, Christie's notion of the ideal victim does not explicitly explore the importance of the media in transmitting knowledge of specific (hate) crimes, and in turn, identifying victims whose experiences exemplify the ideal. It does not account for less-than-'ideal' victims becoming figurehead cases, and so we demonstrate in this article the individual and collective conditions that facilitate such recognition.

Likewise, Christie's typology of the ideal victim fails to consider a range of individual and collective factors that produce non-normative victims incapable of becoming figurehead cases. These non-normative bodies are measured against the normative frame of ableism, which refers to:

> A network of beliefs, processes and practices that produce a particular kind of self and body (the corporeal standard) that is projected as the perfect, species-typical and therefore essential and fully human. Disability then is cast as a diminished state of being human. (Campbell 2001, 44)

Ableism perpetuates the myth the 'perfect' body is the 'fully human' body, and disabled bodies are inferior and as such 'not one of our own'. Hughes (2009, 400) suggests 'the strong, well-formed, non-disabled, masculine body is the benchmark' against which all people are measured.

The Shepard, Byrd Jr. and Lawrence cases helped to initiate global conversations about prejudice, hate crime protections and creating better criminal justice responses. While examples of racist and heterosexist hate crimes, this analysis yields important findings for 'disablist violence', in spite of the absence of a disablist hate crime figurehead case. The most significant case of disablist violence to spark a public imagination about this form of hate crime involved the death of Fiona Pilkington and her daughter, Francecca Hardwick, who was labelled 'intellectually disabled'. Following years of abuse directed at Francecca, Fiona drove to a deserted laneway and killed herself and her daughter by setting the car on fire (Wilkes 2007). While this initiated considerable media attention at the time, it has not continued. Moreover, the public reaction to the case focussed upon Fiona, who was 'driven to kill herself'

(*The Telegraph*, September 29, 2009), and not on the disablist violence Francecca endured over the years. In this sense, 'disability' is deferred, and the sensationalizing of the macabre context ensures it cannot be representative of the ideal victim, and to date has failed to have inter-jurisdictional impact. For these reasons, the Pilkington case is not examined in this analysis. Likewise, while the death of Brent Martin received some attention in the media at the time, and perhaps reached figurehead status of crimes against the vulnerable, it has not had the impact of the figurehead cases discussed in this analysis.[1]

As with Flyvbjerg (2006, 241), in this article, we aim to 'contribute to the cumulative development of knowledge', and illustrate various contextual factors that inhibit disablist hate crime recognition through an analysis of three figurehead hate crime cases. In the following section, these cases are described and then analyzed in relation to a range of individual, social, cultural and institutional factors that contribute to their status as figurehead cases. 'Figurehead production' illustrates the ways in which this status has been *produced* by various contextual, historical and political factors. Later in the article, we contemplate what this analysis means for the category of 'disability' in hate crime provisions. In particular, we consider how disability identity politics positions itself in response to the ubiquitous abjectification of disabled lives.

Matthew Shepard (heterosexist hate crime, USA)

The murder of Matthew Shepard is arguably the most well-known hate crime case. On the night of 6 October 1998, the twenty-one-year old met two men at the Fireside Lounge in Laramie, Wyoming. The two men, Russell Henderson and Aaron McKinney, posed as gay men, and socialized with Matthew leading later in the evening to an offer to drive him home. Matthew was driven out of town, brutally beaten and tied to a fence, and left to die in near-freezing weather. He was found 18 hours later by a cyclist and died five days later in a Colorado Hospital. Shepard's death was torturous; he was pistol-whipped so severely his brain stem was crushed, and the 18 hours tied to a fence contributed to the lethality of the violence, which was exacerbated by hyperthermia. When he was found, there was blood all over his face, except for streaks where tears had washed the blood away (Ott and Aoki 2002).

Figurehead production

A range of cultural shifts was occurring around the time of Shepard's death, and this shaped the public and media reaction, and transformed it into a figurehead hate crime case. The media reaction was instantaneous and sustained, emotionally charged and pervasive (Munro 2014). In the earliest media reports of the incident, reporters flagged that police were exploring whether Shepard's sexuality may have been a factor in the crime (Brooke 1998). Following this, the Human Rights Commission (HRC), a queer advocacy group, released a press statement entitled 'Apparent Hate Crime Against Gay Student in Wyoming Highlights The Need For Congress to Pass The Hate Crimes Prevention Act; Brutality Continues While Congress Lets Bill Languish …' (1998). Linking the incident to debates at the time about hate crime legislation – Wyoming was reluctant to adopt hate crime laws – the media started to frame the case as a hate crime (Brooke 1998). Ott and Aoki (2002) suggest an event becomes a major media news story when there is the potential for drama, and the anti-gay aspect and crucifix symbolism provided 'good melodrama' for the media to pursue. Despite wanting to grieve in private and '… go back to my former career as a housewife and mom' (Thernstrom 1999), the influence of Matthew's mother (and the Shepard family) was also considerable. They played an instrumental part in advocating for the passage of hate crime legislation (most notably the *Matthew Shepard and James Byrd, Jr. Hate Crimes Prevention Act 2009*), and the creation of the Matthew Shepard Foundation, which continues to play a proactive role in fighting against prejudice, 18 years after his death (Matthew Shepard Foundation 2015).

At the time of Shepard's death, the U.S. political and social climate in relation to sexuality was changing. Rock Hudson's death from AIDS-related diseases in 1985 and the Oscar-winning documentary on the 1970s life and activism of Harvey Milk, *The Mayor of Castro Street* (1984) sowed the ground for cultural change. These events prepared heteronormative America for the cultural artefacts that were to follow in the 1990s with the release – and Oscar's success – of Tom Hanks' portrayal of Andrew Becket in *Philadelphia* (1994) and Sean Penn's Oscar success in his 2008 portrayal of Harvey Milk in *Milk*.

Each of these cultural encounters changed the way sexuality was perceived and evaluated; but they also created the grounds for a renewed social activism from conservative and Christian lobbies, including the infamous protest by Westboro Church members at Shepard's funeral. Despite the public adoration of Hudson, and the success of Penn's and Hank's portrayals of gay men, they were not ideal 'victims'. They epitomized the sexual promiscuity and excess of homosexuality, the moral panic over HIV/AIDS, and the 'tidal wave of unprecedented evil' (Tomczak 2015) promoted by Hollywood and the mass media.

In contrast, Matthew Shepard '… became the perfect representation of a nonthreatening face for homosexuality to be juxtaposed against the predatory disease-ridden paedophiles that the religious right created and condemned' (Munro 2014, 11). Shepard was portrayed in media accounts of his murder as innocent and vulnerable, and, importantly, 'straight-acting' or *normal*, making public consumption and compassion permissible. For his abjectification to be deferred, Shepard was portrayed as 'not like the other gays', he was homonormative, or what Seidman (2002) calls, 'the normal gay'. The normal gay:

> … is expected to exhibit specific kinds of traits and behaviors. He is supposed to be gender conventional, well adjusted, and integrated into mainstream society; he is committed to home, family, career, and nation … The politics of the normal gay involves minority rights, not the end of heterosexual privilege. (Seidman 2002, 14)

Shepard's small height, delicate frame, young age and attractiveness facilitated public empathy because he could be anyone's son (Thernstrom 1999). Moreover, the fact he did not die straight away permitted the formation of vigils, prayers and national conversations over his fate, so his story became part of a national conversation about prejudice in America.

Stephen Lawrence (racist hate crime, UK)

Stephen Lawrence died five years prior to Matthew Shepard, but similarly made a national impression on the public imagination in the U.K. On a late night in April 1993, 18-year-old Stephen Lawrence was waiting for a bus home to Eltham (south-east London) with his friend Duwayne Brooks, after they spent the evening at his uncle's house playing videogames. Whilst waiting for the bus, Lawrence and Brooks were approached by between four and six white men,[2] one of whom reportedly called Lawrence a 'nigger'. Brookes immediately ran for his life, but Lawrence, who stood his ground, was attacked and received two stab wounds that severed his arteries and punctured a lung. While Brooks successfully escaped his attackers, Lawrence was only able to run a short distance before collapsing. An ambulance was called, but he bled to death before reaching hospital.

Figurehead production

The immediate media and public reaction to the Lawrence story was markedly different to Matthew Shepard. In the case of Lawrence, the story emerged unevenly before becoming a mounting crisis that transformed the singular event into a national symbolic tragedy (Cottle 2005). Early reports of the incident were fragmentary, with some blaming Brooks for Lawrence's death, but greater media interest followed when Nelson Mandela lent support to the Lawrence family (Pilkington 1993). This also presented the opportunity for Doreen Lawrence – Stephen's mother – to criticize the handling of the police investigation (Pilkington 1993). This led to community marches and protests about racist violence, but it was the decision of the Crown Prosecution Service (CPS) not to prosecute the suspects that presented the 'tipping point' from a singular event to a symbolic focal point about race and racism in the U.K. (Cottle 2005).

Along with community action, the media – especially, *The Guardian* and the *Daily Mail* – became keen advocates in the Stephen Lawrence case, and the story maintained its relevance through the ongoing reporting of the London Metropolitan Police Service's institutional failings (Holohan 2005). Burrell and Peachey (2012) also highlight that the media was intimately involved in the case because of its links to the media's activism against right-wing demonstrations at the time. Its status as a figurehead case was heightened in 1997 when the *Daily Mail* published the photos of five of the alleged offenders, and challenged these men to sue the publication if the *Daily Mail's* claims were slanderous. None of the named men did (Burrell and Peachey 2012). The continuing stories about institutional failings gave the story momentum and catalyzed the community around the Lawrence family. In 1998 (at the same time as the Shepard family in the U.S.), Doreen Lawrence established the Stephen Lawrence Charitable Trust, which continues to play a proactive role in combating discrimination and promoting justice (Stephen Lawrence Charitable Trust 2014). In the same year, the U.K. Government amended the *Crime and Disorder Act* to enact penalty enhancements for racially motivated violence.

Later, the Macpherson Inquiry – an investigation into the case and its handling – precipitated further public discussion about racist violence and the inadequacy of police responses (1999). Following the release of the Macpherson report in 1999, in which the police were labelled 'institutionally racist', a wave of policing and social reforms was instituted (including critical developments around notions of 'hate crime'). The story of Stephen Lawrence was subsequently transformed from a single tragedy to an unprecedented failure of the criminal justice system. Doreen Lawrence continues to maintain a high public profile, and in 2013 was elevated to the peerage (Baroness Lawrence of Clarendon) for her advocacy work since her son's murder.

While the media coverage, Nelson Mandela's comments and the family's advocacy aided in making this a figurehead case, there were other factors attendant to this, and specific to the representation of Lawrence, that made this a figurehead case. For example, Lawrence was presented as a gifted student who had no prior issues with the police (or anyone more broadly), and his family was presented as analogous with middle-class Britain – hardworking and God-fearing (Cottle 2005). In this sense, Lawrence represented a point of departure from the conventional portrayal of black youths at the time (Cottle 2005), including the other, earlier victims of racist hate crimes in the same neighbourhood. Just like Matthew Shepard, who was portrayed *as* straight-acting, Lawrence was portrayed without race (or as an exception to his race) in spite of the factors that led to his victimization. For example, a family friend (and Reverend) stated at Lawrence's funeral: 'As he grew older he began to respect his own blackness, *but he was never aggressive in this* [emphasis added]. He was just confident in who he was' (as quoted in Sharrock 1993). Doreen Lawrence made similar comments very early in the investigation, where she did not want to turn the murder into a political cause (Sharrock 1993). Presenting Stephen without race allowed society to empathize with the inequity and 'inhumanity of his murder' (Cottle 2005, 58).

James Byrd Jr. (racist hate crime, USA)

The reaction to the murder of James Byrd Jr., and the reasons for its figurehead status, contrasts with both Shepard and Lawrence. Forty-nine-year-old James Byrd Jr. was walking home from his niece's bridal shower on the evening of 7 June 1998[3] in Jasper, Texas, when he was offered a lift home by a passing car. Rather than take Byrd Jr. home, the three men – all of whom had white supremacist links – kidnapped him. In symmetry with Shepard, the men drove Byrd Jr. out of town to a secluded wooded area, beat him and tied his legs to a chain connected to the truck. The men drove several kilometres, and while Byrd Jr. was partially conscious during this time, he died after his right arm and head were severed. It would later become known as lynching-by-dragging (Anti-Defamation League 2013). His body was then left in the front of an African-American church.

Figurehead production

The clear echoes of America's history of segregation and racist violence came to epitomize James Byrd Jr.'s death, and in turn, make his murder a media sensation and figurehead case (Petersen 2011). For many, the story and nature of his death seemed surreal; as if it had come from a pre-civil rights era where violence was not only condoned, it was countenanced (Petersen 2011).[4] This, coupled with the sheer brutality and hatred inflicted on Byrd Jr., compelled widespread media coverage, which focused upon the case and the problem of racism in America more generally.

The emerging facts of the case, and whether it could be tried as a hate crime, quickly became a national story (Petersen 2011). Thereafter, the story was sustained by continuing public responses. For example, after the initial reporting of his murder, demonstrations and counter-demonstrations followed quickly. The involvement of celebrities such as Jesse Jackson, Al Sharpton (who attended Byrd Jr.'s funeral), basketball star, Dennis Rodman (who offered to pay for the funeral[5]) and Don King (who donated $100,000 to Byrd Jr.'s children to cover the costs of their education) sustained the public conversation about the nature of Byrd Jr.'s murder. This media coverage was also thought to have led to 'copycat' draggings in other U.S. states. These events permitted further public conversations about race violence in America, and Byrd Jr.'s death mobilized public support for increased hate crime protections in Texas and federally. Byrd Jr.'s family also injected themselves into the public discourse, when one of his daughters became a key advocate for federal hate crime legislation, and his son became an opponent of the death penalty (Petersen 2011). From public and celebrity donations, the family also created the James Byrd Jr. Foundation for Racial Healing, which unlike the Shepard and Lawrence foundations, no longer exists.

Byrd Jr. was decentred from the public discussion following the case, and Petersen (2011) notes that only a faint image of the man emerged over time. Initially, there were vague details reported about his life, but the focus shifted following Byrd Jr.'s funeral. In contrast to the lives of Shepard and Lawrence, which were detailed at length, Byrd Jr. quickly became an archetype of the past experiences and present inequities of African-Americans. Perhaps his age and previous incarceration precluded the construction of Byrd Jr. as innocent or blameless for his victimization in the same way that Shepard and Lawrence were portrayed in the media. The case became an anchor point through which discussions about present and historic racism could be interrogated. In essence, the story shifted from the victim and the violence of the murder, towards the public and their responses. Whereas Shepard and Lawrence became prototypically ideal victims (Christie 1986), Byrd Jr.'s death was used as a vantage point to explore issues of race more generally, and to advance responses to hate crime in particular.

The curious question of 'disability'

The cases outlined above document three instances of racist and heterosexist hate crimes. Each case successfully activated a public imagination that led to substantive discussion, policy transfer and law reform, including the implementation of hate crime legislation, and related policing practices. In this section, some core themes from the analysis of the three figurehead cases discussed above will be considered to highlight some important considerations for the category of disablist violence. The themes presented are not an exhaustive list, but represent the common threads analyzed in the cases examined. These themes also highlight the ways in which cases of disablist violence may have failed to become figurehead. Against this backdrop, the discussion then moves to a framework of analysis of figurehead recognition, in order to identify the factors that make hate crimes 'figurehead' cases (and inform popular understandings of what constitutes a hate crime). The question we are left with, which we turn to later, becomes: What can an analysis of figurehead hate crime cases say about the politics of disability, and the impacts for disablist violence?

Family and shame

In examining the circumstances that contributed to their figurehead status, the murders of Shepard, Lawrence and Byrd Jr. highlighted the influence (and the social and symbolic capital) of their families. In all three cases, the victims' families injected themselves into the investigation, promoted the conditions under which their son/father was undeserving of the violence, and fought for various hate crime protections and social reforms.

In the Shepard and Byrd Jr. cases, their families' efforts helped lead to the passage of federal legislation (named in their honour), and the work of the Lawrence family led to the Macpherson Inquiry – which was 'one of the most important moments in the modern history of criminal justice in Britain' (BBC News 2004). In all three cases, the victims' families created organizations aimed at responding to prejudice, discrimination and violence. Each family played a part in transforming single acts of violence into national symbols about hate crime and prejudice, which contributed to the enactment of important policing reforms and the regulation of prejudice-related violence.

Notwithstanding the 'perfect storm' surrounding such factors as advocacy, growing community acceptance, role of social movements, media and the crime itself, the role of the family and friendship networks of these victims was critical to the outcomes achieved. The presence of a distraught family, and their activism in the face of their grief, created the conditions through which the wider public became invested in change.

Despite recent and extensive media attention and government enquiries on disablist violence in the U.K. (such as the Pilkington case mentioned earlier), the experiences of disabled people have not come to epitomize hate crime (Thorneycroft forthcoming). Nor have they activated a public imagination about violence against disabled people, or the enactment of legislative provisions to respond to disablist violence. A critical factor in these recent disablist hate crimes has been the missing family. In the 2007 Pilkington case, Francecca Hardwick's mother, Fiona Pilkington killed herself and her daughter, leaving only Francecca's 12-year old brother, who was unable to advocate on his sister's behalf. Likewise, in the 2010 death of David Askew, he was a loner with virtually no family or friends to mourn his death (Stockdale 2011; Walker 2011). The few family members he did have also had disabilities (Carter 2010; Disability News Service 2011), limiting their capacity to advocate in a disablist world. As with some LGBTIQ people who have been exiled from their family, many disabled people live isolated lives (Deane 2009).

Another problem is that many family members are offenders of disablist violence (Thomas 2011), leaving no familial support for the victim. Even when the family is supportive and willing to be a subject of the public gaze, other factors exist. For example, following the sexual assault by 11 young men of a 17-year-old girl with mild intellectual disability in Victoria in 2006, the family was reluctant for the case to proceed through the criminal justice system (Walsh[6] as quoted in Thorneycroft 2013). The father stated he was dismayed by the nature of the media coverage (*R v P and others* 2007), and said he 'felt humiliated as a father' (Wenn 2006). Many of the factors relevant to these reactions to disablist hate crimes relate to shame.

Shame, according to Tomkins, Sedgwick, and Frank (1995, 133), is 'the effect of indignity, of defeat, of transgression, and of alienation … [it] is felt as an inner torment, a sickness of the soul'. Distinct from guilt, which is attached to someone's acts, shame 'attaches to and sharpens the sense of what one is' (Sedgwick 2003, 37). Shame is externally oriented, whereby fear derives from one's non-normative identity (Siebers 2008). While Sedgwick (2003, 64) argues that shame is a 'structuring fact of [queer] identity', this is also the case for all minority identities and particularly disabled people (McRuer 2009). Whereas individual and social factors accommodated the family's fight for activism in the Lawrence, Byrd Jr. and Shepard cases, where there was no shame to be experienced (or it had dissipated), this is not the case in the disablist cases described above. Disabled people face significant barriers to social inclusion, and their existence is still essentialized (Siebers 2008). When disabled people (and/or their families) bear considerable shame for their 'impairment', 'difference' or 'non-normative' social identity, it may make it more difficult for family activists to come forth to fight for justice and hate crime reforms.

Celebrity

The Lawrence, Byrd Jr. and Shepard cases also highlight how the power of celebrity is influential at creating media and public interest, and ultimately transforming these singular events into figurehead cases. Wheeler (2013) has documented the influence celebrities have in shaping the public agenda, and suggests they can use their social capital to shift broader cultural beliefs. Several celebrities came forth in each case analyzed, but critically, the most important celebrities came from the same social identity as the victim. Ellen DeGeneres cried while giving a speech at a public vigil for Matthew Shepard (Morris 2011). Nelson Mandela intervened in the Lawrence case and met with Stephen's parents following weeks of police inaction (Pilkington 1993). Black American celebrities were also involved in the public outrage and responses to Byrd Jr.'s murder (Petersen 2011). The intervention of these celebrities was critical in illustrating the link between the victim, themselves and the broader community, and in constructing those lost lives as 'one of our own'. However, in the cases of disablist violence,[7] the absence of celebrity role models or advocates is tangible. This is not surprising, given the lack of celebrities with disabilities, and with the capacity (and willingness) to advocate in the same way, especially in terms of making these victims 'one of our own' when there is such heterogeneity in disability.

The arguments here are not so much about criticizing celebrities who have not spoken out; it merely confronts the reality that in an ableist world, celebrities who are disabled are uncommon (Riley 2005). In such circumstances, it is unlikely that disabled celebrities can come forward to speak out and add their 'face' to issues of disability-related violence. Abjection provides a useful lens to look at the treatment of disabled people in society, and the reasons why no disablist violence case has reached figurehead status.

Abject

No case of disablist violence has been able to reach figurehead recognition, and this is arguably because disabled people are archetypically abject. Notwithstanding the individual and collective factors that create figurehead status, for some disabled people achieving figurehead status is implausible because their existence is rendered unintelligible by their abjection. The absence of a disablist figurehead hate crime case is clear evidence of the distance between the witnessing public and the victim's experiences. While the Lawrence, Byrd Jr. and Shepard cases demonstrate how their abjectification can be deferred (Shepard was portrayed as a 'normal gay', Lawrence presented 'without race' and Byrd Jr. removed from the picture completely), disabled people are primarily constituted *through their disability*. The abject are those denied subjectivity, and abjection describes the process by which people and groups are excluded because they do not conform to normative ideals (Butler 1993). Because 'disability' is the least homogenous of all social identities (Bérubé 1998), it is most readily (and willingly) expunged from subjectivity, even for those who are differently disabled.

The modern liberal subject is only ever temporarily abled and is permanently at risk of disability and its attendant abjectification. The interdependence assumed from disability is the antithesis of the autonomous subject, and the constant peril of disability and dependence is only escaped in principle given it is an almost guaranteed human condition. As such, there is more invested in abjectifying and expunging disabling identities (Butler 1990, 1993). For these reasons, it is difficult for disablist hate crimes to become representative and figurehead because there is too much effort in abjectifying disabled people, pitying them and rendering their existence inferior and non-normative.

'Figurehead' recognition

This analysis has revealed how a mix of individual, social, cultural and institutional circumstances produces figurehead hate crime cases. These cases initiated conversations about prejudice, prompting law reform, and growing tolerance and equality, and assisted in the policy transfer of hate crime provisions. Figurehead hate crimes are important for the hate crime movement, and for the advancement of minority identity rights, as they provide templates that provide explanatory meaning to those who do not face prejudiced violence. Stemming from the analysis of the three cases above and informed by the disablist violence cases already mentioned, a framework of analysis of the necessary constituents for figurehead status are identifiable. They include the presence of family advocacy, the absence of shame, the insertion of celebrity and the suspension of abjection.

This framework assists in assessing the conditions and capacity of a single hate crime case being transformed into a figurehead hate crime case. This is important because it informs how various stakeholders can respond to hate crime cases and act to progress social reforms. It also illustrates how various identity groups are viewed differentially by society. As illustrated by the nature of law reform (including attendant policing practices) and these figurehead hate crime cases, the 'policy career' (Jenness and Grattet 2001) of social movements progresses at different rates and the disability movement has considerable ground to cover before it has the capacity to ignite the same attention. It also illustrates the dissonance between individualized factors and social structures pertinent to individual cases.

Figurehead cases provide us with a rich source of data about conditions of acceptable victimhood, including the conditions under which abjection can be eschewed. Christie's (1986) ideal victim preceded the legislative invention of hate crime, and while accounting for some power imbalance, effectively ignored the conditions where subaltern bodies become representative and figurehead. An important gap in our analysis, and in Christie's ideal victim, is the fundamentally gendered nature of what can be known about crime and victimization. It is not coincidental that all three figurehead cases are examples of 'stranger-danger' violence committed by men against men in public spaces. Hate crime is gendered, and as with disabled people, women are essentialized, and their experiences are difficult to translate as representative or figurehead. Abjection, shame and celebrity are also gendered as illustrated by the lack of representative power of sexual assault victims. In contrast to the figurehead cases, the disablist hate crimes discussed in this article – those that garnered at least some public awareness – were committed by known male and female offenders, within a residential environment, where the vulnerability of the victim is an opportunity for the offender. While these contexts are more likely in hate crimes of all forms, it is the public male violence of the Shepard, Lawrence and Byrd Jr. cases that becomes figurehead.

Christie's (1986) ideal victim was focused on the psychosocial contexts of the micro encounter between victim and offender. In addition to ignoring the role of the media, the media's use of the macabre to 'sell the news' and the representative power of cultural norms about deserving and undeserving victims, extant analyses also minimize the social and political capital of families and communities. The policy career of figurehead hate crime cases is not only about the micro conditions of a criminal encounter; or the media's attention and framing of the event; or the macabre nature of these figurehead cases (or otherwise, there would be many more figurehead cases). From this analysis, we suggest that each of these factors is mediated by family, shame and celebrity, and the extent to which an ideal victim's abjection can be deferred sufficiently to be representative.

This analysis of the Shepard, Byrd Jr. and Lawrence cases may contain no traces of disability; yet, their status as figurehead cases illustrates much about the hierarchies of ideal victimhood and the difficulties associated with identity politics, when the identities at stake are so heterogeneous. What does this analysis say about the construct of disablist hate crime, or hate crime generally? What does this mean for disability identity politics?

As identified by other hate crime scholars, perhaps hate crime is an unhelpful framework given that the conditions under which hate crime is recognizable are themselves ableist, and by extension institutionally disablist. But in departing from the conventional model designed to address prejudiced violence – i.e. hate crime laws – are victims any better serviced by the criminal justice system? Existing provisions for 'vulnerable' adults foreground the victim's 'deficiencies' and responses are aimed at fixing these deficiencies. This leaves the underlying targeted violence and prejudice unaddressed at the individual, institutional and social levels, which, in turn, does nothing to shift the public discourse about disability or disablist violence.

Family and community capital have been found to be critical to figurehead status in the cases analyzed in this article. Can there be lessons learned for disability movements from queer and race politics, which has long ago repudiated essentialist notions (to a large extent, at least)? In particular, in the development of hate crime provisions, identity politics have been an effective rallying point for social and cultural change. Just as with the disability movement now, these early identity movements needed to negotiate representation in the context of heterogeneous experiences. It may be that a new form of disability identity politics is required; one based in shared experiences of abjection rather than corporeality. This analysis has revealed that the hate crime framework creates hierarchies of 'ideal' victims, and that the conditions of this 'competition of suffering' (Mason-Bish 2013, 20) are stacked against those who experience disablist violence.

Conclusion

In addition to the role of social movements, figurehead hate crime cases play an important part in progressing the rights of minority identities, particularly in the area of hate crime law. Various factors produce figurehead recognition, but it remains true that no context has enabled a disablist violence case to reach this status. The reasons are varied, yet this article has identified several themes that inhibit such recognition. As no article has previously interrogated figurehead hate crime cases and the reasons for their place on the public agenda, the arguments in this article represent a starting point. Importantly, this case study analysis highlights several difficulties for the category of disability. It appears that no case of disablist violence can reach figurehead status when disabled people's existence is abjectified, and that this abjection is difficult to eschew.

Notes

1. For more information about these cases, see: Garland (2011); Quarmby (2011); Roulstone and Sadique (2013).
2. Eyewitnesses were not able to identify the number of assailants (Campbell 1993), and only two men have been incarcerated (Laville and Dodd 2012).
3. Four months earlier than Shepard's death.
4. Interestingly, in the Shepard case, a person close to the people involved (including Shepard) allayed the fears of one perpetrator's girlfriend by claiming that 'in the state of Wyoming you don't go to jail for beating on a gay guy' (as quoted in Thernstrom 1999).
5. This offer was rejected by Byrd Jr.'s family; instead, the money was donated to the James Byrd Jr. Foundation for Racial Healing, which was later set up by the family.
6. This is a pseudonym for the name of an anonymous research informant in Thorneycroft (2013).
7. For this article we analysed the deaths of Francecca Hardwick, Brent Martin, Christine Lakinski, Keith Philpott and Steven Hoskin.

Disclosure statement

No potential conflict of interest was reported by the authors.

References

Crime and Disorder Act 1998. (UK).
Hate Crime Enhancement Act 1994. (US).
Matthew Shepard and James Byrd, Jr. Hate Crimes Prevention Act 2009. (US).
R v P and others. 2007. *Children's Court of Victoria*, November 5, 2007.
Sentencing Act 1991. (Victoria).

Anti-Defamation League. 2013. "In Tribute and in Memory: James Byrd Jr." *ADL*. http://www.adl.org/imagine/james-byrd-jr.html.

Asquith, N. L. 2015. "A Governance of Denial: Hate Crime in Australia and New Zealand." In *The Routledge International Handbook on Hate Crime*, edited by N. Hall, A. Corb, P. Giannasi, and J. G. D. Grieve, 174–189. London: Routledge.

BBC News. 2004. "Q&A: Stephen Lawrence Murder." May 5. http://news.bbc.co.uk/2/hi/uk_news/3685733.stm.

Bérubé, M. 1998. "Foreword: Pressing the Claim." In *Claiming Disability: Knowledge and Identity*, edited by S. Linton, vii–xi. New York: New York University Press.

Brooke, J. 1998. "Gay Man Dies from Attack, Fanning Outrage and Debate." *The New York Times*, October 13: 1.

Burrell, I., and P. Peachey. 2012. "How the Press Ignored the Lawrence Story – Then Used It to Change Britain." *The Independent*, January 4. http://www.independent.co.uk/news/media/press/how-the-press-ignored-the-lawrence-story-then-used-it-to-change-britain-6284645.html.

Butler, J. 1990. *Gender Trouble: Feminism and the Subversion of Identity*. New York: Routledge.

Butler, J. 1993. *Bodies that Matter: On the Discursive Limits of 'Sex'*. London: Routledge.

Campbell, D. 1993. "Gang hunted after bus stop race killing." *The Guardian*, April 24: 3.

Campbell, F. K. 2001. "Inciting Legal Fictions: Disability's Date with Ontology and the Ableist Body of the Law." *Griffith Law Review* 10 (1): 42–62.

Carter, H. 2010. "Police Investigate Death of Man with Learning Difficulties Tormented for Years by Gangs." *The Guardian*, March 12: 4.

Christie, N. 1986. "The Ideal Victim." In *From Crime Policy to Victim Policy*, edited by Ezzat A. Fattah, 17–30. New York: St. Martin's Press.

Cottle, S. 2005. "Mediatized Public Crisis and Civil Society Renewal: The Racist Murder of Stephen Lawrence." *Crime, Media, Culture* 1 (1): 49–71.

Deane, K. 2009. *Shut Out: The Experiences of People with Disabilities and their Families in Australia*. Canberra: National People with Disabilities and Carer Council.

Disability News Service. 2011. "The Death of David Askew: Police Force's 'Total Failure' on Hate Crime." March 4. http://www.disabilitynewsservice.com/the-death-of-david-askew-police-forces-total-failure-on-hate-crime/.

Flyvbjerg, B. 2006. "Five Misunderstandings about Case-study Research." *Qualitative Inquiry* 12 (2): 219–245.

Garland, J. 2011. "Difficulties in Defining Hate Crime Victimization." *International Review of Victimology* 18 (1): 25–37.

Garland, J., N. Chakraborti, and S. Hardy. 2015. "'It Felt like a Little War': Reflections on Violence Against Alternative Subcultures." *Sociology* 49 (6): 1065–1080.

Holohan, S. 2005. *The Search for Justice in a Media Age: Reading Stephen Lawrence and Louise Woodward*. Aldershot: Ashgate.

Hughes, B. 2009. "Wounded/Monstrous/Abject: A critique of the Disabled Body in the Sociological Imaginary." *Disability & Society* 24 (4): 399–410.

Human Rights Commission. 1998. "Apparent Hate Crime Against Gay Student in Wyoming Highlights the Need for Congress to Pass the Hate Crimes Prevention Act; Brutality Continues While Congress Lets Bill Languish." October 9. http://www.commondreams.org/pressreleases/Oct98/100998f.htm.

Jenness, V., and R. Grattet. 2001. *Making Hate a Crime: From Social Movement to Law Enforcement*. New York: Russell Sage Foundation.

Laville, S., and V. Dodd. 2012. "Lawrence Verdict: After 18 Years, Justice: Gary Dobson and David Norris Convicted of the Racist Murder of Stephen Lawrence." *The Guardian*, January 4: 1.

Macpherson, W. 1999. *The Stephen Lawrence Inquiry: Report of an Inquiry by Sir William Macpherson of Cluny*. London: The Stationery Office. https://www.gov.uk/government/uploads/system/uploads/attachment_data/file/277111/4262.pdf.

Mason-Bish, H. 2013. "Conceptual Issues in the Construction of Disability Hate Crime." In *Disability, Hate Crime and Violence*, edited by A. Roulstone and H. Mason-Bish, 11–24. London: Routledge.

Matthew Shepard Foundation. 2015. *About Us*. Accessed January 6, 2016. http://www.matthewshepard.org/about-us/

McRuer, R. 2009. "Shameful Sites: Locating Queerness and Disability." In *Gay Shame*, edited by D. M. Halperin and V. Traub, 181–187. Chicago, IL: University of Chicago Press.

Meijer, I. C., and B. Prins. 1998. "How bodies come to matter: An interview with Judith Butler." *Signs: Journal of Women in Culture and Society* 23 (2): 275–286.

Morris, B. J. 2011. "The week Matthew Shepard died." *Counterpoints* 397 (1): 61–68.

Munro, V. 2014. *Hate Crime in the Media: A History*. Santa Barbara: Praeger.

Ott, B. L., and E. Aoki. 2002. "The Politics of Negotiating Public Tragedy: Media Framing of the Matthew Shepard Murder." *Rhetoric & Public Affairs* 5 (3): 483–505.

Petersen, J. 2011. *Murder, the Media, and the Politics of Public Feelings: Remembering Matthew Shepard and James Byrd Jr.* Indiana, IN: Indiana University Press.

Pilkington, E. 1993. "Mandela meets family of London stabbing victim." *The Guardian*, May 7: 4.

Price, J., and M. Shildrick. 1998. "Uncertain Thoughts on the Dis/abled Body." In *Vital Signs: Feminist Reconfigurations of the Bio/logical Body*, edited by M. Shildrick and J. Price, 224–249. Edinburgh: Edinburgh University Press.

Quarmby, K. 2011. *Scapegoat: How We Are Failing Disabled People*. London: Portobello Books.

Riley, C. A. 2005. *Disability and the Media: Prescriptions for Change*. Hanover: University Press of New England.

Roulstone, A., and K. Sadique. 2013. "Vulnerable to Misinterpretation: Disabled People, 'Vulnerability', Hate Crime and the Fight for Legal Recognition." In *Disability, Hate Crime and Violence*, edited by A. Roulstone and H. Mason-Bish, 25–39. Abingdon: Routledge.

Sedgwick, E. K. 2003. *Touching Feeling: Affect, Pedagogy, Performativity*. Durham: Duke University Press.

Seidman, S. 2002. *Beyond the Closet: The Transformation of Gay and Lesbian Life*. New York: Routledge.

Sharrock, D. 1993. "700 Mourn Teenager Killed in Race Attack: Clergyman Attacks British National Party at Funeral Service." *The Guardian*, June 19: 4.

Siebers, T. 2008. *Disability Theory*. Ann Arbor: University of Michigan Press.

Stephen Lawrence Charitable Trust. 2014. *Our Vision*. Accessed January 6, 2016. http://www.stephenlawrence.org.uk/what-we-do/vision-of-the-trust

Stockdale, L. 2011. "No One Should Have to Go Through What David Did." *Inside Housing*, May 13. http://www.insidehousing.co.uk/no-one-should-have-to-go-through-what-david-did/6514832.article.

Swain, J., and C. Cameron. 1999. "Unless Otherwise Stated: Discourses of Labelling and Identity in Coming Out." In *Disability Discourse*, edited by Mairian Corker and Sally French, 68–78. Buckingham: Open University Press.

Thernstrom, M. 1999. "The Crucifixion of Matthew Shepard." *Vanity Fair*, March: 209–214, 267–275.

Thomas, P. 2011. "'Mate Crime': Ridicule, Hostility and Targeted Attacks Against Disabled People." *Disability & Society* 26 (1): 107–111.

Thorneycroft, R. 2013. "Disability Hate Crime, 'Mate' Crime and the 2006 Werribee Case: Exploring the perceived utility of McDevitt, Levin and Bennett's (2002) hate crime offending typology." BA Honours thesis, Faculty of Arts and Education, Deakin University, Australia.

Thorneycroft, R. Forthcoming. "Problematising and Reconceptualising 'Vulnerability' in the Context of Disablist Violence." In *Policing Encounters with Vulnerability*, edited by Nicole L. Asquith, Isabelle Bartkowiak-Théron, and Karl Roberts. Palgrave Macmillan.

Thorneycroft, R., and N. L. Asquith. 2015. "The Dark Figure of Disablist Violence." *Howard Journal of Criminal Justice* 54 (5): 489–507.

Tomczak, T. 2015. "Are You Aware of the Avalanche of Gay Programming Assaulting Your Home?" *The Christian Post*, January 8. www.christianpost.com/news/are-you-aware-of-the-avalanche-of-gay-programming-assaulting-your-home-132277/#kuzkdJzLJii6QqMM.99.

Tomkins, S., E. K. Sedgwick, and A. Frank. 1995. "Shame – Humiliation and Contempt – Disgust." In *Shame and its Sisters: A Silvan Tomkins Reader*, edited by E. K. Sedgwick and A. Frank, 133–178. Durham: Duke University Press.

Walker, P. 2011. "IPCC Condemns Manchester Police over David Askew Death." *The Guardian*, March 22: 11.

Wenn, R. 2006. *Today Tonight*, screened October 24, 2006. Sydney, NSW: Channel 7. Television Broadcast.

Wheeler, M. 2013. *Celebrity Politics: Image and Identity in Contemporary Political Communications*. Cambridge: Polity Press.

Wilkes, D. 2007. "Bullies 'Drove Mother and Daughter to Fireball Death.'" *Daily Mail*, October 27: 1.

Index

Printed in Great Britain
by Amazon

56933150R00099